C000141656

THE CANALS OF
BRITAIN

D.D.Gladwin

Breedon Books
Publishing Company
Derby

First Published by B.T.Batsford Ltd., 4 Fitzhardinge Street,
London, W1H 0AH, 1973.
This revised, re-set and re-illustrated edition published by
Breedon Books Publishing Company Limited
44 Friar Gate, Derby, DE1 1DA, 1994.

© D.D.Gladwin 1973, 1994

All Rights Reserved. No part of this publication may be
reproduced, stored in a retrieval system, or transmitted in
any form, or by any means, electronic, mechanical,
photocopying, recording or otherwise without the prior
permission in writing of the Copyright holders, nor be
otherwise circulated in any form or binding or cover other
than in which it is published and without a similar
condition including this condition being imposed on the
subsequent publisher.

ISBN 1 873626 75 4

Printed and bound by Butler and Tanner Limited, Frome
and London.
Covers printed by BDC Printing Services Limited of Derby

Contents

Prologue

To imagine the coming of waterways, their meaning and their impact, it is necessary to forget the non-stop thrum of traffic outside your door, to forget the television louring in the corner, to remember there was no electric light, but at best a candle and at worst a stinking smoky rushlight, to remember the typewriter was many years away and that thousands of men — not women — painfully wrote out, often in beautiful copperplate, all the details of a contract — and then wrote a duplicate for the file. We must also remember that these men wrote phonetically for English was not standardised. In 1730, the date of the first Act for canalising the Stroudwater, the Jacobite Rebellion had yet to take place in Scotland, the Irish were even then a problem and the Welsh were still proud to be a distinct people. There was no Ministry of Social — or State — Security to look after you when you were sick or unemployed, and the king was a king, not merely a puppet, choosing his government and openly corruptible. George I could not speak English, George II banned his wife from his coronation and George III went a bit odd — but the canals were dug during the reign of all three.

Most important of all at the commencement of the canal era everyone knew his place in the pecking order of society. It is true one could, with a modicum of luck, and more than a dash of influence, work up the ladder. One could, but, and it is a big but, this was a society for men only. Men, whether navvies or gents, ruled the roost, women being for the home.

Still, for all the lack of sewerage facilities, and the poverty, it was a vibrant age, an age of evolution and change.

*****

The foregoing formed the bulk of the original prologue to the 1973 edition of this book. At the time the author was still an employee of the British Waterways Board and firmly believed in the possibility of a renaissance in canal carrying, as did a small proportion of members from the Inland Waterways Association, the Inland Waterways Protection Society and many British Waterways staff. The whole purpose of another body, the Canal Transport Marketing Board, was the retention and promotion of freight movements by water.

Twenty years previously, carrying on narrow canals was primarily hampered by a lack of boat crews, poor wages and, alas, sometimes appalling conditions for the family, forcing men to seek alternative employment, often with the canals perceived arch-enemy, British Railways. The wide boats of the Northern canal network and the Southern rivers still remained economic although the promised widening of bottlenecks in the system seemed to be forever postponed or at best to be built years later than was clearly desirable. Twenty years after the book's first publication both water and rail have almost totally surrendered commercial carriage of goods to the road lobby. But there is still an environmental aspect that has not changed since J.F.Pownall first clearly defined its existence in 1944. New canals, comparable in their design with motorways, would cause no pollution, freight could be carried at remarkably low rates, and they would be open for all pleasure seekers, whether walking, canoeing, fishing or boating.

And it is these latter aspects of canal use that has kept the network existing in 1973 from total extinction. In the last twenty years whole lengths of canals have been re-opened, and routes restored to navigation that many thought were gone beyond reasonable hope, and indeed a whole new force has entered the world of waterways: tourism.

There have been great spin-offs from the changing world, for example, where once Birmingham's canals made their oily, murky, way between factories and workshops, now the cleaner, prettified green fingers wander around the backs of housing estates and blandly anonymous, almost lifeless, 'industrial estates'. Towpaths are clearly defined instead of snaggle-toothed but boringly alike whether in Worcester or Wolverhampton with new, sharp blue bricks replacing the battered old red ones that made a canal 'quaint'.

Pubs were to canal people part of their lifeblood and in *Narrow Boat*, rightly the most famous of canal books, Tom Rolt wrote of their splendour and homeliness (although he doesn't mention that the toilets were so bad many boatmen, oddly fastidious, preferred to use the bushes up the bank) but there has come into the system a form of lager-lout who hires a 12-berth boat, rams 20 or more youths on it who then infest too many canalside hostelrys, seeking the freedom to drink and drive.

So the good and the bad still exist side-by-side, conservationists try to prevent progressives from destroying the very things that canals are believed to give; the owners or steerers of a (relative) handful of 'proper' canal carrying craft, many of which are mobile museum pieces themselves, still carry out an honourable calling. On the other hand some naturalists, blind to common sense, are so intent on preserving a particular species of plant or insect that they try by any means to stop further restoration work on, admittedly, long disused waterways.

The old fascination though still remains as powerful to many canal people as ever, and again I can only quote from 1973: 'Whether canals should remain moribund, advance or die is a matter of opinion and although the story of waterways is given in the following pages together with a few personal opinions, each individual must interpret the facts in the light of his or her own experiences.'

However, if we are to have a canal network that retains all or any of those aspects that first attracted you, the reader, to its charms, its nuances, its ever changing pattern of light, the plants, the birds, even the factories and industrial bleakness that provides such a foil, then beware not only of the foe without, but within. The then British Waterways' chairman, David Ingram, stated on 16 January 1992: 'Our business is the efficient management of the inland waterways system for the increasing benefit of the nation. We seek to expand business on the waterways by pursuing a business approach, providing a safe and high quality environment for customers, staff and local communities, and aiming for excellence in every aspect of our work. The waterways heritage and environment will be conserved, enhanced and made viable for future generations'.

There is precious little room for sentiment in 'efficient management' and without a feeling of sentiment, of going back in time, how can a waterway bewitch and beguile newcomers? Then, too, there is another problem. John Wilkinson and Hilary Peters wrote in *Waterways World* in January 1994: 'We keep a bridge on the Gloucester & Sharpness Canal and have been delighted to see the return of the grain barges *Tirley* and *Chaceley*, running from Sharpness to Tewkesbury. It is a joy to see the canal being used for its proper purpose. Unfortunately, we seem to be in a minority. There are complaints on all sides. So much so that we hear Healings, who run the barges, are thinking of stopping because the nature of the canal has changed. How can we let this sort of thing happen? It is monstrous that comers-in should have more say in the use of the canal than commercial carriers. We don't complain about pleasure boaters, or even anglers, being there, but we do object to them complaining when the canal is used as it should be. 'First things first'.

Do real pleasure boaters complain about commercial craft? Are we to let that miserable minority of snivelling, wittering, 'chrome-plated', idiots who know nothing except 'gin and a flash bird' decide how our canals are to be? Or will it rather, and better, be those who understand?

Acknowledgements

I am greatly indebted to the many friends, colleagues, acquaintances and professional bodies who have been kind enough to provide material and photographs for use in this book. The omission of their names is not intended to be in any way derogatory to their efforts and my thanks are none the less sincere. Among these and deserving of special mention are: Hugh Barker, George Bate, BEM, Arthur Cross, Martyn Denney, L.A.(Teddy) Edwards, Phil Garrett, A.J.Harmsworth, G.Harris, B.Holding, Jack James, F.W.Jones, D.G.Russell, Peter L.Smith, N.L.Thomas, Alf Watton, Captain A.V.West, members of the British Waterways Board, including among others Miss S.Doeg (*Waterways News*), J.Beer (Press Officer), the Section Inspector, foremen and workmen of the Worcester & Stratford section, librarians and staff of the Bromsgrove, Banwell (Som.), City of Lincoln, University of Birmingham, University College of Wales and Worcester libraries, staff at the Waterways Research Centre and Somerset, Southampton, Essex and Berkshire Record Offices, the editors of *Sea Breezes, Marple Rate Payer* and *Record* (Transport & General Workers Union), the Hon. Secretary and members of the Inland Waterways Protection Society and Canal Transport Marketing Board, and finally my wife, co-author in all but name, typist and general coffee-maker. Hers was not an enviable lot.

The above were the acknowledgements for the 1973 edition and to these must be added dozens of people who have enhanced my knowledge of waterway history in the last two decades. Regrettably many of my older colleagues have died and we are no longer in touch with others, but I am glad to say there are still many helpful, real, canal people in the world and I thank you all. In particular I should name: E.C.Amesbury and A.J.Douglas (photographers), M.Black, Eric and Mary Fenton, John Heath (editor and canalman), Dieter Jebens (photographer), Colin Judge, Captain B.A.Lane of Dursley, David Lewis, Alan Lucas, Mike McClelland BCNS, Joe & Ann Morley, Worcester Birmingham Canal Society, Jenny Reah, J-J Wright, Trevor Yorke for the use of his Worcester & Birmingham canal map, staff and officers at Birmingham Central Library, Archives and Local Studies Departments, Black Country Museum, Boxfoldia Ltd, Dudley Public Library, Falkirk District Council Archives, Linlithgow Union Canal Society, National Waterways Museum Archives at Gloucester, Neath Borough Council, Pontypridd Public Library, RSPB, Shrewsbury Public Library, Shropshire Public Library, Staffordshire & Worcestershire Canal Society, Bonded Warehouse of Stourbridge, Waterways Museum, Stoke Bruerne. Malcolm Luty and staff at Media Relations, British Waterways, who I'm glad to say, are helpful to the utmost degree. The editors and their staff at the offices of both *Waterways World* and *Canal and Riverboat Monthly*.

Much of the chapter *At Your Leisure* has relied upon outside contributors, each is acknowledged in the text but I must also mention Judy-Joan Wright who completed the Basingstoke story when Alan Lucas was taken ill.

*****

The financial figures shown in the book have been metricated when conversion seems reasonable but where the comparison involves a few (old) pence they have been left alone, therefore original documents retain their pre-metric figures throughout but one mile = 1.609 kilometres; 3 feet = 1 yard which equates to 0.944 of a metre and 12d = one shilling (1/-) = 5p.

The Specification of a Canal

'**Dimensions Of The Canal.** *The breadth of the canal at bottom is 16' and at the level of the top of the towpath 42', the depth of the water 5', the height of the towing-path and the top of the opposite bank 1'6" above the water surface; the breadth of the towing-path in all cases…to be 10' except under the bridges.*

*_**Bridges.**_ There are 4 Turnpike-road bridges, 24' between the parapet, 10 Parish and Bye-road Bridges, 16' between the parapet, 33 Accommodation Bridges, 12' between the parapet, 2 Junction Bridges one at each end of the Canal.*

*_**Aqueducts.**_ There are 10 Aqueducts upon this branch of Canal from 6-15' span; and one of 3 arches of 10' span each.*

*_**Locks, etc.**_ There are to be 23 Locks, 5 Lets off, 5 Sets of Drop Planks, 7 Waste Weirs, 45 Single Culverts from 2-4' diameter' besides 5 double two-feet and 7 single two-feet Culverts to be made of English Oak free of sap, for the Morasses &c. &c.*

The whole of the Works to be completed in a substantial and Proper Manner to the satisfaction of Mr Telford, the Engineer in Chief, within two years after the signing of the Contract, unless prevented by some accident of circumstances over which the contractor could have no control.'

A History and Description of the County of Salop (1837)

A CANAL IS a physically complex structure. If one looks at any area of land, whether on a map at home or when out driving, and imagines cutting a 42-feet wide ditch through it, all on one level, solely by the muscle power of men and horses, this much will be quickly apparent.

An ordinary field of four acres will almost certainly have a drainage ditch which must be culverted to pass under the canal, or have to be diverted away. Trees, hedges and undergrowth must be uprooted and burned. A barn, table or hut will need to be rebuilt, the farmer's right of access to his other lands may well need to be protected by an accommodation bridge and the bifurcated field fenced to prevent animals straying. All these trivialities must be planned even as the necessity of a cutting or embankment is considered. And these particulars must all be specified, even if not in detail, by the surveyor and his assistant before plans are laid in front of Parliament. And worse, permission must be granted by the farmer or landowner, for if he disagrees it may be that some vast subsequent diversion must be made.

In 1819 Thomas Telford said, and every subsequent engineer of the Birmingham & Liverpool Junction Canal has echoed:

'In passing through Cheshire, the canal was …peculiarly unfortunate, for the marly soil, of which the surface of that rich country chiefly consists, when used for embankments slips and bulges in great masses, and rapidly dissolves when exposed to the atmosphere. From an unaccommodating disposition in some of the landowners, in persisting to prohibit the proper line of canal, these evils were experienced to an enormous and unprecedented extent…'

The landowners' influence at that time is a contrast with the methods now in force; where motorways — a roughly parallel feat — are concerned, nothing seems to be sacred.

Having, one way and another, drawn up a line of the waterway, and the Act for the building passed — details of which will be found in Chapter Two — and some, if not all of the money raised, the work would then be put out to contract utilising small contractors or, often, direct labour gathered for use under the eye of the engineer. The problems for the later canals of shortages of good labour were as bad as they are today, and it is advisable at this juncture to take a sideways look at the politico-economic situation in Great Britain in 1760.

At the time when the Duke of Bridgewater was cogitating on his plans for a canal, the life of the working man went on much as it had done for the last hundred or so years. To walk to the market town — perhaps not more than ten miles away — with the wife and children suitably and relatively well-dressed for the fair day, was the equivalent of our going to Majorca. The strange places, strange faces and strange accents heard! The beer was better, the food sweeter and sun warmer on this day.

The labourer's cottage — and here we refer to a hard-working man in a reasonably affluent part of the county — was small, somewhat lacking, to our eyes, in the sewage department but warm and comfortable. Hire-purchase facilities existed, of course, and were a necessity; typically, boots were made and worn in the spring, payment, it was understood by both cobbler and wearer, being made from the harvest bonus. 'In the sty a pig, in the wife a child, in the furrow a seed' was an apposite description of these men's existence. While the price of flour and beer remained stable against the wages there was little to complain about, things were no better or worse than in their father's day, and he hadn't grumbled . . . True, there were rumblings from some discontented men, but these were little heeded by the mass.

Coalmining was still incredibly primitive, for the basic method was to dig hundreds of little pits in the ground, each with minuscule tunnels leading off. Although many of the early river navigation Acts were centred on mining areas, there was little incentive for a man like Scroop, the Duke of Bridgewater's father, to extend his pits when there were no means, save carts in summer, of shifting the coal to the consumer. Even presuming a dry summer and a modicum of luck, only the best paid of men could afford to buy the fuel, the remaining 80 per cent of the population, living as they did in rural areas, contented themselves with traditional materials — wood, peat or dung.

Corn would be grown in the fields of the villages and milled by the miller. It has been estimated that nowhere in England could one, at that time, be further than ten miles from a water-mill or windmill; a day's journey for a carter. Ironworkers, logically, lived either near the source of iron or of wood, and at least within a reasonable distance of the navigable rivers. the few domestic utensils required by a labourer could be bought from a travelling tinker, or, more probably, from the blacksmith. Bricks and pottery were likewise produced on a day-to-day basis. What little pottery the average householder possessed would be brought by the monthly travelling cart, a superior form of tinker who carried everything from Redditch needles to Scotch yarn. It is noticeable that, excepting the houses of the gentry, most red-brick dwellings were to be found near the brickfields or near a navigable waterway. Napton village and Stratford (with the Avon as its navigation) are good examples. In this context one should not belie the efforts and effects of coastal sailing craft, which provided an excellent intercourse between industrial areas centred around the Trent and what was to become Cobbet's 'Great Wen', London, even by 1750 the latter represented a parasitical growth, inasmuch that very little of its produce was home manufactured. In remoter parts, such as Dorset, mud dwellings were still being erected, elsewhere wood was used.

The cities were growing, a greater import/ export movement meant an increase in white-collar staff and their attendant families concentrated near the great ports and cities. The population figures for Manchester and Salford show this rate of growth all too clearly, growing from an estimated 19,800 in 1757 to 164,000 in 1824.

The population of England and Wales as a whole also increased, but not to the same proportions:

1688	1760	1801	1811	1821
5.5 m	6.5m	8.9m	10.2m	12.0m

Principal imports also increased:

Decade	Corn	Groceries	Total Imports
1750-59	40 (-)*	2,641 (32)	8,325
1760-69	226 (2)	3,863 (36)	10,719
1770-79	421 (3)	3,918 (32)	12,104
1780-89	422 (3)	4,295 (31)	13,820
1790-99	1,168 (5)	7,633 (35)	21,797

*The figures in brackets are percentages of total imports.

This postcard was dated 1913 and shows one of the last primitive fish weirs on the River Avon. However this was a navigation although in 1914, 'There is very little trade done on the river at the present time.' It is now fully restored, and exceedingly busy.

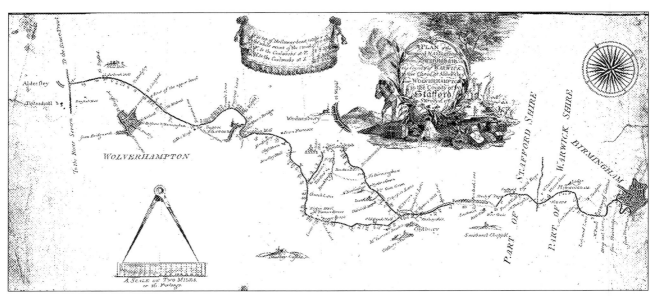

The building of the Duke of Bridgewater's Canal is often cited as a masterpiece:

'This then was the first step taken towards making this very early and useful navigation, but the degree of supineness exhibited by the original undertakers in so long neglecting the execution of the work which has been, and is yet, a source of immense wealth, is most strikingly contrasted by the enterprising spirit and the astonishing perseverance of the Duke of Bridgewater who unassisted, except by the natural genius of Brindley, carried into execution a series of difficult and expensive works which are even at this time unexampled. The general design of these works is, undoubtedly, great, the whole plan shows a capacity and extent of mind which foresees difficulties, and invents a remedy before the evil exists . . .'

But in fact, it was only a part of a natural trend.

Granted, in many ways, it was an improvement on its forebears, of which the Warwickshire Avon and the Stour are examples, neither being entirely successful for either the proprietors or the population served, while the Duke made a good profit. The greatest strength of the Bridgewater Canal lay not only in the ability of Brindley to combine aqueducts and a level line with a wide canal — one where barges of an economic size could be used — but also in the concealed waterways that ran from Bridgewater's mines.

'. . .We pushed up this subterraneous passage (just wide enough for the boat) above a mile . . .other passages lead from this principal one into divers parts of the mountain and recesses cut in the rock suffer one boat to pass another. In this singular voyage it is almost impossible to believe one's self in motion; the rocky passage, arched with brick, seem to be flying from you, and makes the head dizzy, and in returning the distant entrance looks like a bright star.'

Pretty awesome! It is difficult to visualise a dark, groaning, gaseous hole in the earth, where the sole illuminant was a candle. But men worked there — and with a 14-hour day, nigh on lived there.

Having won the coal and placed it into boats there were two ways of transhipping it into the waiting barge — by hand with long shovels that could lift a hundredweight at a time, or by the forerunner of our modern containers, wide boxes with iron straps holding two tons a piece, which were then craned across. Thus far was Brindley a genius, but a mystery that has never been solved, and which bears heavily upon waterways now, is why he should have built the Bridgewater, Derby and Droitwich barge canals of a wide (i.e. in excess of 14 feet) beam, and his trunk canals to a narrow (i.e. 8 feet or under) beam. The long-term legacy of these narrow canals is simply that they are outclassed today and even where a wide canal exists the connecting links are often narrow. The illogicality of the whole thing is even more apparent when one considers that the majority of waterways were built by small, independent, companies with different engineers, any one of whom, it being a British characteristic, could have been bloody-minded and set the trend for a wider canal. This is especially true when one takes the example of the Birmingham & Liverpool Junction Canal whose engineer, Thomas Telford, had already been engaged on the widening works on the Birmingham Canal Navigations Main Line, providing a canal with dual towpaths and superb tunnels, and yet he built the Birmingham & Liverpool Junction not only with narrow locks but with narrow cuttings only capable of taking a single boat. Granted there was some saving in cost both in land purchase and material cost in building a narrow waterway, but in the heyday of waterways, until the coming of the rail-road, this was not a matter of any great importance; having heard of the spectacular dividends paid on the Trent & Mersey Canal it is improbable that shopkeepers or clerks with dreams of making hundreds of pounds overnight would have cared whether the engineer quoted £28,000 6s 2½d or £48,000 6s 2½d.

An even more curious fact is that some canals were built part wide and part narrow. This is the case on the Trent & Mersey — a narrow canal between two (wide) rivers.

'Harecastle (old) Tunnel, upon this canal was constructed by James Brindley for a distance of 2,888 yards, at a level of 197 feet from the highest summit of the hill above it. This tunnel would only permit a 7 feet boat, with a moderate lading, to pass through it, and then only by employing leggers to propel it, a class of men who, lying upon their backs on the freight, pushed against the sides and top of the roof with their feet, and thus moved the boat onwards. The tunnel is only 9 feet in width, and 12 feet in height, and occupied nearly eleven years to complete; and to pass a boat through it occupied two hours. In the year 1824 Thomas Telford commenced another tunnel, at a distance of 26 yards from that already described; its length of 2,926 yards, its width 14 feet, and height 16 feet, of which 4 feet 9 inches is covered by the towing path, leaving 9 feet 3 inches for the passage of the boat; the path is supported by pillars, and the water flows under it. There are altogether 15 shafts sunk, well set out, and the headings so accurately driven, that the whole length may be seen at one view.'

This was not an inexpensive operation, costing in all some £112,681.

The care and attention that was required by the engineer and contractor is apparent even in such a small detail as the specification of bricks and mortar. 'The bricks were made from clay of superior quality, after being triturated by machinery; the mortar was of Barrow lias limestone, ground in a mill, and when set is quite impervious to water'.

Sporadically waterways have made an attempt to improve their service by widening the cuttings, eliminating the odd tunnel and, of course, by dredging. In the case of the Northern Oxford at Hillmorton a new set of locks was installed virtually alongside the existing ones. In the 1930s, with a little financial assistance from the government, the Grand Union Canal Company embarked upon an adventurous scheme to widen the waterway from London to Birmingham. In this case a grant was given by the government to relieve unemployment, and the old single 7 feet locks were replaced by 14 feet models with up-to-date shrouded paddle gearing; but not only was there no attempt to eliminate the unnecessary kinks in the waterway, the tunnels and bridgeholes, and even the passing places, were left as they were so that only at the big flights, Hatton, Itchington, etc., was there any real advantage to be gained when using a motor boat and butty — the two could work together, side by side, rather than the butty having to be hauled behind the motor.

The basic design of a lock does not materially alter whether it is capable of taking craft of 7 feet beam, 14 feet beam or even the big barge locks of the Gloucester & Berkeley Canal (90 feet beam), but the details have altered — or evolved — over the years. The latest style is in use on the

The coming of pleasure craft on to the waterways is often thought of as being something unique to the late twentieth century. In reality, the earliest boat trips were put on the Duke of Bridgewater's canal in 1785 and in the early years of this century, pleasure boating, either on owner-driven or hired narrowboats, had quite a vogue. Indeed it is due to some of these mildly eccentric voyager/writers that we have a living record of now disused canals. Boats have evolved, and continue to do so, with a move away from traditional (narrow) working boat based hull-lines to what are understood to be more canal kindly craft. Interiors have changed immeasurably from basic 4" thick leatherette covered cushions, with food storage underneath, plus a two-burner cooker to today's luxury.

Oxford Canal, Hillmorton, 1950s. Early full-length conversions.

The famous staircase of two locks at Fort Augustus on the Caledonian Canal are seen here in a 40-year old photograph. Proposed in 1726, the first Act of Parliament authorising the building of the canal was passed in 1803. An incredibly beautiful waterway its features include a Benedictine abbey, Invergarry (where Prince Charles spent a day after the Battle of Culloden) Inverness and, of course, the famous Monster which, alas, the Japanese have been hunting for some years presumably as a change from whalemeat. Above the canal, engineered by Thomas Telford and opened in 1822, almost agelessly there looms Ben Nevis, Britain's highest mountain. D.G.Russell.

Kennet & Avon, Widmead Lock. Turf-sided and structurally interesting, the booms which keep boats within the confines of the lock are clear. The gates were in a state of disintegration and the conditions quite disgusting. The lack of helmets date this work. E.C.Paine Ltd.

than as a generalisation, for Beeston top lock is made of cast-iron plates riveted together, as it was found that the lock was positioned neatly in green sand and refused to stay in shape. The River Kennet had turf-sided locks, while a lock on the Caledonian Canal is cut from the living rock with no more than a facing of brickwork. Disregarding such exceptions, neither the sides nor the bottom of a lock are necessarily parallel or flat, more often than not there will be gullies in the base brick or stonework enabling the water, when the lock is emptied for maintenance purposes, to drain into the paddle-holes from the top end. The sill against which the gate abuts will almost certainly be a solid lump of elm standing proud of the bottom. The stonework into the chamber of the lock, if it is a very early canal, will be dowelled one stone to another with iron or lead for the dowels. The part against which the boats' fore-ends will rub will again be of elm bolted with inch iron bolts, occasionally direct into the stonework, but usually to a plate set in the base sill. The sides of the chamber are often battered (too often, in both senses!) and it was stated by an engineer, Mr Cresy, in 1833 that:

> 'It is by no means advisable to make the walls of the lock chamber strictly perpendicular; some inclination, or talus, is always preferable, particularly at the back, whence resistance is required against the thrust of water; and as its filtration is another point of importance to be guarded against; a greater thickness is necessary at the bottom than at the top of the wall, that filtration being greater in proportion to its height. The walls should, however, be perpendicular towards the interior of the lock, at least in that part where the boats mount and descend; the lower part may have the same talus as that given to the boats. The least thickness for the walls at the level of the water is 4 feet 3 inches, in order to allow for a course of beton, as a protection against the filtration of water: as a general rule, the thickness should be equal to half their height, and as the walls become more lofty, their foundations must be spread out in proportion. Inverted arches have been introduced with considerable advantage to

Caledonian Canal where the work of conversion began in 1959 when a pilot scheme, involving the electrification of existing equipment, was tried out at Clachnaharry. Although successful, it was felt that the method could be bettered and the present very efficient electrohydraulic system of operation was evolved. Provision has been made for a system of standby pumping to enable the locks to be operated, although at a slower rate, in the event of a mains power failure.

Old fashioned, manual locks comprise a number of relatively simple units. Firstly, the basic stone or brickwork is itself an object of more devolution than evolution, for old age has too often eroded the sides into a concave shape. One cannot say though that the masonry of a lock will necessarily be brick and stone, other

The Dartford & Crayford Navigation was unusual as the Commissioners only built this lock on the River Darent in 1895, although they were authorised to do so as long ago as 1840. It cost roughly £4,768 to build with, as a generality, boats passing through on the level, except on Neap Tides. Photographed in 1975. M.Denney

By contrast this lock on the Chelmer & Blackwater Navigation can only be called rural, with the fender in the foreground depicting in real life a method of construction found in drawings of the eighteenth century. Paper Mill Lock, 1989.

Grand Union Canal, Bascote 2-rise, 1949.

form the profile of the wall of lock chambers; where there is a good foundation they may commence with a considerable batter or inclination, rising gradually in a curved form, finishing at the top with a perpendicular face; such a wall resembles an arch, from its having the joints and beds of the several stones made perpendicular to their face, which also prevents them from sliding on each other; the triangle of earth, supported by the back of the upright retaining wall, may be regarded as a wedge, of which its own gravity is the acting power, and it is only supported by the re-action of the inclined plane of earth, and the back of the wall, each of which acts perpendicularly to its plane. The breadth of such retaining wall must be always proportionate to the height, and to be of equal specific gravity with the earth, its breadth should be more than $1/3$ of its height. The specific gravity of walls built of brick or stone is a trifle more than that of the earth they support, therefore the dimensions may be slightly diminished.'

Some detail of the fitting of the gates will be given in Chapter Seven, but taking a standard narrow lock with a single gate and double (so-called mitre) bottom gates, even on a perfectly ordinary canal differences can abound. On the Northern Stratford, possessed of 19 operative

Right: Beeston Iron Lock on what was the Chester & Nantwich Canal (now part of the Shropshire Union) is totally unlike any other lock on the waterways system. Superficially it looks reasonably ordinary, but when the contractor came to build it, he found he was in an area of green or shifting sand. Nothing daunted, the engineer Thomas Telford designed and had built a lock made from iron plates riveted together and keyed to the bank.

Left pictures: Each lock not only reflects the surveyor, engineer and contractor, but responds to the geography of an area, with indigenous materials almost invariably being used. The first picture shows the Trent & Mersey's, Shade House, 1969; the middle is Stone in 1966 and bottom is Kennet & Avon, Devizes, 1966.

1830s this was replaced by a pair of locks, the new 20th lock being built differently as the engineer at that time thought differently to his predecessor. The basic reason for fitting double gates at the bottom end is that double gates are capable of withstanding a greater pressure of water than a single gate. The weight upon them forces them back into the quoin and against themselves. It should be mentioned in this context that aside from the thumping of a boat against a lock gate, a full standard single lock of 8 feet drop (7 feet by 70 feet) contains something in the order of 30,000 gallons of water, a not inconsiderable static pressure being exerted by such a quantity. Particular note should be made of the anchor to which the collar strap is attached. Until quite recently it was a rarity to find these set in anything less than a half-ton slab of sandstone or granite. The anchor arms are clawed to a depth of a foot and bonded to the stone with molten lead. About 4lbs of lead are to be found attached to each claw of the anchor. Fundamentally, as can be seen, there are only two items which hold a lock gate in position, the first being the collar, which in the past was invariably greased to add to the ease of swinging the gate, and the heel-post which operates in a ball and socket joint, the correct name for the parts being a box and a pivot. One of the difficulties past and present is that of keeping these gates in alignment

locks, two have lower gates steel-framed as a wartime economy measure. On the Wolverhampton flight of 21 locks, the second up from the bottom has a single top gate both at top and bottom. As first built the canal had a very deep bottom lock which was found to be extremely wasteful in water and sometime in the

Spectacular is probably the right word for this photograph of Foxton Locks on 27 June 1989. newly painted the gates and bridges alike stand out against the sombre, storm-wracked background. Leicester Section, Grand Union Canal.

Left: New and smart was this lock at Rheola on the Neath Canal in 1989. This represents a part of the restoration work being carried out in a traditional style and is a credit to the workmen involved. Middle left, top: Staffordshire & Worcestershire Canal, Penkridge. Middle left, bottom: Beverley Beck, Grove Hill. Middle right, top: Leeds & Liverpool Canal. Greenberfield. Middle right, centre: Brecon & Abergavenny Canal, Llangynidr. Middle right, bottom: Shropshire Union Canal, Beeston. Right, top: Leeds & Liverpool Canal, Barrowford. Right, bottom: North Walsham & Dilham Canal, Briggate.

Even 'ordinary' canal bridges reflect their eras and locality. Monmouthshire Canal, Malpas, 1973.

Once, not so long ago, the sheer variety of shapes and sizes of paddle gearing used on waterways meant that even an experienced boatman might find a type or method of working not entirely familiar to him. Unfortunately there have been accidents to pleasure boaters unused to the use of a windlass, and on occasion the reasons given were that either the windlass eye had slipped on the spindle, or that the gearing was so stiff that the windlass (being jerked) bit back and flew into some part of the persons body or face. British Waterways ever mindful of their responsibilities, nanny-like decided that one pattern of gearing will be used in future; a safe, utterly boring and wretchedly slow hydraulic drum. Safe-to-use, it is, but experience has also shown that where a boat had been hung up on the lock-cill or gate frame the sheer slowness of operation of these Granny Gears add to the existing panic. These illustrations show only a handful of what was once commonplace.

and this is often the only clue that will be given when a lock starts to 'come in'. This, fortunately rare, occurrence may result in the lock sides closing at a rate of up to 2 inches a year.

The apron at the bottom end of the lock is normally constructed of brick, as are the wing walls. The position of the steps used for access to and from boats varies from lock to lock, the design being modified to suit local conditions, especially in cases where a crossover bridge is in close juxtaposition to the bottom gates. It is interesting to note that with the increase in road traffic some of these crossover bridges have been widened and it can be necessary to fit very short,

Grand Union Canal, Bridge 4, Braunston, 1990.

Wyrley & Essington Canal. Huddlesford Junction, Bridge No. 1, 1969.

Oxford Canal, Upper Heyford 'Warning-Low Bridge'. Believed damaged by vibration from American aircraft, 1966.

Coventry Canal. Bridge No. 1. A tug waits for its tow, 1974.

or cranked, balance beams on the bottom gates. Good examples of these are to be found at York Street and Kidderminster Town Lock on the Staffordshire & Worcestershire Canal, where what were once rural lanes are now busy highways.

Bridges can be divided into a number of distinct groups. The first are accommodation bridges. The best known of these are the red brick bridges of the Midlands. Although declining in number now, the red bricks have weathered well

for 160 years, however age and excessive weight is taking its toll and regrettably where they are replaced it is more often than not by some featureless concrete structure, a good example of which is on the Grand Union Canal at Itchington, possibly one of the ugliest but (one hopes) economic to build.

Swing-bridges abound in the flatter parts of the countryside, on the New Junction Canal, although operated manually by chain and pulley they are functional and impressive in their setting. Older and much photographed, due to their proximity to the lock-keepers' 'Georgian' cottages, are those on the Gloucester & Berkeley Canal.

Lifting bridges which vary enormously in size and in manner of operation, have their own problems. On the Caldon Canal the bascule type is utilised, being counterbalanced by weights in a

Above: Long Buckby, Grand Union Canal 1990. The effluent clearly visible on the water had an uncanal-like and rather unpleasant smell; the only drawback in this halcyon scene.

Right: Kennet & Avon Canal. Roadway to the Hovis Mill, Newbury. A fine example of a low-level swing bridge 1953. L.A.Edwards.

box at the top. One bridge had always given much trouble to a local farmer who, finding that it moved under his tractor, removed the iron ballast, thus ensuring that it stayed down! Those on the Welsh Canal have been much photographed, while the twin-arm type on the Southern Oxford is again well known. Some pleasure is given to boats' crews when cruising the Leeds & Liverpool Canal, for when the bridge at Litherland has to be swung, it disturbs the passage of cars on a busy highway and quite

A view of Lock 17, Claydon on the Oxford Canal as it was in March 1977. This group of canal company's buildings almost inaccessible except for the towpath or by boat had been superseded.

Drawbridges represented a relatively cheap means of crossing an artificial waterway and were perfectly adequate for farmers' use. On some waterways, the Stratford-on-Avon for example, it was normal for such accommodation bridges to be left in the open-for-navigation position. When they go out of balance they are absolute pigs and it wasn't so many years ago that on the Welsh Canal one crew member had to shin up a chain until the bridge creaked into life.

Shropshire Union, Wrenbury. Drawbridge No. 21. An open and shut case, 1990.

considerable queues can build up, the expressions of the drivers, to borrow a phrase, are 'wondrous to behold', but most of these bridges, fortunately, tend to be in quiet rural areas. Mention should be made here of one very impressive modern swing-bridge, that over the docks at Bristol. Electrically operated, it is controlled from a crow's nest, and with an overall weight of over 100 tons swings as

easily and gently as a matchstick on a pond.

Crossover, or junction, bridges are accounted for by going back to the days of horse-drawn craft, when the towpath had to change sides. That near the Blockhouse at Worcester on the Worcester & Birmingham Canal has ceased to bear any resemblance to its original design, being now a four-lane highway; any horse venturing to

Right: Another shot of Shropshire Union, Wrenbury. Drawbridge No. 21.

Below: Stratford-on-Avon. Drawbridge Farm Drive c.1905

cross would rapidly be converted into dog's meat. Others long disused, as at Rednal on the Old Ellesmere Canal look quite forlorn with metre-high grass growing between the parapets. The curves of the parapet wall leading to and from these bridges are often graceful but, regrettably, unappreciated. There are three reasons for the towpath changing over. The first, where it is necessary for the towing-path to cross over an arm of the canal or at the junction of two canals.

The second, where having met with difficulties with landowners, the only way the towpath could be built was to construct it on the opposite side of the canal. The landowners lived in fear of boatmen poaching if they had easy access to the fields! The third, which sounds remarkably humane, was supposed to be that in conjunction with a slightly cambered towpath, if the horse had to cross over every few miles it evened out the wear on its shoulders from the towline.

Top and left: Pontgam or Crooked Bridge at Aberdulais Basin, junction of the Neath and Tennant Canals is seen in both 1914 and 1989. Derelict until a few years ago the site was restored by the Neath and Tennant Canals Preservation Society and has been made easily accessible to the public. The boat in the older photograph is curious insofar as a short length of planking is missing on the far side, but it appears to be water-worthy. (93) British Rail.

Left: This photograph at Norbury Junction on the Shropshire Union Canal was taken by an iced-in boatman during the long winter of 1969-70. During this time domestic coal was being lorried into the wharf at Norbury but this nip came suddenly and the boats were trapped a mile or so away from this junction. J.J. Wright

Some of the most attractive bridges are to be found at the tail of a lock. Often in cast iron, they may be there for the purpose of permitting the boatman to run from one side of the lock to the other without crossing the lock gates, alternatively they may be there to protect an ancient right-of-way and, may often now be the only clue to the existence of such. At lock 36 on the Worcester & Birmingham Canal, known as the Clap Bridge, was an enormous slab of stone serving as a bridge. This differed from most, inasmuch as it was not split in the centre as are those on the Stratford and Staffordshire & Worcestershire Canals, but was offset to one side.

There is a strong case for the retention of a number of cast and wrought-iron bridges, if only for their vintage — and fitting — appearance. Some efforts are being made towards this and the

Above: A scene that can never be repeated. The shortened motorboat 'Princess Anne' in the T. & S.Element fleet had developed a leak and at night it was far better to leave it in a lock pound in the Farmers Bridge flight, Birmingham & Fazeley Canal, 1967.

Left: Lancaster Canal, Garstang 1989. Centre: The approach to Mill Lock, Banbury, on the Oxford Canal was always a tedious business, especially with a lifting bridge carrying a busy road to contend with. This roller had ceased to roll years ago. Right: Trent & Mersey, Booth Lane, 1966.

roving bridges over both the arm that once led to Barlow's Yard and over the Oxford Canal at Braunston on the Grand Union Canal, is being well kept up. Others, plainer, are still to be found on the Birmingham Canal Navigations, often marked with both the name of the iron works and the casting date. Regrettably, a number of bridges were knocked down to aid the wartime scrap drive, others having been left derelict when the canal was closed and many neglected ones are bound to fall down eventually. This is an unnecessary form of vandalism, if a beautiful thing exists surely it is better to retain it than let it go by default. Whilst on the subject of preservation, or conservation, mention must be made of the humble accommodation bridge which is also suffering from vandalism by both children and mad motorists, for upon repair

work being carried out no attempt is made to match the indigenous materials, any old 'bodge', seemingly, sufficing. There is no better way of showing the intelligent use of natural local materials than to look at the handsome high-backed accommodation bridges of the Pocklington Canal or the granite of the Cromford Canal or the Bath stone which abounds in Somerset.

Whilst most bridges are plain, in certain circumstances it was necessary for the engineer to pander to the landowners' ideas and to build a bridge which was more pretty than functional. The very nature of a canal, fortunately, made for some restraint. Ladies Bridge on the Kennet & Avon Canal is a more or less normal bridge with fine examples of a stonemason's craft and Avenue Bridge on the Shropshire Union Canal Main Line

Firgrove is only a couple of miles from Rochdale and when this new concrete gem was built to replace an out-of-date swing bridge over the Rochdale Canal it seemed as though half the population gathered not only to watch its testing but to show off their hats, although many were no doubt half-hoping the engineers had miscalculated! Three steam-rollers were used to trundle solemnly back and forth. Rochdale Museum.

is merely an example of the architectural style fashionable at that time. This restraint, however, is not apparent where Drayton Manor footbridge on the Birmingham & Fazeley Canal is concerned. It is a superb example of the nonsensical — nothing more or less than the castle's portcullis, absentmindedly misplaced by Richard Coeur de Lion.

There can be little doubt that motorway engineers are often forced to use considerable ingenuity when providing their accommodation bridges over a canal, and it is not unreasonable to point out that if we had modern canals these motorways could have been kept in their place.

In the specification of the Newport Canal — given at the beginning of this chapter — aqueducts will be seen to play a relatively small part. Best known of all aqueducts is, of course, Pont-y-Cysyllte on the Welsh Branch of the Shropshire Union Canal. Built in 1795 it is unlikely that anything in the engineering field will ever be made to equal it:

'The Aqueduct of Pont-y-Cysyllte is 4 miles from Chirk, over the river Dee, an earthen embankment was pushed

Canal aqueducts by their nature are more often than not completely unnoticed by boaters. For every spectacular structure there are literally hundreds of mini-aqueducts, culverts if you like, but each carries the watercourse over something, whether streamlet or road, river or, in 1994, badger run.

The story of Wolverton Aqueduct over the Great Ouse River is a sad one. Initially the canal utilised a flight of locks to descend to the river and then ascend back to the proper level, while in the meantime the contractor completed his aqueduct. This leaked and eventually its copious down pourings were said locally to represent his tears. Finally it collapsed, to be replaced by this graceful iron structure. Like Pont-y-Cysyllte there is a towpath only on one side and on the other a sheer drop. It is a sport of the local youths to lob stones at passing boats if only to force them to the non-towpath side and to hear squeals and yells of both fear and fury.

Pont-y-Cysyllte Aqueduct, the most famous of the Seven Wonders of the Waterways: 'There is a footpath and handrail alongside the canal, which runs through an economical trough just wide enough to admit a barge. A man told me today how he and other boys used to bathe in the aqueduct. The donkeys that drew the barges were of uncertain temper, and rather than meet them on the footpath the boys would swim to the other side, where there is no handrail, and hang sickeningly over the Dee by one leg until the barge had passed. The boatwomen used to wear voluminous skirts, and when a gale was blowing up the valley they would often be swept off their feet and flattened against the railings. In hard winters the canal would freeze and the boys would skate the whole of the four miles to Llangollen.' The text appeared in the staff magazine Lock & Quay, January 1952. The photograph is dated 1967. The aqueduct continues about its life, more or less as it has done since 1803.

forward until the perpendicular height became 75 feet. The distance between the end of this and the north bank is 1,007 feet, and the river Dee is 127 feet below the water level of the canal carried over it. To construct an aqueduct upon the usual principles, with piers and arches, 100 feet in height, and of a sufficient breadth and strength to afford room for a puddled waterway, would have

Aberdulais Aqueduct carrying the Tennant Canal over the River Neath. The first stones were laid in May 1823, with the engineer, William Kirkhouse, no doubt being pleased that it was completed in less than 12 months, in April 1824. 340' (103.6m) long it is an example of canal engineering at its best.

been, not only extremely hazardous, but expensive. Telford, who had already carried the Shrewsbury canal by a cast-iron trough 16 feet above the level of the ground, formed the idea of doing the same in the present instance, and made a model of a portion set on two piers, with the towing-path and side rails, which was approved of and finally adopted.

The foundation on which the piers are erected is a hard sandstone rock; their height above low water in the river is 121 feet, at the bottom they are 20 feet by 12, and at the top 13 feet by 7 feet 6 inches. For a height of 70 feet from the foundations, they are built solid, and the remaining 50 feet hollow, the walls being only 2 feet in thickness, with one cross inner wall; by this means the centre of gravity is thrown lower in the pier, and the masonry economised. The width of the water-way is 11 feet 10 inches, of which the towing-path covers 4 feet 8 inches, leaving 7 feet 2 inches for the boat; as the towing-path stands upon iron pillars, the water fluctuates and recedes freely as the boat passes. There are eighteen of these stone piers, besides those of the abutments, and the total expense, including the embankment, was £47,018.'

	£	s	d
The embankment cost	8,570	15	8
Masonry	21,162	13	5½
Iron Work	17,284	17	5½
	£47,018	6	7

This aqueduct almost rivals the works of a similar kind left us by the Romans.

Equally well known, howbeit constructed of different materials, are Dundas Aqueduct on the Kennet & Avon, Maple Aqueduct on the Peak Forest, and Almond Aqueduct carrying the Union Canal in Scotland; but how rarely people notice the little ones. Driving under in a car, or even over in a boat, it is difficult to visualise how much of a problem it is to retain a canal in a channel 20, 30 or 40 feet up, and different engineers met the problem in different ways. Some were successful, Brindley's aqueducts carrying the Staffordshire & Worcestershire Canal over the Sow are cumbersome but solid and seem to bulldoze their way across the countryside while Bevan's on the Grand Union Canal at Itchington is hardly recognisable as an aqueduct from the canal bank, but with a river that has a rise of 12 feet between summer and winter levels underneath, it has to be strong. The new aqueduct at Ryland Road on the Birmingham Canal Navigations New Main Line presented modern engineers with some problems, how then must Telford — by then an

'Lobster pot' weir, Stewponey, Staffordshire & Worcestershire Canal.

old man — have felt as he passed the drawings for the aqueduct at High Onn on the Shroppie Canal?

Locks we have already mentioned but those mysterious 'lets-off' in the specification need some explanation. A problem often faced by engineers is what to do with waste water in winter time when the drainage from the fields, roads and houses over-fills the canal. At certain strategic points along the canal pounds (the generic name for a level

Two canals, one living and one dead. Top: Depicts one of the smartly maintained Duddeswell locks on the Grand Union, too many boats moving up causing an excess of water in the upper pound; bottom is the lock at Wansford on the Driffield Navigation, disused other than as a water feeder. The towpath is the jungle on the left, and further back the river was covered by a foul green slime.

between two sets of locks) a set of paddle gearing is installed on the canal bank high above a stream into which the surplus water can be let off. The utility of some lets-off is well evidenced by their clean and well-greased state, others, long forgotten, will often have to be hunted for, through long grass and brambles. Fortunately, they are usually rusted solid, otherwise the results of malfeasance could be unhappy for people living in the valley below.

Drop planks were once provided at all suitable points along the canal bank for emergency use in the case of a breach or burst. In recent years it has been found that the local inhabitants are likely to convert them into fencing posts or firewood and it is now necessary to keep them at British Waterways Board depots.

A waste-weir would be placed above a stream to allow the optimum canal level to be maintained, other than in times of flood, and it is these weirs which govern the depth of water in a canal. Some (control) weirs can be raised by movable boards to provide an extra head of water, either to feed another canal or to allow a flow to the local Water Board's reservoirs, for a good percentage of domestic drinking water, whilst starting its life in the hills, travels a canal before ending up in our taps. As the name indicates a stop lock served to hold the level of one canal higher than the other and was usually installed at the insistence of the first come to ensure that they did not lose any water to the upstart newcomer who was, in their eyes, a potential danger to their water supplies. This dog-in-a-manger attitude was to provide one of the greatest barriers to the free interchange of canal traffic and perhaps more than any other single cause was to lead to the success of railways. From the canal engineers' angle stop locks were nothing but a confounded nuisance. As an example, to reach its junction with the Trent & Mersey Canal the Macclesfield Canal has to cross over the Trent & Mersey by means of an aqueduct and then drop down via a stop lock (Hardingswood) to the lower level, an unnecessary and expensive flyover. The northern Stratford had to build one of the few examples of a canal guillotine lock, at Kings Norton, to placate the shareholders of the Worcester & Birmingham Canal. The gaunt remains of this stop lock look impressive against a sunset and are probably worthier of greater care than they get.

On the River Nene the problem is rather different and guillotine top gates are provided almost without exception to enable flood waters to be cleared quickly. Magnificently built, they are impressive if only for their utilitarian purpose.

Culverts are far from impressive, and more often than not resemble an enlarged rat-hole. Designed mainly to carry field drains or very small streams, the outermost courses of brick-work have probably long since been worn away

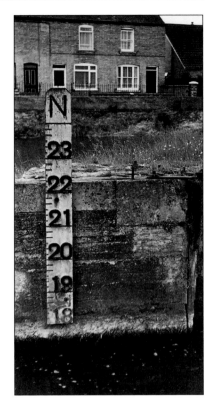

Top: A water-gauge found on the River Welland at Deeping Gate one spring day in 1972. The vestiges of the derelict lock can be seen but the gauge is a not uncommon fitting on both used and unused waterways. The Welland was one of the oldest navigations being first worked upon in 1571.

Middle: Sculpture. An elderly strapping post found by the tenth lock at Atherstone, on the Coventry Canal in 1968. The friction of ropes running round this post have worn it into a strange shape, but how many boat's lines did it take?

Bottom: Canal companies necessarily drew upon existing rivers to top up their supplies or, indeed, to fill reservoirs. The adoption and adaptation of such a waterway incurred a maintenance requirement. This shows just some of the junk on the River Rea in Birmingham that had to be manually dragged out and burned.

and where subsidence is a problem the whole culvert may well be many feet below the surface of the field. Sometimes they can get completely lost, as at Glascote on the Birmingham & Fazeley Canal where a pound between the locks ran dry with monotonous regularity, the cause being believed to be a leaking culvert which had long since been built over by the motor car factories on both sides of the canal. The majority of culverts carrying any quantity of water were built in brick and some, as shown in Telford's specifications, were made of oak. The modern culvert, perhaps carrying sewage or just a stream, will be in prefabricated concrete pipe. To insert this, unless a borer is used, it is necessary to stank off (close) half of the available waterway, dig it up, put in the pipe, rebuild the canal including the clay puddle, reopen that half and repeat the process in the other. The comments of the works foreman engaged upon the job have probably not materially altered over 200 years. Sometimes, too, things go wrong, as on the Grand Union Canal in 1971 when an emergency stoppage was announced because:

'During the construction of a tunnel sewer beneath the canal the bed of the waterway has fractured and it is, therefore, necessary to drain the canal between Castle Lane, Solihull (Bridge 83) and Woodcock Lane, Solihull (Bridge 86) from Thursday, 30th December and it is estimated that the works to the tunnel and the remedial work to the canal bed will be completed and the canal re-opened to traffic by Monday, 17th January 1972.'

When one of the last boatmen to use a horse-drawn craft on the Leeds & Liverpool Canal was asked what was the most important part of the canal, his answer was brief and abrupt: 'T'bloody towpath', and it is here that the change in waterways since their inception has been most marked. Some towpaths have over the years suffered from complaints that their engineers could never have envisaged. In the cuttings on the Shropshire Union Canal the perpetual running of water down the sides has eroded even the rock, in too many other places the towpaths have been broken away by 'shamanglers', but where the fishing from a canal bank is controlled by a responsible club the towpath is, more often than not, in a reasonable condition. The basic foundation of a normal towpath, which can be from 6 to 10 feet wide, will be broken rubble well pounded, behind a foot-thick layer of blue lay at the waterside. On top of this, according to the nature of the locality, we have small gravel or ashes.

The original describes this as 'Whitchurch, on the Canal', but we have to assume Whitchurch, Shropshire, with the milk processing unit to the rear. The splatter on the towpath can only mean one thing!

When commercial craft were about it was the standard practice to tip the ashes from the range, morning and night, into any potholes that might arise — in the days of diesel engines this was probably an atavistic instinct left over from the time when a pothole could tear a horse's hoof, or worse, break his leg. Ashes also gave a good grip when one might otherwise slip and slide around a lock. Early canals had the towpath horizontal, but it was found that over a period of time they gradually gained a slope towards the canal and there have been many, many times when the horse, far from pulling the boat, has been pulled into the water. Conversely, a towpath which is horizontal or sloping to the canal is better drained, and on the later canals where the towpath was cambered away from the water it became necessary to dig a ditch inside of this to carry away the top water, although the lessening of the strain on the horse more than justified this.

These then are the main factors which make up the specification of a canal, save one — and that is that the maximum flow of water on a canal, if it is to remain under control, must not exceed half a mile per hour.

The Cost of a Canal

'THE CALEDONIAN Canal is the greatest undertaking of its sort attempted in the empire. It stretches south-west and north-east across the island from a point near Inverness to another near Fort William. It is chiefly formed by Loch Ness, Loch Oich and Loch Lochy. The total length of the canal, including the lakes, is 58¾ miles; but the excavated part is only 21½ miles. At the summit it is 96½ feet above the level of the Western Ocean.

It was constructed upon a very grand scale, being 20 feet deep, 50 feet wide at bottom, and 122 feet wide at the top; the locks are 20 feet deep, 172 feet long and 40 feet broad. Frigates of 32 guns and merchant ships of 1,000 tons burden may pass through it. This canal was opened in 1822. It was executed entirely at the expense of government, from the designs and under the superintendence of Thomas Telford, Esq., on whose skill and talents as an engineer it reflects the highest credit. The entire cost was £986,924. It would, however, appear to have been projected without due consideration, and promised to be a very unprofitable speculation. During the year 1829, the total revenue of the canal, arising from tonnage dues and all other sources, amounted to only £2,575 6s 4d while the ordinary expenditure, during the same year, amounted to £4,573 0s 1½d. It was, therefore, very doubtful whether the revenue derived from it would ever be able to defray the expenses of keeping it in repair, without allowing anything for interest or capital.'

The following is a detailed account of the various items of expenditure on account of the Caledonian Canal, from 20 October, 1803, to 1 May, 1830.

	£	s	d
Management and travelling expenses	36,691	12	10¼
Timber, and carriage thereof	72,317	1	10¼
Machinery, cast-iron works, tools and materials	128,886	4	7¾
Quarries and masonry	200,014	4	10¾
Shipping	11,719	1	6
Houses and other buildings	5,539	10	6
Labour and workmanship (day-work)	54,209	1	1¾
Labour and workmanship (measure-work)	418,551	16	8½
Purchase of land, and payments on account of damage	47,956	12	9¾
Purchase and hire of horses and provender	3,638	12	2¾
Incidental expenses	2,820	18	10
Roadmaking	4,579	3	6¾
Total cost	£986,924	1	6½

This, then, was the cost of a 'Grand' Canal; the reason for its existence — to convey ships across Scotland; and a prophecy from a writer in the 1830s. The cost was accurate — note the recurring ¼d and ¾d, a punctilious attention to detail that rings falsely in modern ears attuned to nothing less than 10p. As a ship canal it was outpaced in its building by the increasing size of vessels and the fruition of steam propulsion. As to the prophecy this was partly right, in so far as it never served for its designed purpose, and partly wrong for its value in wartime and to peacetime fishing craft should not be underestimated.

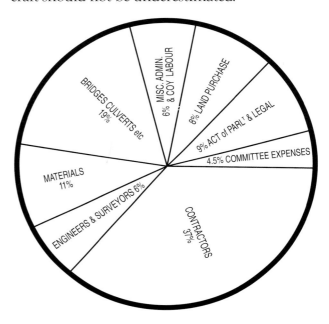

By contrast the costing of the Somerset Coal Canal, shown in the familiar 'orange-segment' fashion, is not final but does show the disproportionate sums that could be expended. Committee expenses appear at first sight to be a trifle excessive. In fact this canal was playing with a mechanical lift invented by one Robert Weldon and specified in his patent No.1892 of 1792 as a 'boat floated into trunk or casoon and lowered by means of rack and pinion'. It was not overly successful and the delays in completion, and hence traffic, led a vociferous minority of the directors to investigate the possibilities of either running a tramway in lieu of the lift (or even the canal) as propounded by Benjamin Outram, engineer of the Huddersfield Narrow Canal, or of an inclined plane. For the former they had to go to the North of England a three-day journey costing, including hotels *en route*, something of

Bottom of the plane. Were the front wheels of the trolley deliberately de-railed to keep it from running away? National Waterways Museum, Gloucester.

Some time prior to 1900 a typical Shropshire Canal tub-boat being used for a pleasure outing is seen with Madeley Court Ironworks to the rear. W.K.V.Gale.

the order of £32-odd, 'to view and investigate the works proceeding'. The shareholders begrudged this money, not surprisingly, for a labourer's weekly wage at this time was about eight shillings, and the 'Proprietors of the Navigation' were, in this case, mainly small men, rather than rich landowners, and doubtless they reasoned that the working of the lift should have been more clearly investigated in the beginning. In the event, in 1800, the lift was replaced by an inclined plane. Two years later the committee begged a further £45,000 to build a flight of locks in lieu of both lift and plane, the remains of which are still extant at Coombe Hay.

It was not until 1910 that the main purpose of the committee's gallivanting was realised, when the GWR closed the canal and substituted a light railway. Other more reasonable committee expenses would include the hire of a public house for meetings — prior to obtaining their Act of Parliament — and the hire of an office or the purchase of same thereafter.

The first meeting of the co-proprietors of the canal from the Trent to the Mersey was held on 30 December 1765, a mere six months after Dr Irasmus Darwin, Josiah Wedgwood, John Wedgwood and Thomas Bentley had first employed James Brindley as surveyor. It was agreed at this meeting that an Act of Parliament for the work should be obtained and, incredibly quickly, by 14 May 1766 this was done. A month or so later we find Wedgwood cutting the first sod. Within a fortnight of the Act of Parliament a general assembly of the proprietors was held, James Brindley being appointed surveyor general at £200 a year, and Hugh Henshall, clerk of the works at £150 a year. It was decided that work must begin immediately on both sides of the proposed Harecastle tunnel and at Wilden Ferry, and furthermore an immediate call must be made on the proprietors for six per cent of their subscriptions. Work began on 17 July 1766.

This was an early waterway and, barring only the usual minor contretemps, it is unlikely that the committee, who were all businessmen, had a great deal to worry about. This was not the case where some waterways were concerned, an example being the Southampton & Salisbury Canal Navigation. Various plans for a canal line had at times been proposed and on 27 December 1792 a meeting was held at the Guild Hall, Southampton, where it was decided to seek five-

Trench Inclined Plane once ranked as one of the 'Wonders of the Waterways' but has been almost totally obliterated, and all that remains is the name used to distinguish different parts of a wholly undistinguished factory estate and the reservoir 'Trench Pool'.

Completed by February 1797, Trench had a vertical rise of 75' (22.9m) and a track length of 669' (204m) but uniquely led a successful life before official closure in September 1921, by which time it was the last inclined plane in service in the UK. The hilly countryside and lack of water in the area precluded the use of orthodox locks throughout the length of the Shrewsbury Canal, and it is worthy of note that the tub-boat canals in this area eventually totalled just over 38 miles (61km). Each tub-boat measured about 20' (6.1m) by 6'4" (1.93m) and carried eight tons of coal. The Shrewsbury Canal also had orthodox locks but with the exception of two later widened at Eyton on the Shrewsbury side of Trench the rest being designed to accommodate three or four tub-boats simultaneously, the standard boats in use not needing to pass over the incline, were particularly narrow and long (long, long boats indeed) at 81'5" x 6'4" (24.8m x 1.93m). The locks were also unorthodox insofar as the bottom end used a portcullis type lifting gate counterbalanced by a weight which sank in a well, the windlass only being needed to assist this movement.

An interesting note on the economy of the plane was that while only one boat could ascend at a time, the traffic being nearly all towards Shrewsbury (i.e.. downwards) counterbalancing with empties rising was almost perfect and once on the level it was claimed one horse could draw 120 tons with only one steersman.

An iron tub-boat recovered from the canal bed and held at Blists Hill Museum. Photograph 1973.

Top of the plane with the mechanism and engine house against the skyline. A pair of tubs are posed for the photographer. National Waterways Museum, Gloucester.

A rather attractive 'working' photograph of the plane c.1915. Visible in the right foreground is one of the extra-narrow Shropshire boats, built to fit tub-boat locks. Shropshire Records and Research Unit.

guinea subscriptions from as many individuals as would give them to pay for surveys. These subscriptions would be counted as representing the first call on the shares which would eventually be issued. Various proposals were made, utilising Joseph Hill of Romsey as surveyor, who quoted a detailed figure of £47,208 17s 10d for the whole waterway; his estimate was accepted on 8 August 1793. A few months later he was called upon to prepare a small plan of the canal, from which an engraving was made and hand-coloured copies given to potential subscribers. This was the normal procedure and

various such maps are still extant — for their time they are remarkably detailed.

By November 1794 Hill had revised his estimate and it had risen to £48,929 16s 6d. This, in a simplified form, was:

	£	s	d
To digging and forming the canal from the Town ditch at Southampton to the Junction in Houndwell and from thence to Northam	1,082	0	0
To 3 Brick Archbridges in the above length will be wanted with a Stone coping and a Road made over them and Graveled	330	0	0
To 3 Drawbridges for Occupation	190	0	0

	£	s	d
To 2 Locks one in the Town ditch the other at Northam should be built with Stone front and backed with Bricks	1,700	0	0
To digging the Canal from the Junction in Houndwell to the Mouth of the Tunnel	210	0	0
To 880 Yards lineal measure in Perforating and making a Tunnel with a Nine Inch Brick Arch at £5 5s per yard	5,060	0	0
To Digging, Banking, puddleing, lining and forming the Canal from the Tunnel at Southampton to the Andover Canal at Redbridge	2,350	0	0
To an Aquduct to be built with Stone at Shirleybrook	230	0	0
To One Culvert at Millbrook Shore to be built with Stone	80	0	0
To 3 Drawbridges for Occupation	190	0	0
To 2 Brick Arch Bridges Coped with Stone and Graveled over them	220	0	0
To Digging, Banking, puddleing, lining and forming the Canal from the Andover Canal to Lockerly nearly in the direction as laid down in the Plan, this will be through various matters such as Peat, Gravel and Clay and Contains 90,136 Cubical yards at 3¼d	1,220	11	10
To Digging, Banking, puddleing, lining and forming the Canal from Lockerly to West Dean, this will chiefly consist of Gravel and Chalk in some deep cutting and will contain 64,120 Cubical yards at 3¾d	1,001	17	6
To Digging, Banking, puddleing and lining the Canal from West Dean to Alderbury Common which will contain about 130,100 Cubical yards at 3½d	1,897	5	10
To 317,100 Cubical yards of Deep digging in Alderbury Common, this I imagine will consist of sand Gravel and some part of a Terraqueous matter and will make no doubt a great deal of Water, this digging taking top and bottom at 6½d. per Cube Yard	8,588	2	6
To 318,162 Cubical yards of Digging, Banking, puddleing, lining and forming the Canal from Alderbury Common to Salisbury and which consists of chalk and Gravel at 3¼d. per Cube Yard	1,870	18	10
To 146 feet of Lockage from the Andover Canal to Salisbury which I would propose to be divided in to 16 or 17 Locks as the Nature of the Land will admit of which will stand somewhat in the manner as represented on the Plan and Section … and will cost £67 per foot Vertical	9,782	0	0
To 15 Arch Brick Bridges from Andover Canal to Salisbury	1,650	0	0
To 16 Drawbridges for Occupation Roads	928	0	0
To 6 Brick Culvers to convey the Water under the Canal from the high Lands	170	0	0
To 8 Trunks to convey the Water to the Meadows and other places	160	0	0
To One Aqueduct at the Test River, one at Dunbridge River and one at the Laverstock River and a large Culver at the Test River to convey the Water to Lord Stawell's Meadows	1,323	0	0
To Turning the River at Butt Green at the School Farm at Lockerly about 200 yards	150	0	0
To Turning the Road at Dunbridge about 200 yards	80	0	0
To 140 Acres of Land	4,480	0	0
To two Reservoirs one at each end of the deep cutting at the Summit on alderbury Common	620	0	0
To Temporary Damages to Lands and Fences, Occupation Roads and unforeseen Accidents	3,366	0	0
Extra cutting in Altering the line of the Canal at Redbridge	250	0	0
	£48,929	16	6

Work then started and all, superficially, was peaceful. However, the committee should not have rested on their laurels, for being alarmed at various hold-ups concerning the building of the waterway they were forced to call in John Rennie, engineer of the Kennet & Avon Canal, to report on the whole of the works. This took place in March, in June they called him in again to have another look. By 1799 the whole of this waterway was in such a parlous condition that the company could not even raise the £21 necessary to pay for yet another surveyor, John Hollinsworth, who had been called in, to have a look at the works, and it is doubtful whether the final survey made by John Rennie in 1799 was ever paid for. The primary cause of the troubles of the Southampton & Salisbury Canal seems to have been Hill's bad first survey.

One of the biggest expenses which, in all bar a few odd cases, was absolutely inevitable, was the obtaining of the Act of Parliament authorising the works to proceed. However, this could, even allowing for all the trivialities involved, be as low as £500, providing there was no opposition and no difficulties arose, but a typical cost of steering

This is the only easily readable page, hereafter Gothic (Black letter) is used.

and preparing and obtaining an Act of Parliament where it was opposed was that of the Wiltshire & Berkshire Canal at £5,795.

In theory there were three ways of laying out a waterway. The first was simply to own the land on which it was proposed, no Act of Parliament would then be required, and merely employ one's own labour. The second was to obtain way-leaves, which involved renting the land through which the waterway was to run; such a route, unless you had the Parish Council in your pocket, must not cross any public highway. The third way was to obtain an Act of Parliament authorising the purchase of the land required for the waterway. Safeguards were built into these Acts, which protected the public right to cross the waterway and laid down the maximum charges that could be made for the traffic. Where there was opposition it was not uncommon for the dividends to be fixed at a given level, the surplus to be ploughed back into the waterway and/or to lead to the reduction of tolls. In practice there were ways around the latter. On the Glamorganshire Canal it was common practice to make the waterway toll-free for three months or so each year to keep the profits down. The proprietors of this navigation were, in the main, local ironmasters or mine-owners, who merely withheld sending their products down the waterway until the toll-free period, with resultant savings in costs to themselves. They adjusted this free period to suit their own requirements, and did not give prior notice of the dates involved.

Prior to obtaining the Act of Parliament it was needful for the clerk, acting for the proprietors, to advertise the intention of the would-be shareholders to apply for such an Act. There were cases where the arrangement could be nobbled by opposition, the clerk conveniently over-looking such a requirement, which could mean a year's delay before the matter could go forward, and sometimes simple negligence occurred. A summary of the bones of obtaining an Act is that the proprietors must be known by a certain name and style, have a common seal and have power to purchase lands, the name of the proposed waterway must be clearly specified, the number of shares defined and the price thereof. Incidentally, assuming one had a £100 share, even if one had already paid £94, should one fail to make payment of the last call of £6 the whole could well be forfeited.

On obtaining the Act powers would be given to enter upon and dig both the permanent and temporary works. This latter allowing for tramways to carry materials or lanes to give access to aqueducts and tunnels. A clause was often inserted binding the company to the line that was laid down in the plans, the deviation distance that was permitted being no more than 100 yards on either side. Surprisingly, although the width of the canal might be defined as being ten yards, land could be bought up to 30 yards on either side. Wharves were also permitted to be laid down and quite often the charges that could be made for loading and unloading were defined. Some items had exemption from tolls — officers and soldiers, horses, arms, baggage, and timber for use by His Majesty's Navy and government stores.

Milestones were a compulsory fitting in order that the tolls might be calculated accurately. Topsoil was protected, having to be returned either side of the waterway. Watering places for cattle could be called for. These, by the by, are anathema to the maintenance men of the British Waterways Board today, the erosive effect of the animals' hooves upon the bank being all too noticeable. Coalmining was often permitted to be carried on underneath the waterway, a rather short-sighted attitude as was found when the Two Lock Line on the Birmingham Canal Navigations disappeared in its entirety down a mineshaft. Steam or fire engines were permitted, if required, to throw the water back up to the top, of any intermediate length. Sewers had to be defined while the right to withdraw water from streams and rivers was often restricted. To protect the proprietors it was laid down that persons tampering with the works were liable to be transported for seven years.

Conveniently for later researchers, two copies of the proposed plan of the waterway and the book of reference listing all the landowners along the route had to be deposited with the Speaker of the House of Commons.

Quite often there was strong opposition — we have already seen that Telford was forced at great cost to the proprietors to divert the line of the Birmingham & Liverpool Junction Canal, and certain mill-owners virtually brought the downfall of the first canalisation of the River Stroudwater by refusing to allow locks to be built, although they were later to take a more reasonable view on the matter; a further Act had to be obtained by the proprietors which still

A beautiful period piece from a postcard dated 1904 showing the unusual locks at Abercynon on the Glamorganshire Canal. Opened in 1794 this ran 25½ miles from Merthyr Tydfil to Cardiff and, remarkably successful, this length was not closed until 1915.

included clauses protecting the mills. One of these reads:

'. . .provided always, That the Owner or Owners, Occupier or Occupiers, of any such Mill or Mills, Shall and may . . .lawfully demand and receive from the Said Company, as a Recompense and Compensation for such drawing up, opening, putting down, or shutting, such Clough or Cloughs, or Flood-gates respectively, after the Rate of Two Shillings an Hour for the First Twelve Hours, and after the Rate of Three Shillings an Hour for every Hour afterwards, that the Mill or Mills on each Pen or Pound of Water shall be thereby stopped or hindered from working...'

Sometimes an Act would permit the waterway to also run 'Rail Ways or Stone Roads', as on the Brecon & Abergavenny Canal. It is also of interest to note that quite often the engineer would himself buy shares, as did Thomas Dadford in that canal.

The fencing of towpaths was most strictly defined and should they not be made the landowners neighbouring the waterway had the power, after a space of three months, to put up such 'Fences, Gates, Styles, Bridges, Arches, Passages, Watering Places and Other Conveniences' as they wished at the company's expense.

Power was given in most Acts for the committee to borrow money, the total sum being clearly defined. One canal that received two Acts and spent quite a lot of money without getting anywhere at all was the London & Cambridge Junction Canal, which was to have run from Bishop's Stortford to Cambridge. The first survey was carried out by Mr Whitworth under the orders of the Common Council of the City of London and a later survey was carried out by Robert Netlam and Francis Giles on behalf of some private citizens. The waterway was empowered to raise £575,000 and if this was to prove insufficient they could borrow a further £300,000 without obtaining a further Act, but, and again it was a very big but, no works were to proceed until £425,250 had been actually subscribed. It was not.

A waterway which was easy and successful in its work might only require one Act of Parliament: the Erewash Canal, for example, received its Assent on 30 April 1777, and was quietly dug and worked thereafter. By contrast the Oxford Canal works required no less than eight Acts of Parliament between 1769 and 1829.

A very small expense to a waterway was that of providing stationery and printing. A number of advertisements were necessary, mainly owing to the relatively inefficient postal service of that time. It will be understood that at the first meeting of the proposed proprietors of a navigation, the amount of the shares would be decided, together with their cost, which we will take as being £100. At the meeting the first call of

£5 or £6 would be made, and further calls made from time to time as the works proceeded, utilising advertisement. Some would be curt in their manner — the Trent & Mersey advertised in *Aris's Birmingham Gazette* in October 1769:

'Navigation from the TRENT to the MERSEY. In pursuance of an Order of the Committee of the Company of Proprietors of this Navigation, bearing Date the First Day of this Instant November, All and every the said Proprietors are required to pay into the Hands of Mr Josiah Wedgwood of Burslem, in the County of Stafford, their Treasurer, Francis Cobb, Esq. in Lichfield; or Messrs. Ashton, Hodgson, and Co in Coleman-Street, London, the Sum of Six Pounds per Cent. of their respective Subscriptions, on the eighth Day of January next; and the further Sum of Four per Cent. on the second Day of February next.

JOHN SPARROW, *Clerk to the said Company."*

Some would be frightening, in effect 'If you do not pay, all you have spent is lost'. Sometimes the secretary's report would be rather sad, for instance on the Southampton & Salisbury Canal, when they were desperately scratching around for money, most of the proprietors, preferring not to sink good money after bad, either ignored notices and letters, or told the committee what they could do. The secretary was forced to report, in 1799, that proprietors had written varied answers to letters, including 'I can only say I believe we have fallen into bad Hands and that I have no money at present,' 'I decline risking any more money in the undertaking of the Southampton & Salisbury Canal' and that only one man, who was totally ignorant of everything relating to the canal, was willing to risk paying up.

Canal-cutting is the first expense that is thought of, although it rarely accounted for more than one-third of the total cost of any one waterway. Various treatments of this matter were possible, some of which depended on the length of the waterway and others upon its nature. When the River Rother was being canalised, Lord Egremont, who owned a large percentage of the land through which it passed, used his own labour force, which he already had to hand for the maintenance of his estates. Its entire length was 11 miles, which made it a radically different problem to that of the Trent & Mersey Canal at 93 miles. A second approach, again more feasible on short lengths, was to allow the engineer to be the main contractor, he being responsible for the hire of labour, supply of equipment, etc. This had advantages to the committee inasmuch as they had only one man to deal with, but it had the disadvantage that if the engineer was a little slaphappy, or was often called away on other works, or was just downright incompetent, they had no real way of checking. The third method was to let the whole work out to one large outside contractor; this was the method favoured later in the railway age. The fourth, and most commonly used, method was to obtain tenders for a given section of the waterway, accept that which in the opinion of the engineer seemed the most satisfactory (not always the lowest, of course) and leave it to the engineer or his assistant to ensure that the work was well done.

The contract, which, using round figures we will say was for £1,000 per mile, would stipulate some matters being in favour of the committee and others in favour of the contractor. It could be that the committee were to find the materials, the contractors finding the men, or, alternatively, the contractor might be responsible for both, subject to the final say of the engineer. The normal system of payment, irrespective of which method was used, was that 10 per cent would be paid in advance and further sums thereafter, as the works proceeded. Of the whole contracted price 10 per cent was withheld for a period of 12 months to ascertain whether or not the works had settled satisfactorily. Usually a built-in float was allowed, whereby the contractor could increase his estimated cost by a given percentage, sometimes as low as 5 per cent and on other occasions as high as $33\frac{1}{3}$ per cent. If, in the opinion of the engineer, the works were not proceeding as they should, the company invariably had the right to take the contractor off the work, continuing with their own, direct labour or using a replacement contractor. The right of the main contractor to sub-contract was usually limited. Clauses allowed withdrawal from the contract in the event of death of a principal within the contracting firm or, if the line of the canal were not in accord with that stated by the engineer, in which case the contractor was recompensed for the work done.

Some contracts which were placed tended to be rather vague, reflecting either the haste with which the work was commenced or the engineer's attitude. Others would go to the point of defining the type of brick to be used in locks, or the number of pieces of lead into which a gate anchor was to be embedded, or might stipulate that only Derbyshire gritstone was to be used for the lock chambers.

Where the contractors themselves

were concerned, it must be remembered that these men were not like McAlpines or Mowlem, the great motorway contractors of today. Usually they were men who had come up the hard way, perhaps being responsible for the resurfacing and maintenance of part of a turnpike, or the building of the local brick- and lime-houses. Some were later to become relatively successful, and the engineer might take them from job to job, knowing that their workmanship was good. Others would dig a few miles of waterway and than fall back into obscurity. Too many went bankrupt.

The price of bread was, to the working man, the governing factor in the cost of living. Its average rate is shown below (all figures are in sterling, per 4lb loaf):

	d.
1760-64	4.9
1770-74	6.8
1780-84	6.7
1790-94	6.6
1800-04	11.7
1810-14	14.6
1820-24	10.0

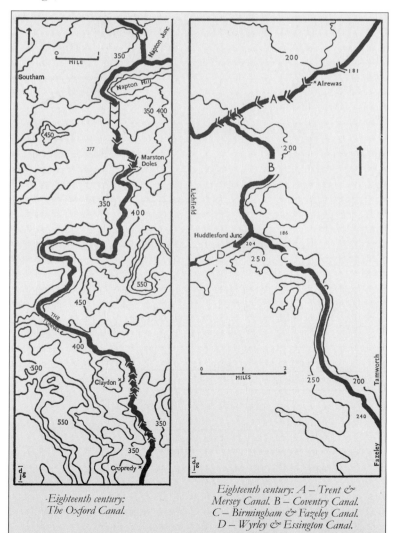

Canals can run with, or against, the lie of the land, and in no way can this be shown more clearly than by their relation to the contours. In these maps (also next page) the contours, locks etc., have been simplified for clarity. All are based on ordnance survey maps with the sanction of the Controller of Her Majesty's Stationery Office (Crown copyright reserved)

Eighteenth century: The Oxford Canal.

Eighteenth century: A – Trent & Mersey Canal. B – Coventry Canal. C – Birmingham & Fazeley Canal. D – Wyrley & Essington Canal.

These figures are based on prices prevalent in London and, prices varied over the countryside, for on 10 November, 1818 we find that in Northampton wheat cost 86s 2d per quarter, in Berkshire 83s 6d, in Oxford 81s, Wiltshire 75s, and in Essex 73s 10d. The local differences quite often can explain some of the short-haul traffic that occurred on waterways, the Wiltshire & Berkshire Canal clearly profiting by the movement of wheat between the two counties. The cost of oats could also have a material effect upon the profit or loss of the contractor. It is estimated that a normal contractor had two horses to every man employed and these animals had to be fed. It is impracticable to give all the economic factors that were involved in the price of works upon a canal, minor items as well as the major could each take their toll. Navvies needed boots, boots had to be made, as the price of wheat increased the miller increased his charge and the flour cost more, therefore the labour to make the boots cost more, higher wages being paid because of the higher prices. The navvy who wore the boots then wanted more money to pay the higher prices for flour and for boots, this later item showing a fluctuation in price from 4s in 1765, 3s 6d in 1785, 4s in 1795, and to a peak of 5s 9d in 1805. It was not only the navvy who wore boots and the men in the brickyards who wanted more money — the men at the ironworks did also. The average lock contains about one ton of iron — paddle gearing, paddle rods, gate anchors, handrails, straps, bolts and other bits and pieces. The iron-master smelting in Wales would find his costs had risen and so all the iron-work would cost more. To make it worse, due to the profit structure of most companies, prices rose out of proportion to the basic effect of putting the boots on the feet of the labourer. Assuming that mining the iron-ore cost £1, the profit would then be based on a total of £3. The iron-master would probably consider £1 profit to be reasonable, making a total selling price of £4. Given an all-round increase in the cost of living of 10 per cent, mining the ore would then cost £1.10, the labour and overheads, etc., the same amount each, giving a total of £3.30. The iron-master still requires his $33\frac{1}{3}$ per cent profit, raising the total cost to £4.40. Thus from small acorns great oaks grow and 10p at the pit-head becomes 40p at the factory door. Allow for proportionate increases in the cost of transportation and contractors' labour, and it will

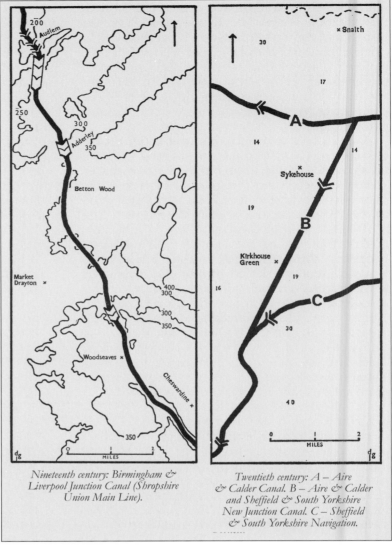

Nineteenth century: Birmingham & Liverpool Junction Canal (Shropshire Union Main Line).

Twentieth century: A – Aire & Calder Canal. B – Aire & Calder and Sheffield & South Yorkshire New Junction Canal. C – Sheffield & South Yorkshire Navigation.

be understood that the poor contractor working on, probably, a 5 per cent overall profit, quickly has his profit turned to a loss. With such inflationary rises in costs the simplest and most obvious way for a contractor to ensure his profit was to skimp the job. However, if the engineer was a reasonable man, he would go back to the proprietors and say: 'This is rather hard luck, the contractors are doing the best they can, everything is going up, will you allow me to increase the contract price by 10 per cent?' He would probably point out that, in turn, the proprietors would gain more revenue by increased tolls. He might also explain to them that to take the contractor off the job at that moment would involve them in more costs, having to employ their own men, find the materials, etc., than would be involved in paying the extra 10 per cent. Telford was quite pugnacious in this approach and he could afford to be so, as he had the confidence of the proprietors and he knew his contractors. Other engineers, Dodd and Giles are two, would make rather feeble excuses as to why the work was not being completed. We have mentioned before concerning the Southampton & Salisbury Canal that the shareholders were growing a little suspicious in 1798, and Rennie then reported, apropos of the tunnel at West Marlands that:

'In respect to the work already done, it is by no means complete, those parts that are likely to stand are ill framed and seem to have been done with little care or judgement . . .In joining the different lengths of Arching together they do not in many places agree, i.e. sometimes one length is sunk more than another . . .At the West end of the tunnel a part of the sheeting for about 16 or 17 yards in length has entirely risen up and the tunnel has sunk about a foot. The whole of this length must be taken out and done anew . . . The sand that has been used for the mortar is perfectly unfit for the purpose, being little better than clay . . .An agent or superintendent skilled in works of this sort should be procured, with an adequate salary, and his whole attention directed to it, not only to see the works are properly executed, but that no improper materials be used . . .'

The engineer, Joseph Hill, was hauled over the coals and he could do little but pass it on to the contractor, Thomas Jenkins, who was told bluntly that he had to put the defective work right at his own cost and that no further payments would be made to him until he had done so. He, in turn, found he could not pay his men or pay for materials and he went bankrupt. Perhaps rather sadly Joseph Hill was two years later a debtor in the Kings Bench prison.

Other contractors found something of the same problem. During the building of the Leicester & Northants Union Canal riots took place in 1793 and 1795, mainly on account of the poor wages being paid, this being an inept endeavour by the contractor to keep rising costs

Alfred Hickman's Spring Vale Furnaces are seen shortly after World War One. This type of cargo is really what canals were designed for — coal, pig iron and flux (limestone) in and pig-iron or castings. The boats were taken out to the coalfield, dumped, the boatman taking rudder, stove, lines and, in winter a couple of overcoats, to a laden boat and working it back, then reversing the process and boarding another laden boat at the works. Birmingham Canal Navigations. W.K.V.Gale

down. On the Wiltshire & Berkshire Canal, Robert Whitworth, engineer and also contractor, stated on 6 June, 1800 that:

'The canal is now open to the turnpike at Dauntsey except for 500 yards from England's land to Chippenham . . .and about 200 yards of the line to the turnpike road in the town of Calne near a mill called Calne Mill. The only work remaining to open Bowd's Farm is the completion of the lock and bridge at Dauntsey, to be done in a few weeks. The canal is cut from Trow Lane to Tockenham and a considerable amount of earth is to be carried in boats, which is most desirable because it is the cheapest mode, and by that time the canal may be made navigable to the turnpike road near Hunt's Mill. Ten boats are on hand. The total expenditure to date is £55,856, this exceeds the estimated price due to the fact that the brick tax has been raised, the price of labour has risen by 20%, and that the diversion of the Calne branch and the tunnel introduced an extra expense of £1,800. Also all coal and stone had to be carried partly overland, but the Kennet & Avon and the Coal Canal expected to be open in three months reducing these transport costs. No difficulty is expected from Hunt's Mill to Abingdon which may be completed in less than two years.'

Even here though the engineer could make mistakes, as we find in a letter from James Johnson, dated 27 January 1796, when he found that workmen had entered his premises and begun to dig for clay. He was a trifle peeved as the company had not even agreed the price of the land, let alone paid any money. When this particular waterway finally opened in 1810 it had cost £255,263 rather than the £111,713 originally quoted by Whitworth in 1794.

Fundamentally, it is true to say that all the early canals were dug by the muscle power of men and horses but this is not to say that machines were unavailable, for we find in the *Monthly Magazine*, vol ii, the following account of the operation of E.Haskew's patent excavator:

'This machine takes the soil from the bottom of the canal, at 40 feet deep, with equal facility as at six feet from the surface! One of them is at work upon the Gloucester & Berkeley Canal. By the assistance of two men only, it removes 1,400 loaded barrows from the bottom of the canal, to the distance of 40 feet, in 12 hours; and is so contrived, as to take up the loaded barrows, leave them at top, bring down the empty ones in regular rotation, and leave them at the bottom. It can be moved along the canal to the distance of 26 yards in 10 minutes, by the two men that work it.'

In October 1793 Mr Joseph Sparrow took out a patent for a machine, consisting of a box with its bottom on hinges, suspended by a sort of universal gib or crane for elevating and discharging the soil dug out of the canal. While in 1796 Robert Fulton, that somewhat eccentric if ingenious engineer, was writing that he had a machine planned which could dig canals and quoted a couple of good reasons for its use. 'But if Such a machine or Any other Can be made to Answer, it will give further advantages by expedition and Set one independent in a great measure of Canal diggers. But in America where Manual Labour is of So much Importance Something to Assist in Cutting would be a most material improvement.' In Britain, although the cost of manpower had risen, there was never any shortage of men and they continued to do the work the way it had always been done.

The first canal engineers avoided cuttings and embankments as much as possible, this being painfully apparent on such waterways as the Southern end of the Oxford and the Northern end of the Stratford-on-Avon, where the waterway will meander around in a great arc to avoid a hillock probably not more than 10 feet high. Neither was there any great attempt to use any soil excavated to make embankments. Assuming that one had a strict engineer the contractor would first remove top soil — as he was obliged to do — and place it somewhere for safe-keeping.

Digging would then commence, the workmen employed on the job being known as navvies or navigators. The navigators usually worked in a gang, having sub-contracted, or undertaken, to shift a given amount of soil within a certain period.

'We now approached the great tunnel, which forms part of the communication, between the Severn and the Thames . . .one end penetrates the hill at the village of Saperton, the other end comes out in Heywood; we turned on our left to visit the former, and saw the shafts busy in several places, at a distance of about 230 yards from each other; by this means they wind up the materials from the cavity and expedite the work. The earth is principally a hard blue marle, and in some places quite a rock which they blow up with gunpowder; the depth of these pits are upon an average eighty yards from the surface. The first contractor received £7 per yard from the company, and the labourers rent it at the rate of about £5 per yard, finding candles, gunpowder, &c., the workers are in eight gangs, having two or three reliefs, and continue eight hours at a time, day and night.'

On later canals where deep cuttings were involved, barrow runs would be utilised, simply a plank laid by the side of the excavation, with a horse-gin, or jenny, at the top. A line would be run from the horse, either via the gin or over an ordinary pulley to a barrow at the bottom of the plank. a navvy would fill this barrow, the horse would move forward at the appropriate command, drawing the barrow up the plank, the navvy guiding it as it went. If horse, barrow or man slipped an accident was almost inevitable. Again, in a cutting, it was the habit of the navvies, in order to save time, to undercut a bank, and not a few were suffocated when the overhang slipped on to them. Blasting through rock was carried out in an incredibly primitive manner; a hole was knocked into the rock, and gunpowder and fuse were pummelled in with a copper or iron rod. The fuse was then lit and the resultant explosion was supposed to loosen the rock. Maiming and death were, of course, attendant risks, for the fuse might go off prematurely, the gunpowder object to the ramming process, the rock not explode in the manner expected, or too short a fuse be used to save time. a casualty rate of one or two deaths per mile was considered reasonable during excavating and passed more or less unnoticed.

I've navvied here in Scotland, I've navvied in the south,
Without a drink to cheer me or a crust to cross me mouth,
I fed when I was workin' and starved when out on tramp,
And the stone has been me pillow and the moon above me lamp.

I have drunk me share and over when I was flush with tin,
For the drouth without was nothing' to the drouth that burned within,
And whene'er I've filled me billy and whene'er I've drained me can,
I've done it like a navvy, a bold navvy man.

I've met a lot of women and I liked them all a spell -
They can drive some men to drinkin' and also some to hell,
But I never met her yet, the woman cute who can
Learn a trick to old Nick or the bold navvy man.

I do not care for ladies grand who are of high degree,
A winsome wench and willin', she is just the one for me,
Drink and love are classed as sins, as mortal sins by some,
I'll drink and drink whene'er I can, the drouth is sure to come -

And I will love till lusty life runs out its mortal span,
The end of which is in the ditch for many a navvy man,
The bold navvy man,
The bold navvy man,
Safe in a ditch with heels cocked up, so dies the navvy man.

Some engineers instructed their contractors that the navies must always be paid in cash, others turned a blind eye to the Tommy Shops. The principle of the Tommy Shop was excellent; goods could be bought in bulk — flour, bullocks, potatoes and beer — and resold to the men at cost, rather akin to shopping in a Cash-and-Carry store today. The practice, more often than not, was very different. The contractor, to avoid having to pay out too much money, might quite possibly pay the men half in cash and the other half in tokens redeemable at the Tommy Shop. He would buy poor quality goods, water the beer and expect to make 100 per cent profit, thus often subsidising the losses on his contract with the profits from his Tommy Shop. The system should have been advantageous to the navvy, for if he started work on the Monday with no money he could go to the Tommy Shop and be given goods on credit, the sum being deducted from his wages; but given an unscrupulous contractor, the navvies' inability to read and the fact that, in all probability, he was the worse the wear from drink, the reckoning at the end of the fortnight or month — on 'Pay Saturday' — might well leave him with nothing in hand, and so perforce the credit bill would run up again.

You boatsmen and colliers all,
Come listen to my ditty,
I'll sing you a song before its long,
It is both new and pretty;
It is concerning Tommy Shops,
And the High Field ruffian,
He pays you with a tommy note,
You must have that or nothing.

With the colliers I begin,
How they pay each other,
Nothing have they but a tommy note,
From one week to the other,
On Saturday when a week's work is done,
And to receive their money,
The High field devil has learned a trick,
To pay them off with tommy.

The boatsmen now I bring in,
That sails from high Fields to Runcan;
The boatsmen an their wives,
They curse him at the junction,
And all belonging to the branch,
That know the art of boating,
Wishing the tiller down his throat,
It would be a means to choak him.

When they had done their Runcan voyage,
And go to receive their money,
One half stops for hay and corn,
The other half for tommy,
Then to the tommy shops we go,
To fetch our week's povision,
Their oatmeal, sugar, salt and soap,
Short weight and little measure.

Saying if we had money instead of this,
Provision we could have plenty,
The profit they get out of us,
Is nine shillings out of twenty,
Then we jump on board the boat,
And the children look so funny,
The voyage we so cheerful go,
till we have eat all our tommy.

There is one amongst the rest,
That knows the art of boating,
He vows and swears a wife he'll have,

So long he has gone a courting,
he vows he will married be,
Come listen to my joke sir,
And when the parson's done his work,
I will pay him with a tommy note sir.

Now we have finished our voyage,
The children look so funny,
For here at Runcan we do lie,
And have eat all our tommy,
Come gear the horse and clear the line,
And jump on board the boat sir,
Both night and day we'll stear our way,
For another tommy note sir.

As we mentioned before, not all the work would necessarily be put out to contractors. Indeed, it might be impossible to get them to quote. Again, sometimes they would have to abandon a contract and such works would be finished by the company. Assuming that the company was far-seeing, it would take on a number of workmen whom it would plan to utilise in the future; thus the company might insist that all the lock gates and stop gates be made at its own workshops, that its own bricklayers be responsible for the bridges and masonry of lock walls. A change of engineer midway through the building of a waterway could lead to many difficulties — the contrast between the northern and southern halves of the Stratford-on-Avon Canal makes it difficult to realise that they were once under the same ownership. The locks and bridges differ radically from one end of the Trent & Mersey Canal to the other, partially due to differing local materials being available, but also to the habit of this company of sub-contracting whole sections of the work to each contractor to do as he wished within the permitted tolerances of the engineer.

Railroads of varying types were an essential adjunct to any waterway during its building for the movement of spoil from cuttings or to embankments and for the movement of materials from the quarry to the line of the canal.

The transhipment basin between rail and water at Moira, on the Ashby Canal c.1918. Coal has arrived from Reservoir Colliery, owned by the Moira Colliery Company Limited.

In the case of a number of waterways it was found advantageous to substitute rail or tramways for part of their intended canal line, the Ashby-de-la-Zouch Canal being one. 'When authority was first obtained, for the making of this canal, it was the intention of the company to have continued the canal to the places mentioned in the title of the Act, with 252 feet of lockage. They, however, adopted railways for all the branches where lockage was necessary. In this case it was partially to save money but equally because they apprehended difficulties in the supply of water'. In the case of the Somerset Coal Canal one feels a certain degree of desperation; after their failure with lifts and inclined planes they were faced with having to build a flight of locks to complete the branch to Radstock. Initially they laid a railway to connect the portion of the branch already built to the main line, subsequently substituting a railway for the whole distance. During the delays in the building of Blisworth tunnel on the main line of the Grand Junction Canal a railway was laid over the hill, goods being transhipped at both ends, but

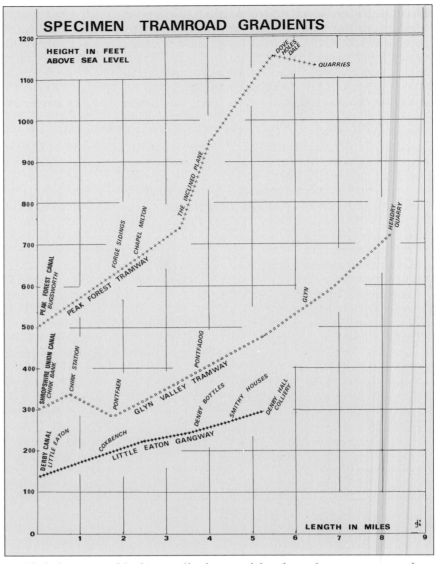

The lockage required for this type of landscape and the volume of water necessary made tramways far more economical to both build and maintain than a waterway.

the complaints received by the proprietors were such that work on the tunnel had to be speeded up with extra shafts being dug to enable the work to proceed from more faces.

The cost of the land which was required for a waterway could vary to a very great degree. quarter of an acre might cost £500 if the owner knew he, or she, could get it; while other landowners were pleased to give the land to the canal company, sometimes being reassured of the benefit to themselves — especially if they were one of the proprietors — or receiving an indirect payment by the canal being 'beautified' where it passed through their land. There is a (possibly apocryphal) tale of a clergyman through whose land it was proposed to cut a canal. He insisted that each of his fields which was to be divided by the canal should be provided with an accommodation bridge to give access from side to side. As the waterway slowly ground towards his land he discussed the first bridge and decided it was not altogether necessary and proposed to the engineer that if the company would pay him half

the cost of the bridge he would be prepared to forgo such a convenience. Oddly, but not unnaturally, one by one, the five bridges were found to be unnecessary provided the same terms were met!

It must be mentioned that some landowners — particularly Quakers — took a very great interest in the navvies who were at work, arranging for a surgeon to call once or twice weekly or paying some small sum to the local cottage hospital where the more battered navvies were sent. In Shugborough House in the Billiard Room can be seen the life-saving set that was issued at the time of the building of the canal; whether it could, or did, save life is a moot point but the thought was there.

'Puddle inspectors and counters of workmen' were two groups of men most vital to the success of any waterway. In theory they existed independently of both engineers and contractors, although more often than not they were appointed at the recommendation of the engineer. The clay puddle in the bottom of the canal is its life and death, whilst counters of workmen were there to ensure that the contractors kept a good number of men at work. Being paid by results the contractors were prone, when they could, to put all their men to work in one section to complete that before paying any attention to the balance. This did not always please members of the committee as they liked to see lots of work going on all at once. That 'penny-packets' were useless on their own was irrelevant — it looked better! Sometimes indeed, a contractor, knowing that an inspection was going to take place, would divert a gang of navvies from the main site to a nice easy spot somewhere, where they could make a big hole quickly; as soon as the inspection was over the men would return to the main work.

Clerks were a necessity, for all letters had to be handwritten, files had to be kept, cheques made out and, most important of all, cash kept in hand, or at least got ready, for pay days. It must be borne in mind that there were very few large banks at this time and a small bank did not keep a large amount of cash on the premises, sending instead to the nearest county town when it was required. If direct labour were employed, 2,000 men might be demanding payment at the same time, and it is on record that the Dragoons were called out to protect the Clerk when it came to pay day. Equally, sometimes the Dragoons were needed when the contractor had to explain to his navvies that there just wasn't any money — either he had gone bankrupt or the money had not arrived from the bank.

These are, of course, only a few items involved in the cost of a canal. Boats were often provided by the company at a cost of about £30 each, stabling could swallow up quite large sums and the party inevitably given at the opening of a canal did not come for free.

'The opening of the Wilts & Berks Canal into the Thames at Abingdon was celebrated there on Friday with demonstrations of joy suitable to the completion of so important a part of inland navigation. At half past two o'clock a body of the Proprietors passed the last lock into the Thames amidst the loud huzzas of multitudes assembled to witness the spectacle. The party then left the canal and proceeded to the Council Chamber where they were joined by a numerous assemblage of gentlemen, including members of Parliament for Cricklade, Abingdon, Oxford, Hereford, Ludgershall, . . . and a partook of a splendid dinner prepared for the occasion . . .The day was spent with great conviviality and harmony, enlivened by many appropriate toasts and songs, and the Company, high gratified, separated at a later hour.'

Fixed Assets of a Canal

'It is with pleasure we congratulate the Public on the Probability of Coal being brought by Water, near this Town, in a few Days; and that the Canal Company have not only resolved to sell the same this Winter at their Wharf for Fourpence Half-penny per Hundred, long Weight, of 120 lb. but to fix the Price of their Delivery in every Street thereof: And in order for the better accommodating of the Poor they have determined to establish Coal-Yards in different Parts of the Town, as soon as possible, where it will be sold in quantities so small as Half Hundreds or less: And, indeed, there is great Reason to believe, that the Price of Coal will come (after the present Winter) cheaper than Four-pence Halfpenny per Hundred; and that the Gentlemen who have the conducting of this important Affair, will use all possible Means to prevent impositions of every Kind.'

Aris's Bimingham Gazette, 6 November 1769

HAVING GOT over their excitement at this lowering of prices, no doubt the populace retired to a nearby-by public house to celebrate, and where better than that situated on a near-by canal — the Eight Locks at Oldbury, the Eagle and Sun on the Worcester & Birmingham Canal, the Junction Inn on the Shroppie, the Boatman's Rest on the Stratford Canal, or one of the innumerable Navigations. But a more regular user of these public houses was the boatman, especially in horse-drawn days. Trips usually started at the company wharf and a day's journey was governed by the location of suitable stabling.

Fodder represented much less of a problem, for an allowance in gauging the tonnage of a boat was always made for its carriage and sufficient for a trip would be carried. Some — a very few — steerers who were on a regular run and whose family was excessive for the cabin accommo-dation used the pubs to stay in overnight. A number of very remote pubs not only came into being with the canal, but were dependent upon it for their living. As the number of boats declined they closed. On the Whilton (Long Buckby) Flight on the Grand Union Canal there were seven pubs in the 1920s, the last of which closed its doors in 1970; the short season of pleasure-craft cruising was insufficient to keep it going. Others, proper boatmen's pubs, which have

Economy in motion on the Welsh Canal at Whitchurch, 1989.

And another view but this time of a pair of boats, each with a forecabin, which could hold two adults or, cosily, four children.

Tyrley Locks on the Shropshire Union Canal in 1966. A true period piece with boat, lorry and car all adding to the time capsule. Peter Smith.

A classical canal photograph containing almost all the elements that still, despite changes, can make a canal trip worthwhile. Braunston and the Lord Nelson pub snoozes on an October afternoon in 1989.

Leeds & Liverpool Canal. Leigh Branch, bridge 4, 1990.

Redevelopment of a public house can be good, insofar as hygienically prepared food from a factory merely needs reheating, seating is comfortable, service fast and the prices reasonable. Conversely because the meals are centrally prepared they have necessarily to be bland and a certain boredom sets in when faced with the same old menu, to a point where one hankers for a good honest cottage pie or 'Giant Yorkshire Pudding with Beef, it may be yesterday's joint re-heated but it is different!
The Brewers Wharf near Merry Hill Centre, Brierley Hill, on the Birmingham Canal Navigations, caters for the local clientele and is one of the Milestone group. October 1993.

disappeared include the Bull & Butcher at Napton (Oxford Canal) although this has now re-opened as The Folly and the Halfway House at Tardebigge (Worcester & Birmingham Canal), leaving this latter canal without a pub for three miles and 36 thirst-making locks! Another hostelry, on the Shropshire Union Canal, even these days finds it necessary to state 'This Public House is open Friday, Saturday and Sunday 11am-2pm and 6pm-11pm' — the publican having other work during the week.

Some, moving with the times, would be unrecognisable to the old-timer, shorn of stables and with yards converted to car parks. Any connection with the boats and boatmen is tenuous, typified by a collection of modern, Japanese made martingales and 'pretty' boat paintings. On the broad canals and rivers of the

north a happier state is preserved and one is certain of, in season, a good fire and cold beer.

The importance of public houses as warehoues on a canal, serving the local populace, is often overlooked. Surely one of the most unusual was on the Wilts & Berks Canal at Wootten Bassett where the cellars of the Bridge Inn were used for the storage of spices. Presumably these must have been for the use of the gentry, but we are told that in 1821 the working class were most distressed through the non-arrival of salt. The waterway was suffering, as was its way, from the drought and nothing was moving.

Some public houses, although dependent upon waterways for their existence are, in contradiction to the old Navigation Wharf or Three Locks, named after outside interests. The Greyhound, the Crown, the Globe and the Praed Arms are all on the canal-side, although the latter was named after the first chairman of the Grand Junction Canal Company.

The vicissitudes of a canal-side hostelry have been many and varied. Some have lost their licenses through declining trade, others following the death of the owner and many have been eliminated by the brewers who have transferred the licence to a modern plastic and chrome palace on the nearby road. The Navigation at the Old Wharf, Tardebigge, on the Worcester & Birmingham was built when the canal terminated at this point, and in its latter days it provided a convenient habitat for the 'leggers' waiting to propel the boats through Tardebigge tunnel. Unfortunately, there were two drawbacks with the usage of this waiting place, the first being that the leggers became intoxicated and some drowned, the second, the logical corollary, was that being intoxicated they enjoyed a good fight and when they extended their fighting to include the natives of the district, the lord of the manor, Lord Windsor, who owned the land whereon the public house stood, closed it, removed its licence and demolished the building. Normally leggers had small brick-built huts, situated at one or both ends of a tunnel, wherein to wait, together with the animals, whether mules or horses, that had been brought over the tunnel. Leggers were official employees of the Canal Company rather than of the carriers or the boatmen and were paid so much per boat, the sum varying according to the distance and time involved. On the majority of canals they were issued with large brass amulets and worked on a rota or shift system, some form of organisation being necessary as the situation could easily arise where all the leggers were on one side of the tunnel. If a boatman was working his boat single-handed he would pay a legger to take the animal across the tunnel, but it was more normal to carry a lad who would undertake this work. George Bate has gleefully told us of one serio-comic adventure that befell him:

'On this particular day my father steered the boat through the two tunnels, while I took the two donkeys over the tunnels. All went well until I got on the top of Shortwood tunnel, there are two clap gates that close the fields from the towing-path, I got through one gate with the donkeys alright, but on getting to the second gate I had to go past alongside the donkeys to open it, and this was when the trouble started. Those donkeys started off at the gallop towards Stoney Hill

with me after them. I never got hold of them, still and docile again, until they had been running as far as the top of Scarfields Hill, Alvechurch. When I finally got to the other end of Shortwood with the donkeys my father was still waiting with the boat — after two hours. Of course, I had to do some explaining and tempers were not at the best.'

When George Bate was alive he and his family lived on the Worcester & Birmingham Canal in a cottage connected with the reservoir, known as Reservoir House. It is situated by the side of the reservoir and one of Mr Bate's duties was feeding water to the reservoir in times of surplus or from the reservoir to supplement the flow going down the locks. His cottage is unusual in so far as it pre-dated the building of the waterway, being purchased from the landowner after the completion of the canal. Another reservoir house in the same vicinity is that at Bittell, it is unusual in being built on an island. To the side there is Jacob's Cut, a short branch leading to the old pumping house, in front is the main line of the Worcester & Birmingham Canal and to the back and the remaining side the Bittell Reservoirs, only one of which has ever served to feed the canal, the other being built to recompense the mill-owner for the withdrawal of water from the local river. Ironically it is only within the last decade that running water has been installed within the house, supplies previously having been fetched in a tank mounted on a cart from upwards of two miles away. This lack of water supply to canal-side properties is not uncommon and was probably of little importance in the days when working boats regularly went up and down and there were local springs to be drawn upon to supplement the well supplies; nevertheless it is of small wonder that lock-keepers preferred the neighbouring hostelry. However, before the days of industrial and farming pollution, cut-water was quite adequate for normal washing and domestic purposes. The lack of toilet facilities is, without running water, obvious, and is a matter which has not entirely changed — not over-surprisingly when it is recollected that maintenance men going about their normal duties on the canal are expected, at the best of times, to use the hedge for such purposes.

That there are sporadic attempts to modernise waterway cottages is undeniable, sometimes to a ludicrous extent whereby all that remains of the original after the rebuilding, at great cost, is one wall. Sometimes the local council will slap a demolition order on the premises and the tenant then moves to a council house; alternatively, if the structure of the cottage is good but the facilities are poor, it may be leased out, or even sold, to someone who is in no way connected with the waterway. Both these states are undesirable, for as each cottage is released there is less supervision of intermittent lengths of waterway.

Rural tranquillity in 1819. The Grand Junction at Stoke Bruerne has changed beyond all recognition since; but the day-boat seemingly laden with hay could fetch a fortune today.

The architecture of a local canal cottage in many ways typifies the attitude and finances of the company which originally owned the waterway. Nowhere is this more apparent than on the main

Left: Church Minshall, Shropshire Union, 1977.

Below: Shropshire Union, Welsh Section, Grindley Brook, 1967.

Each lock not only reflects the surveyor, engineer and contractor, but responds to the geography of an area, with indigenous materials almost invariably being used.

line of the Grand Union Canal, where at the top of Bascote the old toll-house, now in private hands, shows only slight signs of its age in its small windows and soft red-brick shell; while at the bottom of the flight, within a mile, one of the 'new' houses, built by the Grand Union Canal Company in the early 1930s, an excellent house in many ways, nevertheless belongs to the 'suburban by-pass' school of architecture. On the Aire & Calder main line the lock-houses are usually built of stone, somewhat grimed now, and on the neighbouring New Junction Canal there are very attractive swing-bridge-keepers' houses, although as the swing-bridges have become unnecessary the houses are falling into private hands. The barrel roofs of some lock cottages on the southern Stratford Canal are quite well known, but the comments of one man who lived in one tend towards the unprintable, due to the inherent difficulties

Another tranquil scene at Linlithgow on the Union Canal, Scotland. There is another stoplock under the bridge from which this 1970 photograph was taken and a small basin, quay and crane on the left. The Edinburgh and Glasgow Union Canal was opened in 1822 and originally ran from Edinburgh, some 31 miles (50 km), to the Forth & Clyde Canal. D.G.Russell.

in decorating and that great bugbear of most canal-side premises — damp. The 'round-houses' of the Thames & Severn Canal and the neo-Corinthian houses of the bridge-keepers on the Gloucester & Berkeley Canal are also well known.

To say that a lock-keeper's job is to maintain his local flight of locks is both an understatement and is also inaccurate, for in all probability not only is he responsible for his locks but the towpaths above, between and below, the hedges, leak-stopping, bridge brickwork and all the other requirements of any well-run waterway. In time of flood, or during the winter, he might be up all night keeping an eye on the water levels, or he may be patrolling, in the face of the wind, some stretch of embankment that he knows to be weak, and it was in recognition of this that, until comparatively recently, a free issue of coal (upwards of four tons per annum) was given to the lock and reservoir keepers, in compensation for the fact that they would probably need a fire burning all through the night. Although the Truck Acts had outlawed the 'tommy shop' system of payment, there can be no doubt that in many ways the rents of waterway houses were kept at an artificially low level to compensate for the low wages paid. On the other hand if the house has been standing for 200 years its cost must have been paid many, many, times over.

At most entries to navigations will be found a narrow point or 'gut', often taking the form of a lock with, possibly, a building straddling the two sides. This, in one form or another — varying as it did from a primitive narrowing of the cut bank to a solidly-built block of offices — was the gauging, or bar, stop. Any traffic moving along the waterway could be charged a sum specified in the incorporating Act of Parliament, calculated on a ton/mile basis. Typical of these charges are those for the Barnsley Canal shown below:

Wheat, Shelling, Beans, Pease Vetches and Lentiles, Rape, Line, Cole and Mustard Seed, Apples, Pears, Onions and potatoes	6d	Per Quarter for the whole length
Barley	5d	"
Oats and Malt	4d	"
Pack or Sheet of Wool, Dried Pelts or Spetches, Coal, Slack, Cinders, Culm, Charcoal and Lime	1d	per ton, per mile
Limestone	¾d	"
Stone, Iron-stone, Flag, Paving-stone and Slate	1	per ton, per mile
Pig or Old Iron	1½d	"
Cast Metal Goods and Bar Iron	2d	"
English Oak, Timber and Planks	1½d	per Forty Cubical Feet per mile
Elm, Oak and other English Timber	1½	per Fifty Cubical Feet per mile
Fir, and other kinds of Foreign timber	1½	"
Deals and Battens, equal to Thirty Deals, of 12 feet long, 3 inches thick, and from 9 to 12 inches broad	1½	per mile
All other things not before enumerated	2	per Ton, per Mile

Each craft using a waterway was registered in a toll-book, which gave the draught of a boat when laden with *x* tons. Taking this loading figure as being an inch to the ton, allowing for the weight of the craft and its fittings, and adding a certain percentage for dunnage, the basic draught could be 12 inches. A special rod or stick was always held which could be placed on the side of the gunwales, its bottom end being immersed in the water. It was graduated in inches. Thus our imaginary craft being shown to have a draught of 36 inches must, logically, have a load of 24 tons. At some points (The Worcester Bar in Birmingham is a very good example) manning these gauging locks took place around the clock, which necessitated houses for the clerks engaged in these duties. A variant on a gauging lock could incorporate a weighbridge so that the goods discharged from the boats into carts could easily be calculated. Sometimes these would be maintained by the canal company, particularly at a coal wharf where 500 tons of coal might be stock-piled at any one time. By the checking and weighing of all vehicles passing to and from this wharf pilferage could be kept to a minimum. It might even be that the canal company owned the stock-pile of coal and merely held it until required, hence on the Birmingham Canal navigations we

The Junction Cottage at Pontymoel where the Monmouthshire and Brecknock & Abergavenny Canals joined, built in 1814 for the latter company. This property originally housed a vital employee whose duty was to restrict the movement of water from the Brecknock & Abergavenny to the Monmouthshire Company as this was a stop or regulating, lock, the later arrival (the Brecknock & Abergavenny) having to 'pay' the original company in water for each boat movement. He was also a toll-collector, being required to gauge each boat passing uphill and to charge them on a ton/mile basis for their cargo. From 1820 to 1865 two families were living in the cottage (four adults and seven children in all) as duties had been split, one man looking after water levels and the other toll collecting.

find the notices quoted at the beginning of this chapter, and that below:

BIRMINGHAM CANAL NAVIGATION
Navigation-Office, 27 October 1769
'Wanted, for the Use of the Company of Proprietors of this Undertaking, a Number of Carts and Horses, for the Delivery, of Coals in this Town; and Horses and Men without Carts, the Company being already furnished with some of the latter. All Persons willing to enter the Contract with the said Company, will be paid either by the Day, or in Proportion to what Distances they draw, as shall be agreed upon. Apply at the Navigation-Office on Thursday, Friday, and Saturday, the 2d, 3d, and 4th Day of November next, between the Hours of Eleven and One, on each of the said Days.'

Another example of a canal-owned weigh-bridge, together with its tiny toll-house, is at Knowle Hall Wharf on the Grand Union Canal. Obviously, a craft newly entered upon a waterway had to be weighted as an entity, and a good example of a weighing dock may be seen at the Waterways Museum, Stoke Bruerne.

There were a number of fiddles carried out by boatmen and, occasionally, the company might require that the load carried in a craft be completely taken out and weighed on scales. In the case of the relatively soft, top-crop coal carried on some parts of the Birmingham Canal Navigations the complaints of the shipper and of the boatmen were vociferous, for the continual handling could mean the coal being converted into slack which brought a lower price on the market. In an endeavour to overcome this, various hydraulic machines were developed: 'Birmingham, 23 July 1770. We have the pleasure to inform the Public that the Birmingham Boat Company have invented a Method to weigh their boats by Tubes, and by an Experiment made on Tuesday last, they weighed by Scales 30 Ton 09 Hundred into a Boat, and weighed them afterwards on the Proprietors' Machine, and the Difference was only 11 pounds, which Invention is allowed to exceed any Thing of the Kind, and is an Incontestable Proof of the Justness of the weighing Machine.' Another problem lay in the handling of bagged goods, and to this end a machine was developed and actually used, whereby a bag could be slung on the machine a rachet moved one turn and a number would appear on the machines' indicator. If, assuming one were carrying sugar, a couple of bags had gone astray *en route,* the whole art lay in persuading the weighing clerk to allow his attention to be diverted for a moment or two while a judicious application of the foot to the treadle or platform could increase the number shown to compensate. One had, of course, to ensure that one did not press the platform too often. Some coal-wharves tended to be situated in relatively quiet parts of the countryside and it

was not in the least unusual for a load of coal to be discharged overside, the toll clerk taken away to the nearest hostelry by the boatman and, in the meantime, his mate would shovel back on board sufficient for their immediate requirements. It would be illogical to expect a boatman to buy coal, and until the virtual cessation of commercial traffic a certain amount of bartering inevitably took place between passing boats; one perhaps having flour or puree and the other having coal, although no one seemed amiably disposed to the boatman carrying fishmeal.

Wharves, often of great interest to the industrial archaeologist, represent in many ways the history of the waterway but most, with the coming of pleasure-craft and their demands for moorings, toilet facilities, car parks and cafes are now battered out of recognition. The humble farmer's wharf, usually a small wooden staging, has often been eroded by the effects of wind and rain; such wharves dated back to the days when many farmers were one-boat owners, sending away milk in churns, butter in crocks and corn in bags. Cadburys had a number of especially fast dairy craft whose sole occupation in life was to run along the Shropshire Union Canal picking up such churns of milk and butter, discharging them at Tyrley Wharf. A breakdown of carriers functioning on the Worcester & Birmingham Canal around the turn of the century shows nine boats in service owned by farmers whose cargoes were shown as 'farm produce'. On the Grand Union Canal about the same time there were a number of market boats which would pick up fresh vegetables from within a ten to fifteen-mile radius of London and take them to the markets. Milk, euphemistically described as fresh, was brought by the same means and before we scoff at the time taken, say 12 hours to reach the consumer, it is salutary to remember that little, if any, of our domestic milk today is less than 48 hours old when we receive it.

The next type of wharf, of rather more durable nature, is or was that used for handling bricks, timber or similar heavy goods. Of necessity a portion of land would be bought, or leased, from the waterway company and a stone or

Driffield had a navigation to the river Hull at Aike but this was closed in 1947, although most of the navigation remained intact. Seven locks were in use and standard Yorkshire keels carried 50-60 tons to and from the town.
Developers have moved in, and the area towards the River Hull (i.e. south of the main road, A166) looks really most attractive. The north side of the road was quite a different story in 1993.

Another view of Driffield.

brick curbed storage area built alongside the navigation. These items did not, in general, require covered warehousing but necessitated the building of a road. Sometimes this could lead to the wharf being built alongside a lock, which must have been a nuisance, and at other times it became necessary to cut away part of the bank to make a winding or turning place for the boats used.

The next extension to such a wharf would be a short stub arm, leading off from the canal. such arms are commonly to be found, sometimes being used as the local rubbish tip. An interesting example, now disused, is the old Brewery Arm on the Stratford-on-Avon Canal near the Alcester Road Bridge. Originally leading to a malthouse it was subsequently used for the carriage of coal and, to a certain degree, of timber, but ceased to have any purpose in 1900; it is, nevertheless, more or less intact. From such a development would come the necessity for warehousing. As trade picked up this might lead to the growth of a town or village around the place where the wharves were first made. 'Preston Brook, is a hamlet at the foot of the hills, a little south-west from Preston, where the Trent & Mersey and Bridgewater Canals form a junction , it being the place of transhipment of agricultural productions and other goods to Liverpool, Manchester and other places. Extensive warehouses and offices for the different carrying companies have been erected, and a considerable extent of business is transacted here . . .'

The next stage, as the demand extended still further, would be for a boat-building and repair establishment to be set up. In turn the canal company, who might only have kept a small office hitherto, would find it desirable to extend their scope of business, as on the Trent & Mersey Canal where the Etruria Wharves grew from nothing until by the 1830s:

'The various public wharfs, at which the raw materials are landed, and from which the manufactured goods are principally forwarded, are situate on the Grand Trunk

When a canal is almost totally disused, as was the Market Harborough branch of the Grand Union in 1969, seen here at Great Bowden Hall, the snow and ice in the land can thaw while the canal remains frozen, inaccessible to boats.

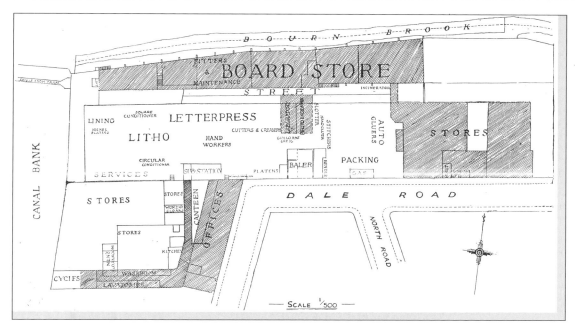

Location and detail of Boxfoldia factory, c.1933.

Boxfoldia Limited were one of the companies that it was hoped would use coal supplied by the Worcester & Birmingham Canal during the war, although the report (Appendix 2) states that this was difficult, previous supplies having been pushed down a shute. With the co-operation of Boxfoldia's managing director and with the help of their publicity executive, Nigel Pedley, research into the company's activities brought to light a copy of a 1933 map clearly showing both the shute and the factories relationship to the canal. A year later we have two letters which confirm another problem affecting canalside properties. The first, dated 29 October 1934, from C.H.Foyle, the managing director, is addressed to 'The Officer in Charge, Police Station, Selly Oak, Birmingham': 'We do not know whether anything can be done to avoid it, but we are having a good deal of our roof glass broken on that portion of the factory which faces the canal bank, and the breakages occur at the weekends. We can only infer that persons must be on the canal bank and occupy their time by throwing missiles at the roof. During the last weekend we estimate there are four large panes broken so that they require replacing. We hardly know the position as actually we assume the canal is private property and there is really no right of way along the canal bank, but perhaps you can make some suggestions to us.' The police reply must have been very prompt indeed, although of course Boxfoldia were a good ratepayer and employer of local labour, for on 31 October Boxfoldia were writing to the Sharpness New Docks & Co, Dock Office, Gloucester: 'We enclose a copy of a letter we recently had to send to the police, and they now inform us that the trouble is not a new one, and that it was experienced before by the Ariel Company. We do not want to put you to any trouble if it can possibly be helped; on the one hand the police say that they will keep an eye on the place and if they catch anybody we will undertake to take proceedings, but if we might suggest to you, would it be possible for you to block up at each end the pathway to prevent the bank being used, or, if this is not practicable, unless you have some standard notice boards which you could easily provide to the effect that the police will take proceedings against stone throwers, we could get one of our artists to write two such if you will give us permission to erect them at each end of the bank.' Unfortunately we do not know the result, but as Boxfoldia were to stay on the site for another 56 years before moving to a £4 million purpose built factory in Redditch during the summer of 1990, we many assume that their representation had some effect.

Canal, near Etruria (which are called Etruria Wharves) and near the lower extremity of Shelton (which are called Shelton Wharves). They have spacious warehouses, sheds and accommodations, and are held by various carrying-companies. A railway, for horse-draught only, extends from Etruria Wharves

Dimensions are of interest, such a craft could leave Spalding, run to Portugal or Spain, collect a 'perishable' load (fruit usually) and bring it right back to the town.

to near the middle of Hanley, about two-thirds of a mile. The principal wharves here are occupied by the following carriers or firms: Hugh Henshall & Co (the company's own carrying-firm), James Sutton & Co (the company's own carrying-firm), James Sutton & Co, Heath & Son, Morris, Herbert & Co, and (at Etruria Vale) The Anderton Carrying Company; Shelton Wharfs are occupied by Kenworth & Co, Mills & Co, and Ebbern & Sons. A large timber-yard and boat-building establishment here is held by Timothy Dimmock & Co.'

The docking of boats for repair or servicing can be carried out in a number of different ways, the simplest being to utilise lines of railway track laid at an angle from the water's edge to a large open-fronted shop, the boats being drawn up with winches, broadside, and being rolled over

Right: Ellesmere Port docks some time in the 1920s. The cranes on the left were hydraulic (water) powered by means for an accumulator.

Centre: Not, perhaps, an 'ordinary' canal craft but this is the Billy boy 'Laurel' being overhauled at Pannell's boatyard, Spalding, around the turn of the century. At one time the Welland was navigable as far as Market Deeping but Spalding, nearly ten miles (16 km) from the Wash was by 1900 the normal head of navigation.

Bottom: Hednesford transhipment basins.

manually if any work is required on the bottoms. The second approach is to use an arm running off the canal, fitted at one end with stop planks, the boat resting on bostocks or stands above the bottom of the arm. After the stop planks or gates have been put in a closed position, a paddle is drawn allowing the water to run away down a culvert. The system is simple but wasteful on water. A later design required the water to be pumped back to the upper level although prior to the advent of electricity it is improbable that the cost of running and maintaining a steam engine for this purpose would have been

One of the worst acts of wanton destruction on the canals was the burning of the Ellesmere Port warehouses by local hooligans on 1 April 1970. Designed by Thomas Telford they were so constructed that boats could load and discharge their cargoes entirely undercover. Once there were acres of docks, warehouses, locks and canal arms where vast tonnages were transhipped. Originally the hamlet of Netherpool within 150 years of the canals opening (1795) the population of the renamed Ellesmere Port had grown to in excess of 60,000. R.Bird.

For many years Thomas Clayton Ltd had the largest fleet of decked narrow boats capable of carrying a surprising range of chemicals, all in perfect safety. The hold was normally divided into two tanks with three hatches to give access and when built new such craft cost almost double that of a standard open boat. Claytons (as a general carrier) commenced operations in the 1840s, carried tar and similar gas works' by-products (albeit initially in barrels) 20 years later, but faced with a decline in trade as gasworks closed and the necessity to relocate due to the M5 passing over their yard (shown here), their last load was carried on 31 March 1966, ending yet another safe, traditional way of moving loads by water. Over a dozen boats are shown here, the nearest motor is probably the 'Tay' (Captain Moore) and the butty the 1935-built 'Pinn'. The butty with her doors closed and showing the style of decoration used is the 'Poyle'. The barrel on the deck of the nearest boat was originally used to store chaff and oats for the horse and in later motor boat days served as a bin for dunnage. P.Garrett.

economic. Yet another system calls for a boat to be drawn into a covered area on rollers or slides and placed in a special jig which enables the boat to be rolled over bodily to a 45° angle, the whole craft being suspended within a steel cage. This has the advantage that the whole of the bottom is easily accessible, no part being obstructed by the stands as in a normal dock.

Obviously, maintenance yards on waterways had a vital function to perform. Until comparatively recently it was normal practice for lock-gates, stop planks and any iron-work required to be made locally and it is sad to reflect that the majority of the old maintenance yards are being leased out to outside interests, often not in any way connected with waterways. In some ways this is logical, as it brings in a greater income and waterways must be made to pay; but whether the extra

Tardebigge Yard, Worcester & Birmingham Canal.
Below, top: Swinging round to the saw-toothed roof on the (then) lockgate makers' workshop. A pair of gates can be seen on board 'Bramble'.
Bottom: The conversion 'Snail' lies at her moorings behind the workshops and stores. Another crane stands by the dry dock to the left.

Top: This drydock on the Rufford Branch of the Leeds & Liverpool Canal has clearly seen better days and equally is obviously designed to take rather larger craft than the pleasure boat kept there at the time of the photograph.

Bottom: In dry-dock at Moorfield, Aire & Calder Canal, during 1971 was a Hargreaves (West Riding) Ltd timber barge. The collapsible wheelhouse is of note.
P.L.Smith

Lock 17, Claydon on the Oxford Canal as it was, seemingly preserved in aspic, in March 1977. The blacksmith's forge and the carpenters' workshops seemed to wait, as patiently as the bricks they were made of, for a new life.

costs involved in buying materials from outside contractors or of hauling them from the nearest main workshops are justified is arguable. Quite often too, these maintenance yards will show the growth and depth of commercial carriage on any one waterway, the oldest building may well date back to the early 1800s, with later additions. They are, almost invariably, dated by specially cast bricks or engraved stones and the dates continue through to as late as the 1920s, these later buildings being built, more often than not, of matching materials howbeit in slightly different styles. Any modern asbestos, concrete or aluminium structures are probably no connection with the canal company. Too often though, the fittings of maintenance yards remain medieval. In the 1950s, when cranes with wooden jibs went out of fashion, they would often be replaced not by modern electrical devices, but by even older iron ones, manually operated. Access to these yards, which dates back to the day of the horse, can prove very difficult with modern articulated vehicles and, indeed, at

some it is necessary to specify the overall length of a vehicle to be sent.

In such yards the ghosts of commercial carrying are still about and most men tend to talk of the 'good old days' when there were 30 or 40 men employed, and busily employed, making and maintaining items for the waterways. The old men also tend to conjure up ghosts: 'I remember old Bert 'iggins in 1810 building a bridge on his own in seven days'. Such improbable stories are common even if real ghosts are not. Any logical person states point blank, and believes, that there are no such things as ghosts, but true canal people are illogical. Most firmly deny that there are such things, and then go on to tell you something odd that happened. The following was quoted, in a perfectly serious book, dated 1860.

'Well, gaffer, yers ago, in the werry middle o' the tunnel, right between Tunstall on the one side, and Kitcrew Kidsgrove junction on the other, two men murdered a woman and threw her body inter the tunnel, and because it wor a deed o' violence, and her life taken from her afore it wor axed fur, that ere 'oman have never lain quiet; but years ago as it wor, she'll appear, sometimes in the form o' a white horse, sometimes like a female without a head; but whenever her comes, troubles sure to foller. Never wor there an accident at the collieries, but the Kitcrew bugget wor sure to come first to tell o' it. Somebody'll die, or be murdered, or drowned in the cut or coal-pit, when that 'ere ghost appears.'

Another story concerns a boatwoman who, it seems, had been a terror to boaters all her life due to the awful language she normally used and who also 'continually indulged in drunkenness and just about everything that was bad.' One day in the year 1875, she began in her frenzy to swear and actually foam at the mouth. She took hold of the tiller and laid it on the deck and when she turned around to swear at the horse the tiller

When the thaw comes it can bring some misery with it. A BWB maintenance boat lies against the hoist at Bulbourne Workshops, Grand Union Canal, one February morning in 1973. Just discernible is the white hull of the one-time inspection boat 'Kingfisher'. It was on just such a miserable morning as this that any boatman felt inclined to 'jack it in', even one's fag got soggy as brasses tarnished within an hour of starting away, let alone the coal and diesel smoke drifting along the cabin top into one's face! Still the sun was bound to come out — wasn't it?

suddenly vanished out of sight, leaving no trace. The canal was searched but to no purpose, and from that day to this it has not been seen or heard of, the boatwoman believing that 'an angel or some spirit filched it.'

Any boatman worthy of the name will tell you the story of 'Spring-heeled Jack' and we relate it as it was told to us many, many,years ago.

'Going back a bit, ain't we my dears, but only to my father's time, when he was working down what was then the Grand Junction Canal. Now you know Cassio [Cassiobury Park] well enough I expect, and you know the Park Lock. Well near there was an old oak, and it happened during a storm this old oak got struck by lightning and me Dad did tell as there were nigh on two hundred keys [windlasses] dating back a long time in the middle of the tree, because yer see it was hollow. It seems the Lord who owned the land at the time when they first thought of building the cut, had in his employment a young and very athletic buck-nigger, and when the canal was dug this Lord did not want it, or the boatmen, and what he done was to have this nigger knock any boatman returning to his boat at night on the head. They had usually had a pint or two, so the nigger easily took their keys and dropped them in this old oak, which caused the boatmen some difficulty when they wanted to work the lock the next day. Because they was a bit dazed from the beer and the clout over the head, and because they couldn't see him at night, him being as black as the very night itself, they thought it was a ghost as done it, and any that was brave enough to chase him never did catch him because he was so athletic.'

Superstitions regarding certain craft abound. When the boat No. 471 sank on the 'Moira Cut' (Ashby-de-la-Zouch Canal) in the early 1900s, the boatman who was inside the cabin was drowned and although the boat was subsequently raised no one would spent a night on it and it was broken up shortly afterwards. The butty boat No.211, ex-Grand Union Canal Carrying Company, does not seem to have brought anyone any luck, there having been a couple of inexplicable drownings from her. Referring again to the 'Kitcrew bugget', we asked one old boatman who had worked the Trent & Mersey Canal all his life whether there was a ghost in Harecastle Tunnel, his answer was simple and to the point: 'No, no ghost but I gets down in the cabin and lets me mate [his wife] steer the boat through — just in case!'

Boats on a Canal

SHOWN below is a random sample of craft types from a BCN Boat Register; 20 times this variety, all of which bar a few — tugs, maintenance boats and the like — were in use for carrying. Obviously some designs played a major part in the history of commercial carriage on waterways, others less strong numerically nevertheless had a duty to perform, perhaps the movement of a specialised item.

Date when Gauged, Weighed, and Measured   21.09.1900
                                  Tipton *Station*

BCN Register No. 17414			
Open Iron *Boat*		*Name* No. 74	
Owner Patent Shaft & Axletree		*Address* Wednesbury	
Extreme Length	70.7	*Extreme Width*	7.1½
Stowage "	62.4	*Stowage* "	7.0½
Draught when light	8.50	*Draught when laden with*	
		38 tons	44.10

Articles on board when 5 beams, rudder, mast
weighed   *Cut up* 10. 5. 27

Date when Gauged, Weighed, and Measured   25.9.1900
                                  Smethwick *Station*

BCN Register No. 17423	*Name* The Empress *No. 15*		
Cabin Wood *Boat*		*Address* Lifford	
Owner G.Griffin		*Extreme Width*	7.1
Extreme length	70.7	*Stowage* "	6.7½
Stowage "	57.4	*Draught when laden with*	
Draught when light	8.00	40 tons	45.92

Articles on board when 5 beams, rudder, mast
    weighed   *Cut up* 16. 3. 34

Date when Gauged, Weighed, and Measured   25.9.1900
                                  Smethwick *Station*

BCN Register No. 17425			
Cabin Wood *Boat*		*Name* The Linnet	No. -
Owner L.B.Faulkner		*Address* Leighton Buzzard	
Extreme length	70.11	*Extreme Width*	7.1
Stowage "	52.1	*Stowage* "	6.8½
Draught when light	10.10	*Draught when laden with*	
		38 tons	47.08

Articles on board when 4 beams, rudder, mast & case,
    weighed   cratch, two stands, 4 planks, 4 stretchers, 2
            barrows, 1 pump, 8 bags of corn, 2 cwt dunnage

Date when Gauged, Weighed, and Measured   28.9.1900
                                  Tipton *Station*

BCN Register No. 17433			
Cabin Wood Tank Deck *Boat*		*Name* The Derwent *No.* 14	
Owner T.Clayton (O) Ltd.		*Address* Oldbury	
Extreme length	69.10	*Extreme width*	6.11
Stowage "	52.8	*Stowage* "	6.7
Draught when light	12.40	*Draught when laden with*	
		36 tons	48.84

Articles on board when rudder, mast & case, tank
    weighed   deck, 5 bags of corn, 1½ cwt. logs

The most common heading in any Birmingham Register is 'Day boats without cabins,' in itself a misnomer, for about 60 per cent of them had a 'hutch' which would hold four men and a stove (for use in inclement weather), but in contradistinction to 'cabin boats' were not (in theory) used for overnight sleeping or to accommodate families. A case was, however, reported in the *Birmingham Gazette* in 1794 when a man of 50, engaged in bringing coal from the collieries, returned to his boat against regulations and perished from exposure, the boat not being equipped with a stove or bed. He had had a number of drinks and death was occasioned, it was thought, 'by the rapid cooling of his body'. It was stated that he was in the habit of sleeping on the boat to save a night's lodging money.

It was these day or 'Joey' boats which then provided the greatest variety in craft design within one general classification, as they do today. One boat in the register, No. 16141, until recently remained in service with Messrs Stewarts & Lloyds at Coombeswood Basin on the Birmingham Canal Navigations. Of orthodox wooden construction, pointed at both ends, and measuring roughly 72 feet by 7 feet by 3 feet 6 inches over-sides, the minuscule cabin mentioned above has always been in danger of knocking itself to pieces in the low tunnel (Gorsty or Gosty Hill) at the entrance to the works, and provision is made, by means of a bung, for the boat to be partially flooded, thus increasing the unladen draught and reducing the freeboard (height above waterline). Obviously this increase in traction is advantageous to a tug driver — all this type of boat being engineless — as the steering is greatly enhanced, and the danger of becoming wind-bound (blown against a bank by the wind) eliminated. Iron boats of a similar class are even more sophisticated, being fitted with flooding taps and permanent plunger pumps. A further development of this flooding arrangement is to be found on some mud-hoppers used for the removal of waste from dredging sites. These have an internal tank with either a 'drop' bottom, for circumstances which permit the discharge of spoil at sea, or a raised bottom, making a double skin. Due to their inherent top-heaviness some form of ballast is desirable; water is economic and easily discharged by electrical pumps.

Nearly all wooden boats, whatever their construction, were fitted with bungs for two purposes other than those above. Firstly, should

The 1950s and 1960s were a time of great sadness on the waterways as commercial carrying slowly fell apart, especially on the narrow canals. Although traffic had been falling away since the 1930s and the number of available boatmen had been reduced, especially as those who had been in the Armed Services realised there was another life, none the less even in the early 1960s there was some degree of optimism. When British Waterways disbanded their narrow carrying fleet in 1963 many boatmen and their families were displaced and although British Waterways did their best to help them obtain other work and houses the culture shock after, in many cases, four or five generations of boating, was to be great. To give three examples. A very boat and house-proud girl went to work in a factory, where her life was made unendurable by the other women, simply because she could not read or write. In another case a previously very clean boat-girl simply gave up when faced with a house and became a dirty slut, with the husband finding friendly faces at the pub better than a stinking house. The third, who was lucky enough to be re-employed on the boat a year or two later, found (having no capital) they could only afford to furnish one room of their lock-house, so they lived more or less as they did on a boat. They ended up a decade later in a mobile home, as snug as bugs in a rug. But the boats went.

Late Register No...............

Date when Gauged, Weighed, and Measured, 13 . 10 . 10

Smethwick Station.

B.C.N. Register, No. 17469

Owner I. M. Dixon **Address** Tardebigge

Cabin Wood **Boat. Name** *Victoria* **No.** 20

Extreme Length 40.6   **Extreme Width** 7.1

Stowage ,, 57.6   **Stowage** ,, 6.8

Draught when Light 7.22   **Draught** when laden with 44 **Tons** 48.82

Articles on Board when Weighed 5 Beams   Rudder

Tons.	Dry Inches.	Difference.	Tons.	Dry Inches.	Difference.	Tons.	Dry Inches.	Difference.	ALTERATIONS. Cwts.	DATE.
Light.	41.75	94	21	22.00		42	2.05			
1	40.81		22	21.05		43	1.10			
2	39.87		23	20.10		44	.15			
3	38.93		24	19.15	95	45				
4	37.99	94	25	18.20		46				
5	37.05		26	17.25		47				
6	36.11		27	16.30		48				
7	35.17		28	15.35	95	49				
8	34.23	94	29	14.40		50				
9	33.29		30	13.45		51				
10	32.35		31	12.50		52				
11	31.41		32	11.55	95	53				
12	30.47	.94	33	10.60		54				
13	29.53		34	9.65		55				
14	28.59		35	8.70					41.60	
15	27.65		36	7.75	95				.15	
16	26.71	.94	37	6.80					41.75	
17	25.77		38	5.85						
18	24.83		39	4.90						
19	23.89		40	3.95	95					
20	22.95	95	41	3.00						

there be no traffic they would be taken to a quiet backwater where the bung would be knocked out and the boat allowed to sink. Like their iron and steel brethren the greatest wear is inevitably 'twixt wind and water', a controlled sinking on to mud is preferable to unwanted perching on

Above: Cromford Canal boat ex-Ironworks, Langley Mill, 1970.

Right: The death of joey-boats. Birmingham Canal Navigations, Soho Branch, Salford Wharf, March 1967. Mainly from the T.& S.Element's fleet; others were sunk beneath the water's surface as the photographer found out when his tug stopped rather suddenly.

Probably on the Tame Valley Canal, and again in 1917, some details of the boats are clear, the ice-boat is on the left, to the rear. The lack of any protection for boatmen is all too apparent. Once this ice melted floods were normal as the locks, themselves heavily frozen, could not easily cope with the loose ice and water-borne rubbish. Waterways Research Centre.

stones which might break her back. Secondly, use of the bung could be made to drain water from the craft if she accidentally sank or was going on dock. Not too long ago an elderly day boat, laden with 35 tons of soft slack sank in the Farmers Bridge flight of locks on the Birmingham Canal Navigations, due to the dislodgement of a piece of oakum. Two alternatives existed after the slack was shovelled out. The boatman desired to have the craft lifted at one end and after removal of the bung, as the water drained out, to let her natural buoyancy assert itself — they will float half full — the leak then easily being stopped; but he was

overruled by the canal engineer who essayed a straight lift which broke the boat's back. After this little could be done except to drag the boat out and break it up.

A second type of Joey boat, No.16211, was listed as a derrick or crane boat, being fitted with a small manual winch amidships with a capacity, probably, of about five tons (three in later years). This boat, albeit with reduced carrying capacity, was in great demand, being still in service in a maintenance role, carrying piles, until 1951. Obviously it had many advantages, not the least being the ability to load and unload awkward

Not a good photograph but one that depicts all too well just how horrendous conditions could be on the canal, especially for 'Joey' (day) boatmen whose only source of warmth was a fire bucket. In the case of these BCN boats there was not even a vestige of a cabin. 1895. Sunday Mercury.

Now quite outmoded as lorry sizes are increased at a breakneck speed (60-tonners being planned) this ecologically kind steel barge of Hargreaves (West Riding) Ltd was seen in 1971 en route to Thornhill Power Station with 70 tons of coal taken on board at Calder Grove Loading Staithes. P.L.Smith

cargoes at remote factories or wharves which were without mechanical canal-side facilities. Fishing unwanted objects from the bed of the waterway would undoubtedly fill in any spare time.

One functional advantage of a Joey boat was that, being double-ended, the helm could be put on either end, thus eliminating the time taken to 'wind' or turn a normal cabin boat.

Day boats with cabins could include a number of classes of craft, ranging from the short boats of the Leeds & Liverpool Canal to the Birmingham area station, or railway, boats. There is a curious difference in the life-span of a narrow and a wide boat, for example craft engaged on the Calder & Hebble Navigation in 1970 were none of them over 30 years old, some that were 35 years old suffered the ignominious fate of being dragged out of the water into a field and being burnt, others have ended up serving as boys' clubs and floating restaurants. Wooden narrow boats, on the other hand, will have had a minimum life, with reasonable care, of 50 years — spending those 50 years in hard commercial graft. Virtually all the cabins on these craft are equipped with stoves, or in more recent days with gas fires, and benches. Some, for reasons of economy, have steel cabins, which being unlined are not very popular due to condensation troubles and maybe one of the causes of the rheumatic and bronchial complaints which often beset day boatmen in their later days.

On the majority of northern canals the cabins are capable of being dismantled, mainly to clear low bridges with the craft when running empty.

The railway or station boats had a long and honourable carrying career, although often outclassed in so far as their tonnage capacity, a maximum of 22, was inadequate. Their fundamental use was within the Birmingham area, taking coal to the various railway yards wherewith to provision steam locomotives.

Others were factory-owned, again carrying coal, running at relatively high speeds. As one might expect a horse-drawn station boat could operate faster and more economically than a diesel-driven motor boat on these short day runs.

Within the field of day boats with cabins could be found the market passage boats, which operated on a fixed timetable through various waterways. The best known, if only for their speed, were those utilised on the Glasgow, Paisley and Ardrossan Canal. In 1820 an advertisement for this waterway route appeared:

'A boat for the conveyance of passengers and parcels leaves Johnstone for Port Eglinton, Glasgow, every morning, Sunday excepted, at 9 o'clock, passing through Paisley at 10, and at 4 o'clock in the afternoon from Johnstone, passing through Paisley at 5. NB an additional boat starts from Paisley at 9 in the morning, every Wednesday (Glasgow market day) and returns the same evening at 6 o'clock in the summer, and 5 in the winter. Fares to Glasgow — 1st cabin 1s. 2nd cabin 9d. Trading Boats on the canal start from Paisley to Port Eglinton at half-past-10 in the morning, and 12 at noon, to Johnstone at 11 morning, and from Johnstone for Paisley and Port Eglinton at 9 morning.'

These packet-boat services were rather more extensive than is normally presumed. The Duke of Bridgewater was the pioneer, his services running from Warrington to Manchester, initially with two passage boats, one being a single-cabined craft and carrying passengers at one shilling (5p) each, the other being a saloon craft with three separate cabins, varying in price from 10d (4p) to 2s 6d (12½p) per head '. . .and it is the pleasantest and cheapest mode of travelling

These four probably unique photographs show one of the most unusual boat workings of the twentieth century. During and after World War One production at the Dunlop Rubber Company's works at Bromford was vastly increased and the labour force trebled. Unfortunately no trams ran in the area and the girls had great difficulty in being on time, having to walk 2½ miles (4 km) each way, each day, from and to Aston Station. In February 1920, after some experiments, a fleet of five boats, each powered by a primitive outboard engine (Hooke's Detachable Motor) were put into service, with a capacity of 100 and moving in all over 1,000 passengers each way each day. The boats now in use (1924) are of ordinary light build of canal boats with sharp bows, and drawing less than 1 foot of water when light. They are housed in with timber, have glass sides, and the necessary gangways for boarding and alighting. They are fitted with electric light, and are heated with hot-water pipes. The inside is fitted with seats, and is warm and comfortable in all weathers.'

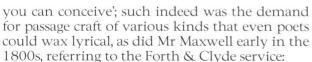

you can conceive'; such indeed was the demand for passage craft of various kinds that even poets could wax lyrical, as did Mr Maxwell early in the 1800s, referring to the Forth & Clyde service:

'For here a cabin at each end is found,
That doth with all conveniences abound,
One in the head, for ladies nine or ten,
Another in the stern, for gentlemen.
With fires and tables, seats to sit at ease,
They may regale themselves with what they please,
For all utensils here are at command,
To eat and drink whate'er they have at hand.'

Long Buckby, then on the Grand Junction Canal when Emmanuel Smith's pair were photographed showing us a typical pair of honest workaday family narrow boats. British Waterways Board.

On this particular service in the course of 1812, 44,000 passengers took the boat from Glasgow to Falkirk, covering 25 miles in three and a half hours; by 1836 the figure for passengers was well over 200,000.

An amusing story is told of a mishap on the Worcester & Birmingham Canal in 1796. It is said that a party of Birmingham people, with a band of musicians, were travelling to a fair on a passage boat and were within sight of their destination when a rush of water overturned the craft. All their paraphernalia, including musical instruments and wigs, floated down the canal; however, nothing daunted, after the retrieval of both band and instruments, they marched to the fair and gave their recital. It is to be hoped that they were able to dry their outsides and wet their insides sufficiently well to compensate. While this accident was a frivolous one, that which took place on the Glasgow, Paisley and Ardrossan Canal in 1810, caused by some drunken oafs, was not, for at least 90 passengers were drowned. The *Flying Post* of 22 November reported: 'One family consisting of husband, wife and two children, were in the water. The husband is recovered, and a child, but the mother and the other child are gone. Another man has lost his wife and several children, and one woman has lost her husband and one or two children. We have indeed a general mourning. In one small street lie nine dead bodies. Some families have lost two children, some an only son!'

In many ways it is perhaps just as well that, other than for purely pleasure purposes, this type of working has come to an end. Sir George Head, a somewhat humanitarian man for the time, did not altogether approve of the horse-management on the Lancaster Canal and in his *Manufacturing districts of England* published in 1835 he writes:

'The proprietors of these canal-boats have endeavoured to establish a theory, which, setting philosophy aside, is surely a bad one for horses; they maintain, that the animal

An almost forgotten view of a butty (unpowered) boat, one that probably 99 per cent of pleasure boaters can not, and will never, know. Grand Union Canal in the 1950s. P.Garrett

works more at his ease at the rate of ten miles an hour, than at eight, or even less; because the swell at the head of the boat is, they say, by the greater velocity, surmounted before it accumulates, whereas at less speed the increase of the obstacle more than counterbalances the diminution in labour. Much depends, at all events, upon the width of the canal, the depth of water, and so forth; but, in practice, I think the experiment fails; I never saw horses more defeated than these, although the stages were usually only four miles. At the end of each they sweated and panted, as if they had undergone a severe burst with foxhounds; there they stood planted as it were, reeling and shaking their tails till led away. We were generally on these occasions very soon out of sight, for on changing the cattle no other ceremony was requisite than merely to unship the eye of each trace from the hook, and fix the other instead; nay, so quick were our movements, that frequently, on whisking round a corner,

Even the most serious of canal users must be charmed by the indiginous life on and in a waterway and the sight of a horse or domestic animal going about their business. Dogs can look fearfully serious as they pass along the towpath, Jersey cattle quite adorable through a hedge and to meet a badger or fox face to face can make a holiday perfection.

Pride, Tennant Canal, 1912. Canals Officer, Neath Borough Council.

a traveller was seen waiting for a passage, and within the space of twenty seconds, from the moment the boat stopped till she proceeded on her way — from the blast of the horn to the sound of the whistle, the packages and our new companion, the owner, were all together gliding away on our voyage.'

Of cabin, i.e. residential, craft it is probably an understatement to say that there were

manifold varieties, as the permutations were infinitely variable. The best known, if for no other reason than their exposure through the popular media, are the pretty, painted narrow boats of the Midlands. Outclassed for general carrying, their movements on the few remaining traffics that were suitable have been stultified since nationalisation. In all probability cabin boats as we know them today did not exist in the early years of waterways when there was little financial necessity for a boatman to take his family on board the craft; for he was, like the coachman and the modern lorry driver, one of an *élite group*, and a good boatman could be sure of finding employment almost anywhere.

The orthodox crew for a horse-drawn single boat would have been one lad on the towpath to guide the horse and an older man to steer the boat. Lock working was almost mechanised, the horse being trained to pull and stop at the required moments. In various conditions and positions he would act as accelerator, brake and clutch combined, in addition to his main function as the motor.

The man and the youth would, on arrival at a staging post, place the horse in the stables and attend to his requirements (if there was no ostler). They themselves would stay at a suitable hostelry, although on some waterways sheds were made available by the canal company for their overnight accommodation. Their wives and children could stay at home in their cottage. Eventually as trade decreased so it became logical for the boat's captain to use his eldest son in lieu of the lad previously employed and when the son grew up and left to take his own boat there was room for the wife and younger children. For financial reasons the wife now found herself steering the boat as it was apparent that economics no longer permitted the running of what was effectively two households, and living on board became permanent. Unfortunately, it is axiomatic that the larger the cabin the less the carrying capacity of the boat, and there can be little doubt that overcrowding did in some cases take place.

Mr John Harris of Falmouth, the 'Cornish Poet', in 1860 asked:

'Seven in a small boat huddled,
With beds, and pots, and cans,
When wintry winds are wailing,
Or summer zephyr fans,
Even from the year's beginning,
Until it endeth slow;
Ye who give laws to England,
How long shall this be so?'

But the statistics relating to the boatmen in the employ of the North Staffordshire Railway Company in July 1875 with two exceptions do not seem to bear out this rather general contention.

Name of boatman	M or S	No. of children	If brought up in boat or not	Age	
J.Butteress	M	6	Brought up in boat	38	Cannot read or write
S.Wilkinson	M	1	"	50	"
J.Curtiss	M	1	"	45	" (child)
W.Taylor	M	3	"	30	"
W.Griffith	M	2	Not brought up in boat	26	Can read and write a little
O.Wooding	M	1	Brought up in boat	50	Cannot read or write (child)
S.Hodgkinson	M	1	"	33	Cannot read or write
W.Clews, Sen.	M	7	"	43	" (excepting one child)
A.Jinks	M	-	"	50	Cannot read or write
W.Clews, Jun.	S	-	"	21	"
J.Curtiss, Jun.	S	-	"	23	"

February 1896 and the Birmingham Canal Navigations New Main Line is seen at its junction with the Netherton Tunnel Branch. Around a dozen horses and 30-40 men are working the ice-breaker. Black Country Museum.

Most ice-breakers follow the same general shape, having pointed bows, a round bottom with a heavy rudder, the primary requirements being the ability to cut through the ice, for the men on board to easily roll the craft and for the steerer to pull the boat back in line when, as they will, it tries to follow a lead or crack in the ice.

However, due to pressure by various 'do-gooders', an Act became operative on 14 August 1877 for the registration and regulation of canal boats used as dwellings:

'After the expiration of twelve months after the commencement of this Act, or if the regulations of the Local Government Board hereinafter mentioned have not at that time come into force, then after the expiration of six months from the date at which they have come into force, a canal boat shall not be used as a dwelling unless it has been registered in accordance with this Act. The owner of a canal boat may register that boat with the registration authority hereinafter mentioned as a dwelling for such number of persons of the specified age and sex as may be allowed under the provision of this Act; and the boat shall be used as a dwelling only for the number of persons of the age and sex for which it is registered.'

Descriptions of narrow-boat cabins abound; usually omitted are the two items which will be found and accepted as essential on any pleasure craft today: toilet facilities (a bucket in the engine-hole being considered good enough for boatmen) and water capacity — for the boatman, two cans on the roof.

For various reasons cabin boats were never widely used in the north, probably the main reason being that tonnage capacity has always been greater and the wages higher. A modern example of the effect of low wages upon craft relates to the boats *Maudie* and *Ada,* both iron cabin boats and now lying on the

Right: The shell of the boat 'Scott' 1968.

Far right, top and bottom: The fore-end of the boat 'Thomas Holt' 1989.

bottom of the Basingstoke Canal. When offered for sale in 1906 they were bought by a man and collected from Nateley where he took his wife and children. Living in the cabins they began to bowhaul the boats down the canal but, unfortunately, a stoppage took place and they had to wait. Whilst doing so they contracted diphtheria; the children were taken to an isolation hospital in Guildford and the parents disappeared, leaving tolls and dues behind them which they could not now pay — their capital had been expended and the enforced layover left them with no money. Eventually the craft sank and was never salvaged.

The average cost of building boats cannot easily be quantified, it rose during times of wood shortage when the Royal Navy, at war, called upon the services of shipyards and their stock so timber ran down. The price of corn, too, had much bearing on labour rates particularly during 1800-50. What we do have is 'an estimate of a Ice Boat 42 feet long, 7ft 6in wide or 8ft, and 4ft 10in deep to top of Wash Boards', given by Mr Thomas (of Walsall?) on 30 October 1834 to the Trent and Mersey Canal Company:

	£.	s.	d.
To 420 feet of 2 inch Oak plank free from sap			
@ 1/- per foot	21.	0.	0.
70 feet of 3 inch Elm Bottoming @ 8d	2.	16.	0.
35 feet of 3 inch Oak Keel @ 8d.	1.	8.	0.
9 feet of Cube Oak in Stern Post		16.	0.
400 feet of ½ inch Oak Sheeting @ 4½d	7.	10.	0.
40 Knees and Timbers from 7 feet to 5 feet long			
@ 5/- each	10.	0.	0.
2 Beams 4 by 12 Oak 7 feet long	1.	2.	6.
56 feet of 2 inc Oak for rocking stage for men to			
stand on @ 1/-	2.	16.	0.
56 feet of ditto for drawing stage to hold the Horses			
and rings @ 1/-	2.	16.	0.
4 Oak beams under the same		12.	0.
2 Uprights to rock, by 10 feet long 5 inch square	1.	0.	0.
100 feet of inch Oak Boards for stern, outboard, steering			
stage, false floor and other jobs @ 6d	2.	10.	0.
Oak Timber	2.	0.	0.
	56.	6.	6.
Iron Work and plating			
400 feet of plate Iron of 14 gauge - will be about 8 cwt.			
weight @ 2d per lb	7.	10.	0.
56 lb of plate nails @ 6d	1.	8.	0.
56 lb of sheathing nails @ 4½d	1.	1.	0.
4 cwt of Bolts @ 4d	7.	9.	4.
Stern Bar, 40 lbs @ 6d	1.	0.	0.
Stern Plate, Thumble and rod @ 2d a lb		14.	0.
2 Guards, 2 cwts @ 6d per lb.	3.	14.	0.
1 cwt of Spikes and nails @ 4d	1.	17.	4.
Ringers, Screws to draw by and other odd Iron Work			
	2.	10.	0.
	27.	3.	8.
Journeyman's price of Building is	15.	0.	0.
40 lb of Strong paper under Iron and Sheeting			
@ 6d	1.	0.	0.
1½ barrels of Tar pitch, oil and grease	2.	12.	0.
1 Bundle of Oakham		17.	0.
Total	£102.	19.	2.

It is not our intention here to give technical descriptions of boat types — these may be found elsewhere — but it is not inopportune to quote a description of how typical craft were built on the Basingstoke Canal at Ash Vale during the period 1918 to 1949. Barges were built on the boathouse side of the canal, repairs being done on the other side, because it was easier to chain winches down to the trees for winching out operations. Barges came off the production line at approximately one-year intervals and there were two main types: 'Reso's' and 'Oddn's'. Abbreviations used to indicate residential boats, accommodating two people, and odd barges with no accommodation, used on day work. Most had transom sterns and would load 75 to 80 tons on the Thames, carrying 50 tons to Woking; they were built of English oak with Columbian pine bottoms. The construction, to Mr A.J.Harmsworth's personal design, embodied many features which had proved to be sound practice, giving strength and long service, and they were all moulded chine (i.e. two turn-up planks) which made the barge easier to steer in the confined channel of the canal. With bottoms of 2½ inches thick pine and 1 inch deal sheathing inside, the chines were 3 inch oak, the sides 2 inch oak with ½ inch oak sheathing inside, frame 4 inches by 4 inches oak, crooks or knees 4 inches by 7 inches and floor timber 5 inches. Overall they measured 72 feet 6 inches with a beam of 13 feet 10½ inches.

According to Mr Harmsworth the distinguishing marks were the almost straight stems and booby hutch cabins with 12-inch thick wash-board for'ard and 9-inch wash-boards aft. Most had iron bollards, one on each quarter. The building started with the laying down of the bottom planks inside the corrugated iron barge-building shed, deal sheathing was then nailed across and floor timbers spiked down, stem and stern posts erected, followed by the knees, timberheads and crooks. Next two turnup planks were fitted and the sides planked up, steaming to give the requisite curve where necessary. Once this was completed the gunwales, coamings and decks were put on, the flooring in the hold put in (the false floor) and the fitting-out done. Some tar and paint and the barge was ready, except that water was pumped in on several consecutive days before the launching in order to swell up the bottom planks. The barge was jacked up, skids were placed underneath and greased. On the day of the launch the barge was lowered until it just rested on the top of the skids and before the jacks could be removed, two struts — one at the head, one at the stern — were put under and the whole weight of the barge taken on these. On the count of three the struts were simultaneously knocked out by men with large iron bars, the barge dropping down on to the skids and sliding into the water broadside on. After launching the new barges were taken across the canal to have rudders fitted, which was done by dropping them on with a chain hanging from a tree branch. The final touches, such as the fitting of hatches and supplying of tarpaulins, were made at this point. The whole operation would have been completed within four months.

The basic causes of the decline in residential craft are not difficult to establish. Disregarding any official attitudes that exist, the conditions in cabins are no longer acceptable to women. Even if they are prepared to forgo their television, washing machine and other domestic appliances, they will not willingly live on almost non-existent wages. The average take-home pay for the captains in 1963 was something to the order of £8 per week with wives and children giving their labour free. During the British Transport Waterways regime, tonnage rates were calculated for all trips on the narrow canals, and a few are quoted below; a maximum payload for a pair was 55 tons and overall working time averaged by then not more than two-and-a-half linear miles per hour.

Detail of ex-Erewash Canal Carrying Company's butty 'Cedar', seen in the colours of her last commercial operator, Seymour-Roseblade of Leicester, during 1967. She was later converted to a trip boat.

From	To	General goods per ton rate	Total rate inc. 95% cost of living bonus at 7th March 1960
		s. d.	s. d.
Brentford	Tring	1. 11.	3. 3.
Brentford	Wellingborough	3. 1.	6. 0.
Regents Canal Dock	Leicester	3. 8.	7. 2.
Regents Canal Dock	Brentford		2. 0. nett
Bournville	Brentford	3. 10.	7. 6.
		Bowhauling 2. 6.	Bowhauling 5. 0.
Birmingham	Nottingham	2. 7.	5. 0.
		Bowhauling 5. 0.	Bowhauling 10. 0.
Southam	Birmingham	1. 5.	2. 9. / Fly money 6s
Coal per ton			
Coventry and Newdigate	Dickinson's Mills	2. 5.	4. 9.
Griff	"	2. 6.	4. 11.
Baddesley, Orchard and Mancetter	"	2. 7.	5. 0.
Amington, Pooley Hall and North Warwick	"	2. 9.	5. 4.
Measham	"	3. 0.	5. 10.
Northampton	Greenford (Coke)	2. 4.	4. 7.
Light running payments per boat			
Birmingham	Amington and Pooley Hall via Fazeley	8. 4.	16. 3.
		Bowhauling 5. 0.	Bowhauling 10. 0.
"	Amington and Pooley Hall via Braunston	15. 0.	29. 3.
"	Measham via Fazeley	18. 0.	35. 1.
		Bowhauling 5. 0.	Bowhauling 10. 0.
"	Measham via Braunston	15. 0.	29. 3.
Hawkesbury	Weston Point	26. 8.	52. 0.
Croxley Mills	Measham	45. 6.	88. 9.
Leicester	Bulls Bridge	33. 4.	65. 0.
Fly Money (General)			20. 0.

Fly working here means working the clock through, although as most flights were padlocked at 7 pm this was obeyed more in spirit than in the letter. One boat captain, lying at Broad Street Wharves, Wolverhampton, was told to go forthwith to Anderton Basin on the Trent & Mersey Canal, a mere matter of 82 miles and 54 locks, which journey he performed, admittedly with only a single motor boat, in 23 hours. On arrival he staggered up to the superintendent's office only to be told 'Oh, the goods have gone by lorry!' Tut-tutting philosophically, the captain went back to his boat and slept.

There is a tendency in modern economics to find that a tug plus a number of towed or pushed dumbcraft, with the boatman going home by motorbike every night, is far better than residential boating. About a hundred years ago the Aire & Calder Navigation, faced with the severe competition of railways, instead of buckling under made an all-out effort to compete by dredging, lock-lengthening and building up the facilities at the port of Goole. All assisted, but the key factor was their engineer William H.Bartholamew, for not only was he a good engineer but also a man of fortitude and vision. Small wooden tub boats had been tried on various canals, but they had only been mediocre in practice, probably because the horse lacked suitable power, and therefore no great future had been envisaged for this method of transportation. The Aire & Calder Navigation had thousands of tons of coal to transport, and a method of moving vast quantities in bulk, quickly and cheaply, would be of great advantage. Steam tugs were now making an appearance, and these, utilised properly with an efficient tub boat, could be the answer to all their problems. The earliest tub boats (more popularly known as Tom Puddings)

The story of the Calder & Hebble is complex but designed and engineered by the famous John Smeeton it was opened in stages during the 1770s as a mixture of river and canal navigation. Never updated to the lock size of the Aire & Calder (despite being leased to them) none the less craft up to 57'6" (17.5m) x 14'2" (4.3m) can navigate from Wakefield to Sowerby Bridge.

At the Bottom lock of Double Locks, Dewsbury there is the Dewsbury Old Cut once giving direct access to the River Calder, but with modernisation this was truncated to terminate at Savile Town Basin. Flyboats were permitted to work through locks at night, and paid extra fees for this. The dog sitting on the lock gate walking plank looks pleased with his lot in life. A curiosity of the Aire & Calder Navigation Company's permitted tolls is that they included Pigeon Dung, Rape Dust (1d per ton per mile), Apples, Pears, Onions and Potatoes (every 32 Pecks being 9d), Wheat and other listed cereals which were quoted at 6d for '8 bushels, Winchester Measure', and 'Bad butter or grease' at 4/3d per ton per mile (i.e. 13.2p/km). A malodorous mixture! Peter L.Smith.

mobile. These hoists of gigantic proportions lifted a loaded compartment boat out of the water and tipped its contents directly into the holds of a ship. Because of age the first hoist was dismantled in 1920, the second to be dismantled was removed as recently as 1969. The remaining three hoists, one of which is mobile, still survive, but although in 1969 one of the hoists was given a general overhaul to ensure its satisfactory working life for many years to come, they are now disused.

of the Aire & Calder Navigation made their appearance in 1860 and were able to carry between 10 and 15 tons each. The locks on the canal had been enlarged to a length of 215 feet and were 22 feet wide with a depth of 9 feet. With the size of the locks so greatly improved it followed that the Tom Puddings could be of a large size and were developed until they became a steel construction, 20 feet long and 15 feet wide and able to carry between 35 and 40 tons of coal each.

The ends of each compartment boat were designed so that each boat was cunningly attached to its neighbour. While in motion no side movement occurred howbeit it was still possible to navigate around bends in the waterway. Towed by steam tugs in trains of 19 the total average tonnage moved per trip was 740. William H.Bartholamew received the satisfactory sum of ½d per ton royalty for all coal transported by this method. Continual progress was made, regular trains of Tom Puddings made their journey to the port of Goole. This unique compartment-boat system and shipment of coal, along with the rise of the Goole Steam Shipping Company, brought the port into prominence as one of the more important ports in the country, despite the fact that it is 50 miles inland from Spurn Point. Five 52-ton Compartment Boat Hoists were erected at the port, one of them being

From the early days a towing piece was used, called a Jebus, to eliminate some hydrostatic problems. It is a specially built bows-only section of a barge and was pushed in front of the tug when the tug was towing empty compartment boats. When the boats were loaded the Jebus towed in front of the train, behind the tug. This enabled the water pushed back from the screw of the tug to separate before the loaded compartment boats. Without this device the action of the water pushed back by the tug against the wall of steel of the first compartment boat, which when loaded extends some 7 to 8 feet below water level, had some adverse effects on the handling and propulsion.

Tom Puddings were, and still are, loaded by gravity chutes, with one exception of note. Coal from St John's colliery, Normanton, some two or so miles from the navigation, was loaded directly from the colliery screens into the boats. They were then transported on special railway trucks to and from Stanley Ferry Basin. The trucks with the compartment boats on top were lowered down a slipway into the water, where the compartment boat floated off, or on if empty, to be pulled out for loading. A steam tank locomotive was used both for transporting the trucks and compartments to and from the colliery, and, by means of a system using pulleys and ropes, for trucks using the slipway. During

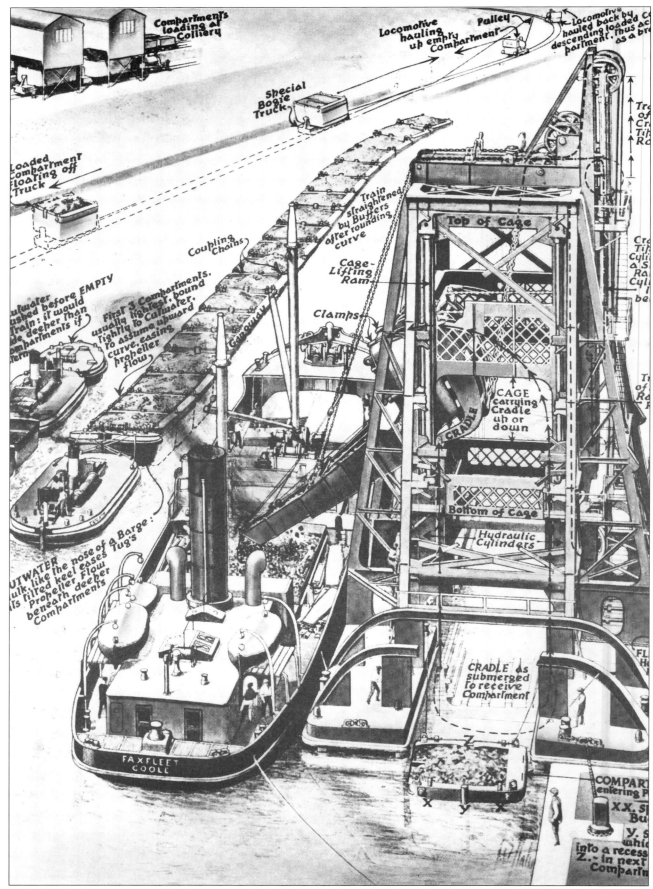

The hoists at Goole were so simple to use in conjunction with the 'pans" or compartment boats of the North-East waterways, but in the 1990s it is considered more ecologically efficient to use fleets of lorries.

This view of Runcorn, shows a good variety of craft going about their business c.1900. The narrow boat on the left seems to be laden for market work with a barrel and two crates of (probably) live fowl. The barge, like the others on the left middle distance, is a normal Bridgewater Canal craft measuring about 70' (21.4m) x 14'9" (4.5m). On the right are a pair of steam tugs, required for craft entering the Manchester Ship Canal. The Bridgewater is, of course, famous as the forerunner of the 'canal age', being promoted by Francis Egerton, 3rd Duke of Bridgewater, known subsequently as 'The Father of the Canal System.'

Goole, as a town and port, owes its entire existence and prosperity to the adoption of the area as a port by the Aire & Calder Navigation. With a population now around 20,000 it is difficult to realise that only 150 years ago it was just a desolate wasteland by the River Ouse. Postcard dated 1916.

Above: The last two Rochdale Canal barges rotting away, Manchester 1970.

Left: At an unknown location in 1990 a laden barge shows both her majesty and environmental value as she swings into a ridge-hole. Media Relations, British Waterways.

1942, subsidence had adverse effects on the railway line in the vicinity of the colliery, and as the expense of making good was considered prohibitive the practice ceased.

British Waterways, who took over the Aire & Calder Navigation upon nationalisation, continued the use of Tom Puddings, new diesel tugs named after Yorkshire collieries being obtained to replace the former steamers. Seven tugs were used with the compartment-boat fleet, six for towing trains and one permanently at Goole used for 'shunting' operations at the hoists. The number of compartment boats in use over the years has fluctuated, the total in service finally being reduced to 450. Compartment boats in the past have, besides being used on the Aire & Calder Navigation Main Line, been used on the Barnsley Canal (abandoned 1953) and the Calder & Hebble Navigation.

By contrast the Leeds Industrial Co-operative Society held a distinction which no other retail Co-operative Society could possibly equal. They were the proud owners of a fleet of canal barges and a waterside depot. Unfortunately their traffic, with the coming of smoke-less zones, declined,

A postcard of the 1920s shows a gaggle of laden craft (including the 'John Tom') laid up for Sunday upstream of Bank Dole Junction on the Aire & Calder Navigation. The lock lies behind them and the Tar Works to the right. E.Fenton.

but since the 1930s they gradually eradicated their standard barges replacing them instead with tugs and dumb barges.

Nowhere can the death of barges and boats be better shown than by the statistics of the number of barges passing under Royston Lift Bridge on the Aire & Calder Navigation en route to the Barnsley canal:

1943	1944	1945	1946	1947	1948	1949	1950
856	674	542	703	124	54	15	4

Nevertheless, the outlook for waterways in so far as commercial carrying of this type is concerned is not entirely gloomy. In 1967 the British Waterways Board considered replacements for their rather elderly craft in use on the Sheffield & South Yorkshire Navigation. it was not felt that individual 100-ton barges, each requiring one or two men as crew, would be economic and instead, at the end of 1969, orders were placed for nine compartment boats, each of 150 tons capacity, which can be pushed two at a time by a new type of tug. To give manoeuvrability an outdrive system, the German Schottel propulsion unit, was utilised. The first was launched in September 1970 and, after trials, she delivered her first consignment in December of that year.

This new tug was, functionally enough, called the *Freight Pioneer*, a far cry from those names of early craft — *Rosa Ann, Elizabeth, Rachel* were probably names of wives or children, others, *Independent, Perseverance, Unity,* typified their owners' ambitions or philosophies with *Live and*

Let Live, Chance, or *Look Up*! Flowers too, were popular, *Tulip, Rose in June* and *Marigold* were pretty enough for a 'rough old barge'. Battles — at least those we won — and the royal family had their share, *Waterloo* and *Princess Mary* are but two. Towns and rivers were extensively used, sufficiently so for two classes of craft to be named after then, but they were not always very imaginative, *Bawtry* and *Bognor* vie with the *Diglis* and *Smethwick* for prosaism. One likes the idea of a boat called the *Hope II, Lord Babs* or the odd *Algebra*. The succinct *Bee* conjures up visions of a light fly boat while the *Happy Return* must have had a cheerful enough crew. Did the captain of *Nelsons Valour* take heart when iced-in one January in 1909? Seemingly so, for this wooden fly boat, built in 1894 was still around in 1971. Like seamen, canal people prefer not to change the name of a boat, although a modification as with *Ivy* to *Hedera Helix* is permissible and indeed *Why Not?* Certainly *Willie and Bertie* will not mind, although the *Imp of Tradition* might object!

One little-known episode in the lives of some craft resulted from their being dispatched from the green fields of England to less salubrious parts of France during World War One. One eyewitness, then Sergeant (Inland Water Transport Corps, Royal Engineers) later Captain (M-N) A.W.West stated in a letter to Turnpike Sailors Ltd that:

'In 1915 with IWT tug As88 I towed two narrow boats from Mills & Knights Dry Dock, Rotherhithe to Calais — from there to Abbeville on the Somme — we had a very rough passage and I was pleasantly surprised what good little sea boats they were. Later on in 1916, I was detailed for a special job of towing floats of high explosives up to the batteries on the Nieuport-Dixmuide front with the *M.L. Geranium* — it was then I met those narrow boats again, they used to go up a small canal that ran through a forest, and load great heaps of thickets for trench supports. The IWT nicknamed them the *Robin Hoods*. I can assure you they did a fine job. I received a special commendation — and so did your NCOs in these advanced front line jobs. The engine was on the top of the cabin. Although it was very hot up the line at times, I think we all preferred it away from the discipline of the base. As long as I got my cargoes to the guns I was left alone!'

One wonders where the boats ended up. Other canal craft were later to be used, during World

This card tells a story.

War Two, on the retreat from Dunkirk. At least one is still extant, proudly bearing a bronze plaque to commemorate the occasion.

Crews on Boats

'In this year 1783...The flame broke out at Etruria. A boat laden with provisions stayed at the wharf there, and the goods, as it was supposed, were for use in the Potteries. But as soon as it was found they were destined for the Manchester market, this simple fact was interpreted into a design of the owners to enhance the price and scarcity of provisions. Word of this was conveyed to Shelton and Henley; and the result was the collection of a vast mob which hastened to the scene of action. The boat meanwhile had gone on its way, but it was followed to Longport, seized, brought back to Etruria and with another boat which had just come up the locks, was rifled of its contents. These were sold at such prices as the mob pleased. An endeavour was made to give an air of justice to this daring act, by handing over the proceeds to the captains of the boats; but the real spirit of the rioters was shown in the attempt made to rifle and fire several houses to other mischief...Two men were subsequently arrested...Both were tried and convicted, and one named Stephen Barlow was executed.'

Life of Joshua Wedgwood (1866)

THE ABOVE was a rathxer grim experience for the boat's captain, but to his credit he, who could so easily have joined in, tried to resist.

During the general strike of 1926 a number of day boatmen found themselves unwilling accomplices of the strikers. Small groups of colliers in Birmingham had leased plots of land at £1 a time and making a 'winning-hole' or 'bell pit' extracted as much coal as they could, selling at 18s (90p) per ton to the boatmen. Obviously this black-legging was regarded with an unfavourable eye by the strikers. Initially the boatmen shovelled ashes and dirt from the towpath on to the load, giving the impression of carrying rubbish, the said tactic also permitting a lower rate of tolls. Once wise to this subterfuge the strikers lay in wait one day at the top lock of the New 'uns (Farmers Bridge 13) and, turning the horses loose, gave the boatmen two alternatives, sell the coal or be sat on. Some sold, some swam, the upshot was the same — the coal was sold for what it would fetch and the proceeds were given to the boatmen.

One day in the middle twenties a boat-owner found that the flight of locks he wished to traverse was closed for an emergency stoppage. He thereupon decided to lay up in the private basin above the top lock. 'Sorry, Mr Smith,' said the owner, 'you can't stay here.' Not unnaturally, for he knew the man well, Smith asked him why. Jerking his head the owner walked around the corner of the warehouse and asked Smith how well he knew his butty (mate). 'He's good,' said Smith, 'he don't go a-baccering (idling) along the towpath, but keeps a good eye on the horse.' The owner grunted, 'Leave your boats if you must, but tek him away — he's the biggest rogue on the cut, used to work for me until he sold me horse, boat and harness. Got three quid for the lot, and

nine months after (in jail), but I dain't get anything back.'

In 1910 the father of a friend of ours wanted to wed a lass. He was a day boatman and born in Pelsall and she was a miner's daughter from Walsall, only six miles away. Their wedding took place with an armed (bludgeons and staves) guard of boatmen to protect them. Five men were arrested including the father-in-law who openly stated in court that he wasn't going to have his well-brought-up daughter marrying a boatman. About the same time, a long-distance boatman, operating between London Docks and the Northampton Mills — wheat in and flour out — fell in love with one of the miller's daughters. There were 60 guests at the wedding and afterwards a new boat showed the attitude of this father-in-law. So whence comes the disparity?

It is usual in this day and age to regard boatmen as rather 'quaint', and a lot is talked and written about their honesty, uprightness, illiteracy, their hard life, their clothing and so on *ad nauseam*; something to be stared at. 'Fancy living in one of those cabins, how did they do it?', something to be treated as a pariah — 'Come away from those barges, they're dirty!'

The simple truth is that bargees and boatmen were, from 1760-1860, basically much as any other people of the labouring classes, with a few of their failings and more of their virtues. They had as much to put up with after 1860 as a 'tied' farm cottage tenant, for, too often, they did not own their own boats but worked for a 'boss' without union or other protection. On the day boats life was harder for the captains than for the long-distance boatmen in terms of conditions and the work involved to earn a day's pay, but far easier for the family as they had a roof over their heads. In the same context it must be admitted that unless the boys of the family joined their father boating they had to go to work in a mine or factory as early, in 1846, as nine years old. By contrast the family of a long-distance man automatically started work as soon as they were old enough to push a gate or lift a paddle and most had only one ambition — if a girl, to marry a boatboy, or even a canal man 'on the bank' (usually a lock-keeper); if a boy, to have a better boat and horse than his father.

There was a certain degree of interchange between men on the banks and men on the boats and, in general, we shall speak of them collectively as boatmen, for the better class of 'company' employees who were engaged in maintenance work could hop on a tug and go off for a couple of days, handling the tug as well as the regular boatman could. Again for the purpose of clarity, we do not propose to distinguish between boatmen and bargees, all men who worked on, in and about inland waterways had many things in common.

Some were dependable:
'We, the underwritten, being the Engineer, Inspector, Foremen, Hagmasters and Workingmen , employed on the works of the Grand Junction Canal, highly sensible of the blessings of our free Constitution and truly loyal to our King, think ourselves called upon, as Englishmen, to stand forth in support of our Laws and Property, and that of our Honourable Employers: and do therefore, associate, under the following Rules and Articles, which we request our worthy Engineer, Mr Barnes, to transmit in our names, and on our behalf, to the Marquis of Buckingham, Lord Lieutenant of the County of Buckingham, with our loyal request that he will lay it before the King, with our firmest assurances that we will spill the last drop of our blood, in the cause of Old England, against all foreign and Domestic Enemies.'

Some were jolly if we are to believe the evidence of a china plate held by a boatman friend of ours:
Pickford, Beach and Snell's, are jolly lads & true ones:
Kenworthy & Worthington's you'll likewise find true blue ones:
Wakeman, Green & Ames, amiss you'll never find Sirs,
Holt's Crocket & Salkeld's will sail fast as the wind Sirs,
True harted & jolly ones you'll find with Heath & Crawley,
Sturland's Henshall's, Alkins too, can likewise

Numerous methods of toll evasion existed, this was just one. For comparative purposes the stone would carry a toll of 25p per ton per mile, the pipes £2. Some short workings could miss tollhouses entirely, but paid a low bulk rate if declared honestly. Like passengers and rail conductors today a state of war existed between boatman and toll-collector! Waterways Museum, Stoke Bruerne.

COVENTRY CANAL NAVIGATION.

CAUTION.

On FRIDAY, the 17th day of MAY inst., HENRY WOODWARD, the Steerer of a Boat, was brought before the County Magistrates, at Coventry, charged with endeavouring to

EVADE THE TOLL

PAYABLE TO THE

COVENTRY CANAL COMPANY,

In respect of several Cases of Pipes which he had secreted in his Boat laden with Road Stone, on the 1st instant, and was CONVICTED of the offence, and fined in the mitigated

Penalty of 1s., and £1. 0s. 6d. expenses.

THIS IS TO GIVE NOTICE

That all Persons offending in a similar manner will be proceeded against under the Bye-Laws of the above Company, and the whole PENALTY OF FIVE POUNDS prescribed by the same sued for, and in addition

THE WHOLE OF THE CARGO IN THE BOAT,

Although partly consisting of Road Stone, will be

Charged with Tonnage.

BY ORDER,

CHARLES WOODCOCK,

CLERK TO THE COVENTRY CANAL COMPANY.

Coventry, May 25th, 1861.

use their mauley,
So likewise can the Boatmen all, & drink their can of flip, Sirs,
They'll drink there grog, & toast their lass, & then thay'll Crack their whip Sirs.

Some were viewed askance: 'The boater has not the intellectual quickness of the London thief; but his purely animal life, devoid of all spiritual and almost all social influences, has produced in him a low and coarse animalism.' Some had a rough old working life in the bowels of a colliery or tin mine, moving boats by hand from the working face to the transhipment point from whence another boatman would pick it up.

'The mode of entrance was by means of a bucket in which I was let down to a depth of 70 yards, when we come to a canal, which runs for a considerable distance in a subterranean channel . . .at this canal I got into a barge . . .which was made to advance by the boatman pushing against small staples fastened to the roof . . .in this way I travelled more than ½ mile . . .having returned to the barge I was landed about ½ mile further at another mine.'

Yet another class of boatman who had to haul his boat along staples or pegs was the tub boatman employed in Somerset and Devon, where the canals abounded in tunnels but were bereft of leggers.

With the virtual cessation of commercial

The very end of regular, historical, narrow boat carrying came in 1970 when, as can be seen, the butty 'Ara' was discharged at Dickinson's Paper Mill, Croxley. M.Black.

Trent Navigation Company
CONDITIONS OF SERVICE.

A uniform weekly wage (per week of 7 Days) will be paid, as per scale below, and no Voyage Money.

All Boatmen will work to the order of the Foreman at Hull, Newark or Nottingham, or of the Tug Captain as the case may be.

Hull Boatmen will not be expected to work on any boat but their own when at Hull, nor when at Newark, until after the expiration of 24 hours after their arrival at Nether Lock.

All Boatmen will assist when required in any lightening or discharging which may have to be done on the passage up or down.

Sunday work will be required only when the tide or other circumstances render it necessary. The Foreman or Tug Captain to decide when such work is necessary.

Horsemen will (subject to the rules of the stable) work to the instructions of the Foreman, or, when on a journey to those of the Captain of the Boat.

SCALE OF WAGES.

HULL BOATS	Captains,	30s.	per week of 7 days.
DITTO	Mates,	24s.	,,	,,
LIGHTERS	Captains,	24s.	,,	,,
DITTO	Mates,	21s.	,,	,,
HORSEMEN,	- -	24s.	,,	,,

When the Tug, Boat or Horse with which any Man is engaged is detained for a longer period than three days owing to ice, flood, fog or wind, such Man will be paid one-half his usual rate of wages, after the expiration of such period of three days while he continues to be engaged with such tug, boat or horse.

Seven days' notice on either side to be taken or given in order to terminate the service. Such notice to expire on any Thursday.

February, 1895.   BY ORDER.

traffics over the majority of the country's canals, a large number of boatmen have been forced to take jobs on the bank with the various nationalised bodies that have had control over the waterways, or they go into a factory. Some are successful, ending up as a tug driver, with the dredging team or working for a hire-boat company. A very few boatmen have been, or are, on the canal simply because they know no other life. George Harris, who at one time or another has worked for every carrying company, told us one day:

'To be quite honest with you we went back boating because we couldn't find nowhere to live, and that was the only way to get somewhere. I think that even now if a good many of these boat-people could get a house they wouldn't be boating, although you get a good many who can't settle down on the land, I mean a boatman don't like regular work, and another thing, if a boatman was to go over to the factory to work they have a foreman over them, which they have never been used to. I mean, they have always been used to their own life and their own tinpot way of going about and they won't be told.'

Some canal men favoured charging up and down one route, the Shroppie perhaps, loading oil at Ellesmere Port and running to the depot at Wolverhampton, a nice easy three days' journey. Or they might prefer the coal run from the collieries on the Coventry Canal to Dickinsons Paper Mill and back, ten days for the round trip. Others roamed the canals and if there were any odd jobs, whether it be at Market Harborough, Nottingham, up the Erewash or on to the Leeds & Liverpool Canal, all were grist to their mill. Some boatmen would never go near the Manchester Ship Canal, while others found some pleasure in being towed, five or six pairs behind a tug, across to No.9 Dock for loading. One boatman's claim was that he had been on every waterway, barring the Droitwich Canal, working at various times for the Severn & Canal Carrying Company

operating out of Gloucester, Samuel Barlows out of Braunston on the Grand Union Canal, S.E.Barlow at Glascote on the Coventry Canal, F.B.Lycett & Son from Sneyd Wharf on the Birmingham Canal Navigations, Willow Wren Canal Carrying Company from Hayes Wharf, London, the Anderton Canal Carrying Company from Northwich and Kellogg's from Manchester. In the process he garnered a wife and four children and, to add a little variety to his life, picked up four 'deaders' on his propeller, one at Leighton Buzzard (Beds.), two near Worcester and one at Walsall. He had a brother scalded to death on a barge whilst laid up at the 'Starvation Buoys' on the Thames. He had worked under various systems of payment on a regular wage, on trip money, or a combination of both and the one liked least where the company deducted £5 per week from the wages, theoretically placing it in the bank to cover the provision of and loss of equipment; for the boats were hired out on a bare-bones charter to the boatmen who were responsible for providing their own ropes, cans, chimneys, diesel fuel and even if they broke a shaft they paid for it — 'If your engine blew up you came awfully near to being bankrupt.' As recently as the late 1950s wages for a week's hard work could be only £6, and the next week £28, and then perhaps nothing for three or four weeks.

Canal boating has its own perils and compensations. During World War Two one pair of boatmen working for Fellows, Morton & Clayton, loaded up with aluminium and were ambling along peacefully on a moonlit night on the Shropshire Union Canal when a German hit-and-run raider dropped a few bombs near enough to shake them. It was not until they reached Birmingham and had their ears pulled that they found out that because they had not clothed up (being under instructions to take the aluminium through at once if not sooner) the aluminium ingots had created a beautiful mirror. A number of boats were lost during the bombing of London docks, including the wooden motor boat *Robin* at Limehouse. Fortunately the crews were lurking under a crane at the time.

Boatmen have, among people who know no better, a reputation for being taciturn when going about their occupation and garrulous when in a public house, perhaps the truth lies between the two. One boatman friend of ours, still alive, has probably committed most of the sins in the calendar at one time or another, petty pilfering, absconding with debts, fighting and saying 'rhubarb' to authority, but he had never drunk a drop of alcoholic liquor in his life. 'Boatmen,' said another to us one day, 'are the friendliest people imaginable — amongst themselves!' On the other hand, "The first salutation a boater meets you with is, "Gaffer, wat's the time o' day? Can you gie us a match to light one's pipe?" and if you oblige them in that or any other little thing, you have won them over, and after this they will be very open and free, and will fight to death for you, if need be. " Some, like most householders, take enormous pride in their home, their boat.

'The spotless neatness of the little cabin, and the last polish bestowed on the brass fittings, are characteristics they frequently have in common with the pleasure yachts of our upper circles. It seems that only on the water can one learn how brilliant a polish brass will take...The exterior decoration of these boats is noticeable, and evinces the pride taken in their appearance by the owners, who repaint them with the gayest colours as often as they can afford to do so. On the outside of the cabins are painted two or four landscapes

Canals as they were built to be used. Motorboat 'Jaguar' and butty 'Achilles' laden with 52 tons of coal about to leave Winkwell Top Lock, on the Grand Union Canal, in April 1969. Professional handling and well kept boats. M.Black

Norbury Junction, Shropshire Union Canal an the motor boat 'Alton', owned by the Narrow Boat Trust is en route to the River Weaver with domestic coal in September 1976. The steerer is Martyn Denney.

(usually river-scenes) of which they are proud enough . . .The smartness of the cabin part of the barge is often the more striking, from the fact that the load it bears is of a very opposite character, as coal, which is perhaps the most common freight.'

Others were perhaps not so particular, either in painting or sanitary habits.

'Their habits are filthy and disgusting beyond conception. I have frequently seen women in a half nude state washing over the sides of the boat as it was moving along, out of the water of the canal, upon the top of which has been floating all manner of filth. They wash their clothes - those that do wash - out of the canal water, and instead of being white, or near to it, they look as if they had been drawn through a mud hole, wrung, and hung out upon the boat line to dry . . .Swearing and drunkenness seem to be the two ruling passions . . .Swearing is taught to the children before anything else; nearly every sentence begins with an oath, and finishes with blasphemy . . .The women are coarse and vulgar, and, if anything, can outdo the men in resorting to obscene language and disgusting conversation.'

However, to put this kind of report in perspective one must not forget the conditions existing in, say, a Leeds slum:

'With broken panes in every window-frame, and filth and vermin in every nook. with the walls unwhitewashed for years, black with the smoke of foul chimneys, without water, with corded bed-stocks for beds, and sacking for bed clothing, with floors unwashed from

Motor boat 'Thaxted' and butty 'Betelgeuse' together with their proud crew in the 1950s. (P.Garrett).

year to year, without offices . . .while without, there are streets, elevated a foot, sometimes two, above the level of the causeway by the accumulation of years, and stagnant puddles here and there, with their foetid exhalations, and excrementitious deposits on all sides as a consequence, undrained, unpaved, unventilated, uncared for by any authority but the landlord, who weekly collects his miserable rents from his miserable tenants.'

The human hand seen under a microscope is one mass of living, heaving, life, no matter whether you use 'Sprightly Snow' or 'Purple Yamac' and there are still a number of houses where neither is used and where bugs are to be found. Even in the 1970s there have been found places where babes were playing on the floor while little white maggots ambled up and down between the floorboards. In the close confines of a cabin such uncalled-for livestock make their proximity terribly uncomfortable and the practice when taking over a 'change-boat,'the boatman's regular motor boat or butty boat being under repair, was to ensure that it had been fumigated.

In the early 1870s there were a number of 'do-

Braunston 1963 and the boats look dull and drab after the great freeze of 1962-3 which decimated the state-owned fleet. Few, if any, boats were able to move for 13 weeks and the new British Waterways Board, as successors to the British Transport Commission on 1 January 1963, were able to be rid of all bar a handful. (M.Webb).

gooders' who found that their presence in the emergent nations was unpopular and so they turned their attention to canal people. One found it astonishing to hear 'You must look for yourself, or you will get pitched into the cut' when he asked such questions as, 'When was your boat bugged and cleaned?,' 'Do you tie up on Sundays?', 'Can you read and write?', 'How is it you stare so?' and 'Why is your horse so thin and can scarcely walk along?' Some of the nitwits

Virtually every type of river craft is visible here behind the sailing ship including trows, lighters and a narrow boat. The hulks on the right are rather sad. Collection B.A.Lane.

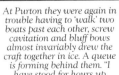

At Purton they were again in trouble having to 'walk' two boats past each other, screw cavitation and bluff bows almost invariably drew the craft together in ice. A queue is forming behind them. "I have stood for hours up forward as look out. In freezing weather I have been so cold I have had a hard job to get warm again . . .Our feet seemed always to become the coldest. I have been dressed in layers of overcoats, balaclavas, scarves and gloves and still become miserably cold".

Top left: Decks were always cleaned of salt, mud and sand between Sharpness Old Dock and Purton bridges, often at 5am, and never later than first light. B.A.Lane *Top, centre left and below:* The same scene in the winter of 1962-63 and (315) looking aft. 'Regent Swift' was one of the 'small' (Stourport) tankers. B.A.Lane. *Top, centre right:* When the canal had frozen hard . . .I remember trying to pass a loaded vessel when I was negotiating the canal and was empty. The ice was piling up in front of him and under the bow of my vessel until it stopped us both. Then we had to get in touch with the nearest bridgeman and have a tug sent to our assistance. He had to break the ice and pull one of use past the other.'Top, right: At The Pilot Captain Lane stands in the middle of the Severn one day in winter 1962-63. At least his load (50 tons of petroleum spirit) was unlikely to freeze. *Above:* Running trials with the Regent Robin, newly built at Charles Hills yard, Bristol. A few years work and the plating will give between the knees, rust (that insidious enemy) will make its mark, and anything that cannot be folded down will have been swept overboard. Collection B.A.Lane.

Severn Tanking *is the title of a book by Captain Basil Lane (published by The Forest Bookshop, Coleford, Gloucestershire) and one which gives a view of river work that can never be replicated. The following photographs are reproduced with the permission of both Captain Lane and his publishers. Normal 'static' photographs cannot capture the sheer variety of conditions met on a day to day basis as, for example, few passengers clutching a camera would have been on board an iced-in canal-boat, let alone one halfway up the Severn.*

As a navigation the first Act to regulate the river was passed in 1503 while others of 1531 and 1772 were 'for making and keeping in repair a Road or Passage for Horses…between Bewdley Bridge and Coalbrook Dale.' Thirty years later the length of towing path had shrunk to between Bewdley Bridge and 'the Deep Water, at Diglis, below the city of Worcester.' Strangely bearing in mind that gangs of men were normally used to tow barges and trows 'Vessels Haled by Men' were exempt from towpath tolls. Apropos of the 'Deep Water', the river-going canal boatmen always reckoned the half-mile from the racecourse to the Dog & Duck Ferry was the deepest stretch. But realistically it was not until the coming of steam tugs and self-propelled barges that the Severn men could carry the loads with ease in both directions.

The tankers started operating to Gloucester in 1925 and to Worcester and Stourport in 1927. Lock dimensions limited craft working to Worcester to 137' (41.8m) 22' beam (6.7m) and a draught of 8'0" (2.44m) while the smaller boats working upstream to Stourport could not exceed 89' (27.1m) long x 18'11" (5.8m), the dimensions of Bevere Lock. Captain Lane saw the traffic at its heaviest through the war until 1945, when the network of pipelines and the development of a means of pumping different fuels through the same pipe without contamination led to a decline. By 1967 there were 'about seven of us that stayed to the end, aboard the only three craft left that were working. The 'Regent Wren' running to Gloucester and the 'Regent Robin' and 'Swift' to Stourport. Then very suddenly, they were moored up with the others in the old dock at Sharpness until they were sold.'

'There was no room for mistakes. Everything was done with commonsense and good judgement. To dock at Sharpness fully loaded was a very tricky business, especially if there was a big tide. It was as much as we could do to hold the craft in the flow of the tide. We would come up the river, arrive off Berkeley Pill and then swing between either the Berkeley Pill and Sharpness (There is a navigation light here termed the swinging light). Then we would head in towards the shore. In the run of a 30 feet tide. Our speed was only about six knots, or about four knots if we were towing. We then dropped with the tide, or held close to the shore to wait and watch for the signal for us to dock into Sharpness. The signal was hanging on the yard arm, or if it was after dark, a light shone on the signal mast. When we saw the signal to dock, we had to pull out into the tide and gently drop back. We would then skim the South Pier with our bow, and pull into the lock waters behind the Pier…Then we would give the engines everything we had to pull into sharpness. We then skimmed the South Pier with our bow, we were never more than a foot from it.'

Previous page, bottom right, upper: "Never again will any craft go out of Gloucester docks without locking. On an occasion of record floods, I once took the 'Regent Jill' out of Gloucester dock into the flooded River Severn. The water in the dock and the canal was level with the river and all four lock gates were open. Following me out that day was the 'Regent Lady', then the 'Regent Swift' …After the three craft had cleared the lock, the lock gates were closed. Then the river stop gates were put into place as the river was still rising, and within the hour it was three inches higher than the dock and canal.' 2 April 1955. The low freeboard of these craft (6"-12"/15-30cm) led to their nickname of Severn Submarines. Gloucester Citizen; lower: From a polaroid but unrepeatable, 'Regent Wren' pushing up through Worcester Bridge with negligable clearance. The power station behind has long since been demolished. B.A.Lane.

who went around making inquiries (their descendants are still employed in the nationalised industries today!) were fired with a religious belief. Edgar Wallace in his Sanders of the River novels castigated the missionaries who went out to teach the heathen about Christianity, omitting to acquire such fundamental requirements as a knowledge of the native language and the local customs. They preached to boat people in the same manner and having an axe to grind they chose the least salubrious craft and crews to question. In 1874 one such made the profound statement that 'For many years the name of 'Bargee' has been synonymous with ignorance, coarse vulgarity, and even murderous brutality', and, appealing to Victorian virtue, his conclusion was that:

'We shall, as a nation, have something to answer for some day for neglecting to protect the boatwomen and children. We seem to forget that in taking care of the children we are also providing for our own safety. We seem to forget that in taking care of the children we are giving physical stamina to future generations, instead of propagating a race of short, stunted, decrepit, pale, sickly men and women, who become aged at 50 … Let us take timely warning, and rescue these miserable women and children from the physical degradation, moral pollution, and unhealthy atmosphere they have to endure in those hot, damp, close, stuffy, buggy, filthy and stinking holes called boat cabins.'

By 1879 matters had obviously reached a climax:

'The boat system of inland navigation has gone on increasing year by year, until at the present time it presents one complete network running through the length and breadth of the land, from the centre to the circumference, of something like 4,710 miles in length. On its surface are over 25,000 boats, carrying human beings of all ages, together with filth, mud, manure, and the refuse of our large towns. Some of the cabins are models of neatness, and a man and two youths might pass a few nights in such very comfortably. Others are the most filthy holes imaginable; what with bugs and other vermin creeping up the sides, stinking mud finding its way through the old leaky joints at the end to the bottom of the cabin, and being heated by a hot stove, stenches arise therefrom enough to make a dog sick. In the boat cabins — 'hell holes', as some of the women call them — people of all ages live day and night. Fathers, mothers, sisters and brothers, sleep in the same bed and at the same time. In these places girls of 17 gave birth to children, the fathers of which are members of their own family . . .It is really sickening and disgusting to witness habits indulged in by these useful people that animals would pass by.'

It is true that the majority of boatmen could not read, but they would become aware of what was being written as things could be read to them. If you went to the inhabitants of a town with a population of 25,000 say, Bromsgrove in Worcestershire, Fleet in Hampshire, Gainsborough in Lincolnshire, Loughton in Essex or

'If you ever have the chance to go up the River Severn and through the Worcester Road Bridge, do look up and see the evidence of deep gauges and ruts in the stonework. I once lost one side of my wheelhouse because I dropped too far to my starboard side. The wheelhouse was folded down, but was resting on the bollards, so it was propped up a little. The corner caught the bridge and hey presto, glass and timber flew everywhere.' Not so here as 'Regent Lady' passes through during the floods of January 1959. Worcester Evening Post.

The decked narrow boat 'Spey' of Thomas Clayton (Oldbury) Ltd laden with gas-oil was forced to carry out its own ice-breaking in January 1959. Believed to be near Greets Green Basin, Birmingham Canal Navigations. Dudley Public Libraries.

Inverness and you told them that their houses were the most filthy holes, they had bugs, they committed incest and were lower than animals, you might possibly find a few of whom this would be true but how would the other 24,950 feel? Might not they grow a little taciturn?

A common practice that no boatman liked was for a minister of the Church to stalk on to the wharf, unsmiling and without a pleasant word, and step straight on to a boat intent upon asking silly questions. A far better approach was through the 'Boatmen's Chapels', set up at most of the terminal points of waterways. Basically places of worship, they made a pleasant change from the nearby pub and one could always be assured, especially where the Salvation Army were concerned, of a pleasant word, a drink, sometimes even a meal and a game of dominoes. Whether these chapels were successful in their early days — most were founded after 1860 — is a matter of opinion. One minister-writer berated them, saying that with 60 boats tied up in the basin on a Sunday and only two or three families going to the chapel they were a total failure. On the other hand there are many extant letters written by, or for, boatmen in appreciation of the kindness they received. The upper middle class may have been, in the Victorian era, the backbone of England but unfortunately they had a tendency to regard those 'of the lower orders' as 'not being quite the same as us', and some of their proposals must have been the most unsympathetic that could have been dreamt up. 'Could not little singing parties be made up out of our elder scholars and teachers to visit canal wharves, back slums, and prisons . . .capable and willing to talk to the boaters and others in language they can understand . . .which would, in my opinion, go

further towards drawing the boaters and 'jail birds' to the church.' One can imagine a boatman, having worked through the night, whacked out, sleeping in his cabin being awakened by a 'little singing party'. No doubt his attitude would confirm that which they already presumed to know. Queen Victoria, by contrast, showed a more practical approach. 'At the commencement of this year a poor boatwoman, with a husband and three little children, had an addition of three other little babies added to their stock in the cabin. Her Majesty the Queen, who is always spoken of by the boaters as one of the best women in England, kindly sent the usual bounty of £3 given on such occasions.'

Needless to say, over the years boatmen have developed a dialect of their own, although even this varies from region to region. Some words are relics of the early nineteenth century, others debasement of common words. 'Gullontyne Lock' for guillotine lock, 'I dain't gew', 'Hackerdock' for aqueduct, are among the latter. If a pleasure craft steerer is told by a boat's captain to 'hold in' he should move towards the towpath, for waterways do not have port and starboard as at sea, but an inside and an outside. 'Check yer moter' means to slow down, derived from horse-drawn days when the horse, by checking, would take the way off the boat. A corner or bend is always 'a turn', if slight it is 'a little turn', if severe 'a big turn'. To a canal boatman all weathers are much of a muchness, except the east wind and that is 'a lazy wind, it gews straight through yer, cos it carsn't be bothered to go round yer.' Locks, wharves and other appurtenances of a waterway have, over the years, attained different names to those shown in official records, the best known being Sutton Stop for Hawkesbury Junction,

Right: Wartime volunteer boatgirl. The Geographical Magazine, London.

Right, bottom: A boatman of the old school.

Far right: Shropshire Union Canal, Wheaton Aston 1962. M.B.Sagitta (ex-Grand Union Canal Carrying Company, fleet No.80), Captain Bill Littler. Plates and polished brass are visible through the doors, but the traditional brass chimney bands are missing.

In the same year an example of what was to be almost the final flowering of narrow boats is seen on the Ashby Canal. The fibreglass 'blue tops' were easy to fit compared to traditional tarpaulins but unwieldy to handle in a high wind! Motor 'Collingwood' and traditional butty 'Angel'.

In 1989 at Beeston, Dorset looked in better condition than she had done for a good few years.

Dorset went to Midland Canal Traders but is seen here in semi-retirement during 1965. The beautiful fine lines of the fore-end are clearly visible. M.Webb.

The motor Dorset was originally built for the Anderton Company, passed to the Mersey Weaver & Ship Canal Company with their fleet in 1954. In 1958 British Waterways purchased the residue of the MW craft, which by then were in pretty awful condition.

named after a family of lock-keepers who lived there. To a boatman Flowers Lock is better known than the Top Lock, Bascote of officialdom. 'Footies Wharf' is another name for Tibberton wharf on the Worcester & Birmingham Canal, the family after whom it is named claims to have had no less than six generations living simultaneously in boats on the waterway at one time. 'Maffers' for Marsworth is probably a laziness, but the 'top of 'ampton' is the best way of describing the top of the flight of 21 locks at Wolverhampton. If traversing the main line of the Grand Union a boatman would refer to the 'Nag's Head Three Rise' (locks nos 34-6) named after the local hostelry. Number 50 on the other hand would be Bush or Barkers lock, whilst number 52 could be called 'The Crooked Billet' or 'Awkward Bills' or 'Old Neds' — the latter being derived from Ned Adlum who worked as a navvy when the cut was first dug. 'Sweeps' commemorated Eli Oliffe, once a chimney sweep, who later kept the famous 'General Boatmens Stores' alongside lock 55, Berkhamstead. The three locks at Winkwell — Irishmans — gained their nomenclature following the death by drowning of a lock-keeper of Irish origin. Not only were lock-keepers and pubs commemorated but at number 80 we have heard the names, Walker's, Beasley's and Cherry's, three one-time Canal Company overseers who had previously lived there. Denham Deep (No. 87) is the deepest lock on the Grand Union, whilst Widewater (No.86) is a logical self-explanatory name.

As the true boatmen fade from the scene (most of them lying in Braunston churchyard) so a new generation is coming to the water and with a new type of boat. Many start off with a small cruiser and dream of the days when the canals were canals, viable, living entities, and it was possible to work a boat making a living in the process.

Twas up in Birmingham so I do hear say,
A boat by the name of the *Rosemary* lay,
She was clothed up and painted in traditional style,
But she hadn't carried for a very long while.

Along came a boatman the old boat to see,
Says he here's a craft that is useful to me,
'I'll load her with coal and to London I'll steer'
said the boatman to the owner, 'if I take her from here.'

The owner said 'Yes' the boatman 'Okay',
And into the cabin he went straightaway,
He lit up the stove, cleaned cobwebs and mould,
And he polished the beam til it shone like fine gold.

He sang as he laboured far into the night,
Got up in the morning before it was light,
He put the rusty blowlamp on the cylinder head,
'Tis a fine day for boating' the old boatman said.

He primed up the engine, a prayer in his heart,
And kicked on the flywheel to see if she'd start,
With a bang like the noise of a ten-pounder gun
The aged Bolinder started to run.

He cast off the fore-end at the counter he stood,
As *Rosemary* shook herself free of the mud,
With tears in his eyes says the boatman, 'We may
Get right down to Coventry for the end of the day.'

On dark stormy nights round the fall of the year,
If the beat of a Bolinder distant you hear,
It's not Claytons *Stour, Youmea* or *Tay*,
It's the ghost of that boatman and the old *Rosemary*.

Goods in Transit

ONE OF THE complaints of all railway traffic managers was to the effect that 'traders are wont to leave their goods in our wagons, on our sidings, for an excessive period; in effect providing cheap warehousing.' This difficulty was also well known to the owners of day boats, for the boat might lie three or four days with no demurrage paid before the recipient was prepared to discharge the cargo of coal or slack. Long-distance carriers were better organised and should there be any difficulty in unloading, say, because of Wakes Week, the goods could be off-loaded into a warehouse and transmitted onwards at a later date. As the cost of labour — until the late 1930s — was negligible and rates minimal this satisfied everyone. But should a small carrier be forced to leave his goods at another company's warehouse the story was different, sufficiently so for polite but useful forms to be printed. On the Duke of Bridgewater's canal, traffic and hence the warehouse congestion was such that boats had often to wait for days to unload, and were then charged for the time they had occupied the basin! One cannot but be astounded at the complacency and over-bearing attitude of a wealthy company when it is reported that in 1828: 'Notwithstanding the number of tons of flints and stone unladen weekly on the Duke's quays, and the present improved state of machinery, the primitive process of weighing by hand has not as yet been replaced by a better. Every individual stone passed through an ordinary scale. The machine is placed on the quay, and the stones are slung out of the vessel by a rough sort of crane.' Often too, the canal companies were very retarded in providing wharfage facilities when a traffic developed.

Loading wharves were scattered up and down the Coventry and Oxford Canals, all in use until the late 1920s, and boats might have to call at one specific wharf or have to hunt for a load. On the Coventry the first stone quarry was at Mancetter where loading was by means of a shute, the location being known to boatmen as 'Tipitsy Wide 'ole'. After that there were the Able Stone Quarry, loading again by means of a shute, and a quarter of a mile on, at the Anchor Bridge, the Gees Stone Quarry relied on loading overside. This meant shovelling the chippings into the bottom of the boat, 20 tons being a load. A two-mile run then to Spring Wood and Boon's Stone Quarry near Nuneaton. A mile on you came to the Punch Bowl where refreshments would be

National Coal Board 823
North Eastern Division.
No. 6 Area.

Delivered to Captain ...
Vessel ...
On account of ...

BANK UNIT STAITHE

QUALITY	T.	C
Slack	72	.
TOTAL	72	.

For NATIONAL COAL BOARD.
Signed ...
WEIGHMAN

Standard Tonnage ticket issued to boat captains. 72 tons of slack.

taken before inhaling that inexorably foul dust that came down with the chippings from the shute at Judkin's Stone Quarry. If you were not loading there you went on through the bridge to the 'Black 'ole', a dark blue granite quarry owned by the Midland Granite Quarry Company. Even if you could not get a load there you still had one more chance at the Griff Granite Quarry a short way on. Sometimes instead of taking this granite down the Oxford Canal you would turn right at Braunston on to the Warwick & Napton Canal Navigation an then you paid tolls at Wigrams Turn (Calcutt). The permit you garnered there enabled you to proceed to Warwick Junction and on to Warwick Basin where the only means of discharging was by hand. Boatmen reckoned to get 20 tons of chippings out of a boat in three hours. If you were going on past Warwick to the Rising Brook Bridge and along the line of the Warwick & Birmingham Canal Navigation there was another gauging office at the bottom lock of Hatton, there you were gauged again and issued with another permit which would take you to Camp Hill. All this wasted time and effort was a matter of course and singularly unprofitable to both canal company and boatman.

One displeasure often found was the variation in the density of water which could materially alter the apparent load on a craft. To quote a boatman: 'With this boating I reckon you carry a lot of tonnage for nothing. I mean you go down to a place like Brentford and you load up a load of deal, you can mark your boat with the tonnage that's on it and then you go to a place like Pooley, back of Coventry. You can bet your boats deeper at Pooley than it was with the proper weight on, because of the water you carry more for nothing there than what you do anywhere else.' Obviously there were many disputes over the correct tonnage in a craft and, fiddles disregarded, the toll collector was the ultimate power in the land.

'The engineer will also have to make provision, while the canal is digging, for stop-bars at the several intended toll-houses, or other places where it may be necessary to stop barges in the night, or in the case of any dispute about their lading: these bars are composed of a large baulk of fir timber floating on the water; and a small arch capable of containing such a floating beam of the proper length is provided under the bank, so that when the trade on the canal is required to be stopped, the toll-clerk has only to draw out the beam by means of a cord, attached to it, until its end enters a recess in the opposite wall, and then to lock the beam fast.'

Naturally, most toll clerks were unwilling to undertake such a final move. Visualise, if you will, a dark and gloomy night somewhere on the Birmingham Main Line, eight o'clock of a winter's evening, the toll clerk makes up his books, a thump on the door and he goes out to see the boat captain whose craft he has just stopped for the sake of a ton, and who knows what might happen? 'During last year nearly eighty boaters were confined in Stafford Gaol

A boat registration plate in use on the Birmingham Canal Navigations, craft could have three or four of these (for different canals) riveted in clearly visible locations.

— nearly all of them young men under thirty years of age — for various offences, principally thieving; and at the present time there are eighteen undergoing sentences in the gaol.' It was not in any way uncommon for a toll-keeper, whose house was sufficiently remote, to be attacked when carrying home the dues he had received — fortunate were they who lived in a toll-house on the island in the middle of the canal. Others occasionally embezzled the loot, a singularly unprofitable occupation for which they almost automatically got seven years' transportation if caught.

Reverting now to wharves — it must be understood that not all wharves had out-of-date equipment, the bigger companies might have cranes, howbeit of the manumatic pattern, but geared so that one man could, with relative ease, lift five tons at a time. At a mill, granary or timber yard there might well be covered-in accommodation, rather akin to a railway station canopy, whereunder the boat could lie protected from the elements. In turn there would be an overhead hoist, often steam operated. Covered accommodation was essential for some perishable items which tended to be packed in sack-bags and could not always be put in the main warehouse immediately. Particularly noticeable in this field was Cadbury's old 'Waterside' Works, at Bournville, (now a housing estate) where once four boats could lie simultaneously under cover for the handling of cocoa beans or chocolate crumb. Flour was yet another 'protected' load, which all too often had to be 'humped' on board, one sack (of 120 lb.) at a time on the boatman's back. Due to its characteristic of becoming a hard inert mass — 'lumping' — this was almost a more unpopular exercise than loading sacks of wheat. A number of boatmen are never seen without shirts, having picked up a form of dermatitis on their backs from carrying wheat, the chaff getting ground into the skin. Brown, or demerara, sugar was another 'humped' traffic, and one which called for the most careful clothing-up (covering with a tarpaulin) on the boat. Some works would, if lacking in a canopy, decline to unload the craft in inclement conditions. Chests of tea also required this kind of coddling, while loose wheat is known for its flourishing growth in the humid conditions of a poorly covered-in boat. Bulk salt had its own tricks; often carried in open boats and merely shovelled out on to an open wharf the wastage must have been unnecessarily high. Apropos of some of the more valuable bagged loads, one essential adjunct to the trade was a good standard of boatmen, and it is known that at least one very good and profitable run, lost ostensibly due to a change of transport pattern, was in fact withdrawn due to the uncontrolled, unhygienic habits of a boatman's children and animals.

A few goods, specifically timber and wheat,

Rural tranquillity on the Kennet & Avon Canal at Kintbury, three miles east of Hungerford. Lock 78 lies in the background. The Kennet & Avon Canal is one of the great restoration successes, being brought back from dereliction to be re-opened by Her Majesty The Queen on 8 August 1990. As the British Waterways Board said: 'The restored canal is for all to enjoy; whether holiday boaters, anglers, canoeists, nature ramblers or families taking a quiet stroll. It is rich in historic buildings and structures, many listed, and is especially noted for its wildlife. The towpath is being improved to a high standard to benefit all, including visitors with disabilities.'

were (some long time before the Americans thought of the word) palletised; the timber being cased, while 20 or 30 tons of wheat were laid into the boat inside a wooden framework, strengthened and equipped with eyes for lifting by crane. Steel bars, rods or strips were commonly bundled, being held together with wire or steel bands which frequently came adrift when being craned overside from ships in the docks. If they survived that, not a few went overboard at the other end! Some wharves are very scarred indicating that they have been utilised for rubbish and scrap, the former being tipped directly on board if a boat were ready, if not a dumper truck would scoop it on board. Discharge, once by shovel, is now mechanised using a crane and grab. Scrap, profitable but loathed, inevitably comes away from its bands, and has to be loaded on, bit by bit, by hand. Mouldering rusting heaps on obscure city wharves often denote the point at which a cheesed-off boat captain 'jacked it in' and went home.

In later years modern factories brought electric hoists into service and either a continuous Archimedean screw or a conveyor belt had some specialised usage.

Looking through a list of wharves, produced by Fellows, Morton & Clayton in 1918, the concentration of them within a few miles of Birmingham is proof enough of traffics. On the London run we have firstly the Birmingham Bar Stop Lock and Toll House, two furlongs away at Fazeley Street are the Warwick Public Wharves, another 400 yards to the warehouses, wharves and offices of Fellows, Morton & Clayton and, virtually next door, one lock up on the Bordesley flight of locks, the City of Birmingham Gas Works, Adderley Street. At the Top Lock are the public wharves at Sampson Road and Bordesley Toll Office. On the ten-mile pound from thence to the Top Lock of Knowle we come to wharves with famous names, Jones, Manley & Co., timber merchants, the Birmingham Small Arms Company, toolmakers, City of Birmingham Refuse Disposal Depot, Alldays & Onions, engineers (and *inter alia* makers of quite fine motor cars), Symmonds Bros., the City of Birmingham Stone Depot, the not very appositely named Golden Hillock Road and Birmingham Small Arms again at Small Heath. at Hay Mills we find Pontifex, engineers, Whitfield, iron-founders, and Derringtons, brickworks. At Yardley there was the coal wharf of the once famous carrier T.Boston, then Yardley tunnel wharf, an almost worked out gravel-pit and three coal wharves, Yardley Road, Francis Road and Lincoln Road. Continuing along the same cut we have public wharves at Olton and Solihull, together with the Solihull Gas Company's own

coke and coal depot. Next is the complicatedly named Catherine de Barnes Heath Wharf — abbreviated by boatmen to Catley, or Ketley, Barnes. If by this time, still only eight miles out from Birmingham, you have a thirst and have missed the Anchor at Solihull, the Boat at Ketley Barnes will restore life. Another five wharves occupy the next four miles from the Bottom Lock of Knowle and at Heronfield three overnight accommodations are shown (for horses, not men), the Kings Arms, Ivy House and the Cat-in-the-Window. Three furlongs on the Old Black Boy offered similar accommodation, then on round to Hatton Toll Office and you pass another eight wharves — a total of 36 in the 20 miles from Birmingham, and Hatton Asylum half a mile away has yet another!

The Warwick & Napton Canal from Budbrooke, Junction, where it met the Warwick & Birmingham Canal, through to its junction with the Oxford Canal at Napton, offered a plethora of wharves, all too many, alas, now disappeared. Your weighbill might direct you to Warwick Locks, Cape Locks or Bayleys' Two Locks — but all are one and the same. The next wharf, not inappositely was the Warwick Union Warehouse! Guy's Cliff, Nelson Dale, the Bakehouse or the Mill at Emscote might all call for your services; coal, coal and more coal. Next came the Leamington & Warwick Electric Power Station the Corporation Tip, Leamington Gas Works and the Midland Electric Light Company. Nelson & Co needed slack at their oil mills, whilst Sidney Flavel used both iron and coal to manufacture his range of gas and coal-fired stoves. The fifth wharf from there — five miles from the Junction, was the Radford Old Brewery and very welcome it was!

In the thick of the locks, the six-rise of Radford, the four of Bascote and the ten of Stockton, nine wharves are interspersed, including the Cement Works, one of the last traffics that was operated under the loving hand of the British Waterways Board. Another five wharves and the Toll House at the top of Wigrams three-rise (Calcutt) was in sight and another 14 miles were completed.

To give some idea of the work involved at a toll-house it will suffice to say that in 1925 no less than 117,000 tons were handled at Stewponey, giving a revenue in excess of £4,000 all collected in dribs and drabs. Typical tolls which the collector might have to extricate, not necessarily in cash, for many would be debited to either the Carrying Company or the consignor, are shown here, drawn from the toll book at Windmill End, Birmingham Canal Navigations. These tolls appear to be those applicable from 1908 to the railway groupings of 1923, remaining, of course, constant throughout the period.

From	To (via)	Distance (miles)	Article	Toll per ton in old pence	Special toll per ton
1. Atlas Tube Works	Withymoor Station	½	tubes	0.60	
2. "	Bumblehole Tip	1¼	mud	min. 1s 6d	plus 1d per ton
3. Bumblehole Branch Top	Selly Oak Wharf	8¾	slag	6.875	
4. "	Worcester Canal	8¾	slag	5.375	
5. Bishton Bridge	Coombs Wood Colliery	3½	sand	3.975	plus 125% extended voyage
6. "	Webbs Green, Halesowen	5	manure	4.50	
7. Coombs Wood Tube Works	Autherley	13¼	tubes and spelter	11.625	thro' traffic
8. "	Berkeley Street	13½	spelter	16.35	
9. "	"	13½	scrap brass	18.65	
10. "	Canal Depot Langley, Titford Canal via Bradeshall and Oldbury Locks	12¼	spelter	15.4625	
11. "	Stour Canal via Blowers Green and Black Delph	10¼	iron	9.7625	
12. "	"	10¼	tubes	6.125	Gloucester traffic
13. Dudley Wood Lime Kilns	Webbs Green Farm	5¼	lime	4.625	
14. Fly Colliery Basin	Stour Canal	5¼	coal	7.35	
15. "		5¼	Coal	6.00	B.Pearson & Co. A/c
16. "	Langley Forge via Netherton Tunnel	—	"	14.50	W.H.Matty & C. A/c
17. Gawn Colliery	Minworth Top Pond via Netherton Tunnel and Farmers Bridge	22	slag	13.75	
18. Gorsty Hill Co. Wharf	Stour Canal via Two Lock Line Black Delph	5¾	coal	9.55	
19. Gawn Colliery Basin	Whitton Turnover Bridge via Netherton Tunnel, Toll End and Perry Barr	14¼	blast furnace slag	12.8125	T&S Element A/c
20. "	Boat and Slipper Wharf via Netherton	7½	slag	9.25	
21. Halesowen Wharf	Smethwick Stour Canal (Gloucester) via Black Delph	11¼	iron	9.625	Tunnel and 1d in addition if crane is used
22. Hawn Basin	Coalite Works Wednesfield, via Netherton Tunnel, Factory Locks, Horseley Fields Junction	15¾	bricks	16.7875	
23. Knowle Colliery	Pensnett Canal via Park Head Locks	4¼	iron stone	4.5375	
24. "	California Brick Works via Netherton Tunnel and Bar Lock	—	coal	9.00	
25. Lodge Farm Canal Company's Basin	Waterfall Lane	3	timber	6.60	
26. Marine Works	Rowley Gas Works	2½	rubbish	3.00	
27. Netherton Iron Works	Knowle Colliery Basin entrance to off side	1¼	dredgings	2.75	If emptied into canal 5s per boat in addition
28. "	Gorsty Hill Wharf	—	coal	2.85	Exclusive of wharfage BCN apportionment 6d special
29. Old Hill District	Stour Canal for Kidderminster only	—	bricks		
30. Pennant Hill Colliery	Spon Lane Wharf via Netherton Tunnel and Spon Lane	5¾	coal	13.55	
31. Rowley Pottery	Warwick Canal for London via Netherton Tunnel and Farmers Bridge	11¾	Pipes and sinks	10.875	through traffic
32. Springfield Basin	Bell Pond via Netherton Tunnel and Toll End	11	undressed road stone for repair of roads	11.00	
33. "	Winsom Green Workhouse	9	Kerbs and setts	12.1	
34. Two Locks Top Lock	Rowley Stop Ovens	2¾	fire-bricks	4.30	
35. Windmill End	Primrose Hill Wharf	1¼	slag	Minimum 1s 6d and 1.00d per ton	
36. Warrens Hall Colliery	The Pensnett Canal via Netherton and Park Head	—	coal	2.85	stoppage at Primrose

All the opposite figures are pre-decimalisation. There were 1,455 entries in the book but certain factors are evident from these few entries. For example, from Bumblehole to Selly Oak Wharf, both points on the Dudley Canal (3), is 1.5d higher than that for traffic of an identical distance to the Worcester & Birmingham Canal (4); this was the drawback previously referred to. The toll from Bishton Bridge to Coombeswood Colliery (5) allowed for transhipment *en route*. Coombeswood Depot Works (7) to Autherley represents an agreed rate for traffic passing on to the Shropshire Union Canal, (8) and (9) show the differential between two different traffics, being a case of what the traffic would stand. Again (11) and (12) show a different rate applicable for local and through traffic. Traffics working from the Fly Colliery Basin led to quite a few upsets (14) and (15), the preferential rate was only legal if there was sufficient guaranteed tonnage to keep tolls at an overall low level; carriers paying the higher rate were prone to kick up a fuss when such preference was known. The cranage toll of 1d (21) was per ton, and was designed to cover the cost of labour operating these manumatic devices. (10), (17), (21), (22) and (31) show relatively long-distance workings. (27) sounds rather odd but probably allowed for infilling of an unwanted arm. Birmingham Canal Navigations apportionments had been granted over various routes for traffic originating and terminating on other canals, alternatively the loads could be for use by the engineers of the Birmingham Canal Navigations for which special rates were granted (29). The differential between (32) and (33) is interesting, showing again the taking of the traffic for what it would stand. One of the advantages with the Birmingham Canal Navigations was that if one waterway was stopped up there was nearly always an alternative (36). Gorsty Hill (18) is the original spelling, taken from the toll register, the 'r' being dropped these days. Significantly a number of the waterways mentioned are no longer navigable, including (10), (18), (22), (23) and (32).

The different type of goods carried and the varying destinations might not at first sight be surprising on the Birmingham Canal Navigations, but there was little difference even on straight up and down canals. A toll register for the Worcester & Birmingham Canal during a quiet month, February, at a time when traffic was already in decline (1924) shows that 38 boats were gauged, having an average load of 28¼ tons. Some boats already had their toll tickets and entries were merely made to cover the return working.

From	To	With	Destination	To load	No. of craft
Gloucester	Old Union Mills	Grain	Cannock Chase Collieries	Coal	1
'	Severn Co's Wharf	Sugar	Gloucester	Empty	1
Diglis	Birmingham	Empty	Lowesmoor Wharf	Coal	2
Gloucester	Old Union Mills	Wheat	Gloucester	Empty	2
'	'	"	Framilode Conduit Colliery	Coal	1
"	"	"		"	1
Tewkesbury	Grahames Wharf	Flour	Tewkesbury	Empty	3
Gloucester	Severn Company's Wharf	"	Gloucester	"	1
"	"	"	"	Sauce	1
"	Central Mill	Wheat	"	Empty	2
Gloucester	Old Union Mills	Wheat	Cannock Chase Colliery	Coal	2
"	Coventry	Maize	-	-	1
"	Severn Company's Wharf	Chocolate	-	-	1
"	Coventry	Maize	Worcester	Coal	1
"	Chester Street	Deals	Cannock Chase Colliery	"	1
Worcester	Birmingham Canal	Elm Boards	Lowes-Moor	"	1
Gloucester	Tipton	Carbide	Gloucester	Empty	2
Not specified-through ticket			Hardwicke	Coal	2
"	"		Gloucester	Empty	2
Gloucester	Severn Company's Wharf	Sundries	"	"	2
"	Coventry	Barley	"	"	2
"	Cape Arm	Sawn Wood	Cannock Chase Collieries	Coals	1
"	Midland Mill	Grain	Glascote	Coal	1
Not specified-through ticket			Frampton	"	1
"	"		Diglis	"	1
Gloucester	Old Union Mills	Wheat	Bournville	Slack	1
Not specified – through ticket			Cannock Chase Collieries	Coal	1
Gloucester	Chester Street	Deals	Whitminster	"	1

In the period pre-1850, as post-1930, most traffic was in the hands of large carriers and competition was fierce. From Nottingham in 1832 Thomas Pickford & Co and Robert Marshalls combined to offer services to London, Liverpool, Manchester, Derby, Bath, Bristol, Hull, Birmingham and 'nearly all parts of England by fly boats, daily'. If, however, you wanted to send your goods to Derby, Grantham, Liverpool and all intermediate places, Samuel Thorpe would be pleased to accommodate you. Robert Barrows offered a service every Tuesday and Friday night to Liverpool, Manchester, Newark, Gainsborough and all parts of the west of England and Cheshire, while German Wheatcroft & Sons went similarly

For a riverman, Captain Lane in conversation is always complimentary towards narrow or 'long' boatmen, for when they were laid off due to falling traffic through the Worcester & Birmingham, and Staffordshire & Worcester canals they joined the lighter and tanker firms where 'they told us tricks of how to work the river above Gloucester, many things we had not heard of or tried.' The narrow boats here are a mixture but the heavy guards and built up bows of a river-going butty are shown in the middle, light, craft. The rearmost of the two steamers is the Penmount of Falmouth. Collection B.A.Lane.

but 'several times a week'. Rather improbably, John Simpson advertised that his boats went to Gainsborough, Hull, Cromford, Mansfield, High Peak Railway, Retford, Liverpool and all parts of Scotland and the west of England. Deacon Harrison's fly boats, on the other hand, found sufficient traffic to run solely to London every Monday and Friday.

In *Aris's Birmingham Gazette* on 9 November 1807, Mr Pickford advertised 'expeditious canal conveyance by fly boats on the line of the Coventry, Oxford and Grand Junction.' On 8 February 1808 the Wolverhampton Boat Company, operating from that place to London, offered 'expeditious canal carriage' and on 2 April 1810 we find William Judd & Sons offering to carry your goods by water from Birmingham to Sheffield or Derby. Some carriers, not unnaturally, favoured certain routes — where there were alternatives — and put forward incentives why they should both carry and use these routes. Thus out of Birmingham in 1820 it was claimed:

'Boats from the wharfs within the town; Birds, Whitehouse's, Robinsons and Crowleys, are capable of delivering goods in London one whole day sooner by the latter route (the Stratford) than they can do by the other (the Warwick & Birmingham) and the merchants and ironmongers in the metropolis are hereby informed of that circumstance. The boat owners by proceeding on this route are necessitated to advance a small sum of immediate money, for tonnage, more than they do on the other route, to counterbalance that, the boats are exempt from the wear and tear of passing through twelve locks, and an extra day's expense; therefore when both circumstances are taken into consideration, the expenses cannot vary much either way, and to the London merchant one day is, at times, of the utmost importance.'

In 1860, when the railroads already had a stranglehold, a few of the carriers in Cheshire were pleased to advise of their existence. From Chester boats went daily to Liverpool, Manchester and Ellesmere Port. William Clowes, wharfinger, would be pleased to be of assistance at Wardle. At Audlum the Shropshire Union Railway & Canal Company found it sufficient to state that they operated to all parts, but Mr John Jones, the local wharfinger, apart from handling the SUR & CC's boats was pleased to place orders for transport with Mellor, Castle & Co, daily to London. At Congleton we had the Bridgewater

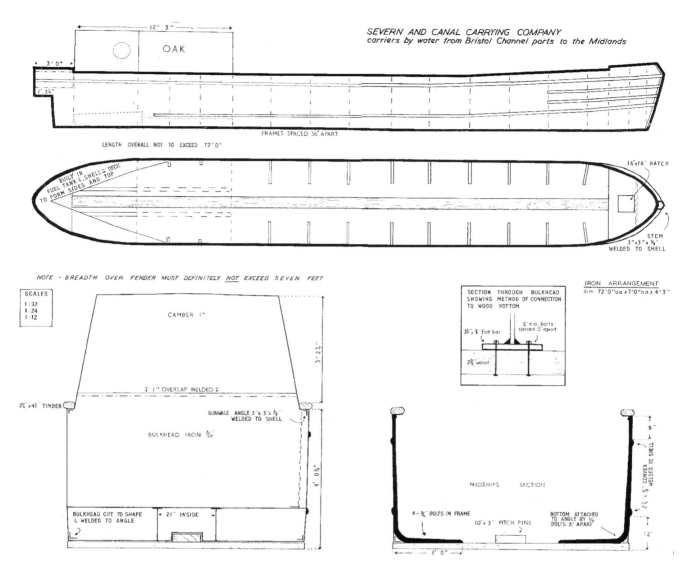

SEVERN AND CANAL CARRYING COMPANY
carriers by water from Bristol Channel ports to the Midlands

OAK

12' 3"
3' 0"
1' 3¼"

LENGTH OVERALL NOT TO EXCEED 72' 0"
FRAMES SPACED 36" APART

BUILT IN FUEL TANK & SHELL & DECK TO FORM SIDES AND TOP

16"x16" HATCH
STEM
3"x3" x ⅜"
WELDED TO SHELL

NOTE – BREADTH OVER FENDER MUST DEFINITELY NOT EXCEED SEVEN FEET

SCALES
1:32
1:24
1:12

CAMBER 1"

3' 2¼"

1" OVERLAP WELDED

GUNWALE ANGLE 3"x 3"x ⅜" WELDED TO SHELL

2¼"x4¼" TIMBER

BULKHEAD IRON ³⁄₁₆

4' 0½"

BULKHEAD CUT TO SHAPE & WELDED TO ANGLE

21" INSIDE

SECTION THROUGH BULKHEAD SHOWING METHOD OF CONNECTION TO WOOD BOTTOM

3½"x ⅜" flat bar

⅝" dia. bolts spaced 5" apart

2¼" wood

IRON ARRANGEMENT
dim. 72' 0" o.a. x 7' 0" o.a. x 4' 3"

MIDSHIPS SECTION

2¼" x ½" CONVEX WELDED TO SHELL

8"

4 - ¾" BOLTS IN FRAME

10"x 3" PITCH PINE

BOTTOM ATTACHED TO ANGLE BY ⅝" BOLTS 5" APART

12"

2' 0"

Trustees offering a daily service to Manchester, Liverpool and the Potteries, whilst the Manchester, Sheffield and Lincolnshire Potteries Railway Company went 'to all parts by canal and rails'. At Middlewich it was sufficient to state, 'The North Staffordshire Co's Canal (The Trent & Mersey, or Grand Trunk) passes through the town. At the wharf near the principal street commodious warehouses have been erected for the reception and transmission of merchandise. Mr Thomas Ball, Wharfinger.' Also represented at Middlewhich were the Bridgewater Trustees, Grand Junction Canal Company, Shropshire Union Railway & Canal Company and James Cockshott. Ellesmere Port, Macclesfield, Stockport, Sale, Altrincham, Lymm and Runcorn all had their share of carriers. There were services from Dukinfield: 'Boats leave the Wharf Inn, Wharf Street, for Hyde and Marple, daily at 10.40am and 3.30 and 6pm'; from Hyde: 'Swift Packets leave the Navigation Inn daily for Manchester at 11.40am, 4.20 and 6.35pm'; and Runcorn: 'The Countess Grosvenor Packet Boat leaves the top locks, Monday, Wednesday and Friday for Manchester calling at the intermediate stations',

these services being run on the railway pattern.

Looking through old carriers' lists is a fruitful but rather sad proceeding, for all too many of the places listed are no longer served by water let alone by boats. John Howell was once pleased to offer services 'regularly' from Birmingham to Measham and Ashby, Pickford & Co to Newcastle, Leek and Simpson, Hyde & New would be pleased to accommodate you on Tuesdays, Fridays and Saturdays to Derby, Cromford or Malton, all by water. George Swain went three times a week to such places as Melton Mowbray, Market Rasen, Pocklington, Horncastle, Cromford, and Pinxton. German Wheatcroft were pleased to state that boats left 'every Tuesday, Friday and Saturday from Derby to their Establishment at Buckland Hollow, whence goods are instantly forwarded'. John White-house's fly boats went to Shrewsbury while Worthington & Co operated services, in conjunction with other carriers, to St Helens, Lancaster, Kendal, Ashton, Oldham, Barnsley, Bradford, Bolton, Bury, and Halifax. At Shardlow, George Moor ran the pub, acted as the farmer and was agent for boats. At Pinxton Messrs William

Josiah Wedgwood & Sons Ltd.

Eperson of the Boat Tavern and Joseph Riley of the New Inn would be pleased to carry your goods, provided of course that it was out of hours.

Some carriers were rather vague, running occasionally or as the demand was felt, others were more particular. From Leeds to Selby the Aire & Calder Company boats were offered every evening 'Sundays excepted' (naturally) 'where they arrive in 12 hours and deliver their cargoes on board a steam packet which sails every morning and lands packages at Hull at the same pm.' The Union Canal Company ran from Leeds to Liverpool daily, in four days, with '40 vessels engaged'. From Dewsbury, Joshua Kenyon let daily '12 at noon', from Huddersfield, Widow Welsh & Sons were pleased to operate to Manchester 'daily in 24 hours'. From Ripon to Hull, Martin Keddy & Co would carry your goods twice a week 'in one bottom'. The bugbear of water carriage in later days at least, was that goods often had to be transhipped with damage and loss occurring.

A rather curious footnote to the above list is that 'The market boats which attend Hull market once a fortnight generally come with goods and passengers on that market day (Tuesday or Friday) which falls nearest the full or new moon, being the period of spring tides, the markets on such days are thence called 'full boat days'.' Obviously the intention here is that the full moon should have its well-known effect on ladies at the sales.

Maintaining the Status Quo

IN 1840 the statement 'A stoppage of traffic (up the canal) is a thing most to be avoided.' was first written down, but stoppages are unavoidable and can be divided into two types. The first is the unprogrammed stoppage, usually brought on by the weather or by bank erosion: 'July, 24th 1769. Early on Saturday morning last, a little beyond Winsome Green (*sic*) in the Birmingham Canal Navigation the Earth fell suddenly in and Killed John Lester, one of the Workmen, occasioned, it is thought, by the heavy Rains on Friday Evening.' A straightforward accident may occur, as when an English elm fell into the Welsh Canal near Irish Bridge just prior to the Easter Bank Holiday — a singularly inopportune time!

DOCKS & INLAND WATERWAYS   SOUTH EASTERN DIVISION EXECUTIVE

LOCK GATE PROGRAMME 1950

Lock site and No.	Estimated cost			Total cost	Material in stock	When carried out and remarks
	Material	Labour	Stoppage			
Hawkesbury 1.	£89. 15. 4	£43. 10	£74	£207. 5. 4	Yes	July/August New Top Gate. New Timber Fits. Repair to lock side coping. Will mean two stoppages to complete. Work to be done on Sundays.
Hillmorton 4.	£55. 10. 0	£45	£65	£165. 10	Yes	July/August Fitting two new timber breasts to the existing bottom gates. Gates will be taken into the Yard for the work to be done. Refitted when ready the traffic will not be delayed at these double locks.
Banbury 29.	£220. 15. 3	£88. 12	£75	£384. 7. 3	Yes	August New double bottom gates. New timber fits.
Heyford 35.	£209	£70	£69. 10	£348. 10. 0	Ordered Dec. 1949	August New single bottom gates. New timber fits.
Watford 3–4	These three locks require cast iron hollow quoins to replace old timber. Gates will stand over for another time.					
4–5	Work could be carried out as traffic permits, and delivery of new hollow quoins.					
6	It is estimated that the stoppage cost per set would be £80.					

The other, an example of which is shown above, is the 'programmed stoppage.' Prior to nationalisation it was traditional to hold these over the Bank Holidays. A gang of men, up to a dozen in number, reinforced by boatmen who had perforce to lay idle, would work a 12-hour day, or, should conditions demand it, shifts through the period until the job was done, irrespective of the complexity of the works.

In the cases shown above it will be seen that the stoppages were held in mid-summer, giving the advantages of longer daylight hours and more or less guaranteed weather. With the traffic emphasis having changed to summer-season only usage by pleasure craft such stoppages would be anathema to the governing body of British Waterways and programmed stoppages are now held between mid-October and mid-April. For both workmen and the quality of the

work done such a change is unfortunate. During a stoppage at Long Buckby on the Grand Union Main Line (Whilton Flight) in the late sixties, conditions were so appalling that men found it necessary to shovel snow from the site before work could commence. Even the local cement company demurred at providing 'ready-mix', as their waterpipes and sand-hoppers were frozen. The fact that the job was finished on time speaks well for the stamina of the men concerned, although the economics of such work carried out in the period of shortest days and poorest conditions probably do not bear examining.

The works to be carried out on such a lock stoppage vary from lock to lock and canal to canal, and one interesting variation concerns the presence, or otherwise, of the foreman. In general, British Waterways Board foremen were ex-craftsmen 'made-up', and if they were interested in stoppages they would be present, if not, then they would probably be occupied elsewhere. In the latter case the responsibility for the work tended to fall on the (wide) shoulders of the carpenter. Until the early 1950s it was usual for lock-gates to be made at the section yard, an involved job which could be guaranteed to keep the carpenters warm throughout the winter. A form of lock-gate, the existence of which is often overlooked, is the so-called safety-gate, which is fitted at the end of a valley or where the canal is high above the countryside on an embankment. A typical waterway utilising these is the Worcester & Birmingham Canal, where along the summit there are eleven sets. Basically they are like a pair of lock-gates, often situated underneath a bridgehole, and the theory is that if there were to be a sudden drop in water they would 'come to'. Unfortunately, due to vandalism it is necessary now to keep them chained back, although there have been occasions when these chains have been sawn off with singularly ill-effects upon craft which did not anticipate and could not see a pair of strong wooden gates just on the waterline. All these gates were closed during the last war, when bombing was in progress and, in fact, the aqueduct at Bournville had a direct hit from a bomb. Had the gates not been closed a large area of Bournville and Stirchley would have been washed into the rivers Bourne and Ray. In 1972 it was necessary to de-water the one-and-a-half-mile-long pound between Kings Norton and Cadburys, Bournville. For this purpose the safety-gates were utilised to retain the water, but, far

Put a dozen or so workpeople into an ordinary narrow lock chamber and it looks crowded, two dozen fill a lock on the Kennet & Avon, but here it would take a hundred to have much impact. One problem, though, is that it is not entirely clear just where this is. The original notation on the back gave the location as Sykehouses (Aire & Calder Navigation) but the structure appears wrong. Whatever and wherever it is certainly impressive. Peter L.Smith

from being instantly usable, work commenced on clearing them on 28 January and continued thereafter until the actual de-watering on 14 February. About 100 tons of rubbish was removed, necessitating the employment of a dredger-driver, discharger-driver, tug captain and various labourers, together with the relevant craft. To compound the loss of time both the dredger and discharger-drivers, men in their mid-60s, were taken sick; there was no one else on the section who could drive either machine so a man had to be borrowed from another section.

In many areas old methods and equipment have lingered far too long on waterways. The hand method of scooping water from the lock chambers continued until relatively recent days, and in fact is the only way to put the finishing touches on such work today, but where there was a long pound a manual pump was utilised around the turn of the century. Made of timber and iron it would be lowered into the lock by stop planks, and a stage fixed for the men to stand on. After priming the pump six men would start swinging the handle and pumping away. After half an hour it was, of course, necessary to relieve them with another six men and so on, until the lock was empty, which might take anything from two to four hours. It is not surprising that songs and ditties were sung to keep up the rhythm. These were often sea shanties, and if the words were not generally known one man would set the pace by calling out the words.

A typical steam pump which came into use during World War One necessitated iron suction pipes, the fitting of these being described as a 'heavy mauling job'. Fitted to a boat, this craft would be floated up to the bottom end of a lock and the overall time required to pump out the chamber was reduced to one hour, providing that the stop planks fitted tightly and were kept well racked with fine ashes.

The next improvement, at least on the Worcester & Birmingham Canal, was when the superintendent procured an engine out of an old car from the local schoolmaster. This was a very early vintage 2½hp De Dion, mounted on a chassis with ironwheels, an improvement albeit still with iron suction pipes. Later, another pump utilised an Aster engine, also from an old motor car. The first pump with flexible suction pipes, following the trend on this waterway, was powered by a BSA engine removed from a car!

Mechanisation on many waterways also reached the sawing division around the turn of the century. Prior to this all such heavy timber cutting was put out to contract, being sawn by roving gangs who used an enormous crosscut saw, one man working from above and the other standing in the pit below the timber being cut, the man above making the lead stroke and ensuring the saw was kept square. One essential requirement for these men was plenty of cider and beer.

The bricks used on a waterway normally came from local sources, but if the canal fell into railway hands or the local brickworks closed

Although used elsewhere this photograph appears to be unique. It depicts a stoppage inside Blisworth Tunnel on the Grand Union Canal, and shows the temporary tank or dam used to give a safe working area. Areas of repair to the brickwork are quite clear; the heat of the naptha lamps must have at least made the job a little warmer if no less stuffy. British Waterways Board.

down some variety can now be found amongst the coping stones. Locally, a half-mile stretch shows bricks dated between 1870 and 1900 from Joseph Hamlit, West Bromwich, the Earl of Dudley's Coneygre brickworks at Dudley Port and from William Morris of Oldbury.

Typical of the maintenance work carried out by bricklayers is the widening of weirs or, in recent times, when a stop lock has been done

away with, raising or lowering them throughout the length of a waterway. It will be understood that on a summit or any intermediate level should one weir be lower, even by so little as half an inch, than the others, it will always be running and wasting water. In areas where there is extensive mining, subsidence often necessitates the raising of weirs, on some occasions as much as three feet over a number of years. The Wyrley &

Left, top: Bitterness of unpaid labour. These men are 'diddling' for coal during the General Strike of 1926. Illustrated London News. Left, bottom: It is invidious to contrast one generation with another, but whether George Bate, BEM, would have been so proud to display his medals today is doubtful. Foreman carpenter, Worcester & Birmingham Canal, he was first employed in October 1914 loading salt boats, having left school before he was even 13, but after doing several jobs, including that of a rivet warmer 'at Christmas 1915 my father ordered me to give in my notice. He wanted me to work with him making lock gates and doing repairs and maintenance on the Worcester-Birmingham Canal.' Promotion was hard for with the shortage of men during World War One 'the blacksmith wanted me as a striker; the plumber and fitter, as a mate; and I did any number of jobs until the soldiers returned from overseas' and under the rules of the day 'a lad worked until his employer thought him competent.' In 1973 George, who although self-taught, was a marvellous writer said 'my working life on waterways had been a long and varied one. It's been interesting and it's a good open air job. Change it? Why should I?' Middle: Portrait of a real canalman. Right: Anderton gearing receives attention from George Beech, lift attendant in 1966. British Waterways Board.

Essington Canal, as built, was a contour canal, keeping to the level of the surrounding ground, but this ground has subsided over the years and the canal banks, having to remain constant, are rebuilt high above the neighbourhood. The bricklayers' handiwork is very apparent here.

Like most canal tradesmen, bricklayers have not necessarily served an orthodox apprenticeship, working instead with different older men until the trade had been learnt. for the first two years of his working life one (now retired) bricklayer acted as the general tea boy for the gang he worked with. His first job in the morning was to sweep out the boat and have the 'kittle a-billing' and the tea cups, not mugs, together with the teapot, sugar and milk, laid out ready for the men when they arrived. For the extra time required he was not paid by the company, nor by the men, but he was rewarded — it was required that he buy all his own tools, but instead of having to do this, as a recompense for his services, the men gradually built up a collection of tools for him. The cabin of their boat, which it must be stressed they had regularly and exclusively, was painted blue and white with carpet laid on the floor and palliasses on the benches. No man was permitted to enter the cabin with muddy boots — relics of this practice are still to be seen among older hands today —

the men carefully wiping their feet before getting on board. Each man had his own cup and saucer and paid 6d (2½p) a week into the common tea fund, the lad being responsible for all purchases. However, sugar was 'freemans', as this was a traffic operated on the waterway, while milk was obtained from local farmhouses in exchange for coal, acquired by some means. While the men had their tea the lad would get the tools from the front cabin and lay out those he thought each man would require. When they had finished their tea he would, again, sweep out the cabin, wash up the cups and saucers, hang the cups on their hooks and generally make himself useful. Each man brought his own 'bait' in his 'snap tin' for lunch, some would have a hunk of bread and cheese, or cold bacon, others would need their food cooking for which the lad was responsible — on the understanding that there was never any need for him to bring his own lunch. One or two of the men, he recalls, would go up the bank and bring back a rabbit, which he had to skin and paunch ready for the men to take home. As the years went on he was promoted and the new lad took over his duties. Rather curiously the last job he had before retirement was to rebuild a pump house, the original of which he had helped to build 50-odd years previously.

Before commencing the serious, heavy, work

In the days when most maintenance work was carried out overside the icing of canals could have one knock-on effect, insofar as when the lengthmen's boat was frozen in they could only carry out hedge-cutting, often conveniently near their homes!

Many years ago a gifted photographer, Eric de Mare, wandered around the parts of the canal system that were open in a leaky pontoon with a home-built cabin powered by rather erratic motors. He loved the sight of weatherworn wood and rope-worn ironwork. Few of these beautiful scenes can be found today, partly because they reflected individual canal ownerships and regrettably because modern senior managers appear to have lost sight of the requirements of people who traverse canals. Too much is now standardised. Buckby Locks, Grand Union Canal, 1989.

ones of 25 rungs or longer ones of anything up to 36 rungs; house and cottage doors; window frames and little 'odds and bobs' including painting and figuring the gauging sticks for the toll clerks. Among the odds and bobs one lad '... used to have to take the men's time sheets and works repair report every fortnight, usually on a Tuesday afternoon to Stoke Prior (walk down the canal-side from Tardebigge), carrying a locked leather dispatch case containing the time sheets, etc., and deliver to the Engineer, a Mr W. Griffiths, who lived on the wharf at that time.'

Blacksmithing was another trade essential to good maintenance on waterways. Iron or steel being bought in, in the rough, rod, flat bar, square bar or tube, as needed. A day's work might be the making of paddle rods, these having to be heated at one end until they were red hot, flattened and a slot cut into them to allow for the insertion of the cotter pin which retains the rod within the rack mechanism. When they had cooled, the other end would be tackled, a flat bar, which was bolted to the paddle, being forged (latterly welded) on to the rod. We are told that it was far easier for a skilled blacksmith to knock a one inch circular hole into a red hot piece of steel half an inch thick, than it is to drill it nowadays. New

of carpentry on a waterway, the younger apprentices would make, in a matter of months, such items as 'horse and donkey supporters' to be handed over to the saddler to fix in the harnesses; water scoops; wheelbarrows in two sizes, small for navvies and larger one for dredgers; ladders, short cranks would be needed for the steam tugs, castings of racks, pinions and safety catches had to be cleaned up and made to fit. Bolts would be manufactured as required. A bugbear to modern maintenance workers is the fact that all too often when a replacement nut or bolt is required the existing one, far from being a Whitworth or BSF standard thread, is one produced by a set of taps and dies which some long dead blacksmith had made for himself. As a sideline the matching of boat hook to shafts would be carried out. A weird modern tendency, failing a stock of old-fashioned rivets, is to buy and cut down coach-bolts, leaving the head and such shank as is required for the job, the end merely being peined over. This is hardly an economic or craftsman's procedure, the blacksmiths of yesteryear must turn in their graves. In fact as far as the blacksmith was concerned nothing should ever be 'put out' that he could possibly, one way or another, make up in the workshops. There are still a few blacksmiths on waterways, carrying out this honourable trade and one we knew, far from being the burly strong man of fiction, sweating madly over his forge, was, instead, a small, loquacious, happy man who did not rely so much on the strength of his back as on the skill of his fingertips.

A latterday requisite of at least one canal maintenance man was a knowledge of electricity, in so far as he was required to maintain the private telephone system operated by most independent waterways. It is said that when the National Telephone Company came into being they rode around to most waterways suggesting the installation of telephones here and

A poor photograph, but a rarity insofar as it shows the inside of a navigation company's workshop. Supposed to be on the river Welland at Spalding, it may in fact show the workshop of the long disused River Lark Navigation.

Right: Walsall, Ryders Green.

Below: Thurlwood Steel Lock, No 53 on the Trent & Mersey Canal when brand new, 1958. British Waterways Board.

A most unusual photograph taken on the Worcester & Birmingham Canal in February 1963 by the then foreman, Stan Turner, this shows the 'company' van parked on the ice by Tardebigge Workshops, with the ganger 'Billy' Mills, stopping it from sliding away.

This photograph was taken in the vicinity of Wolverton, on the Grand Union Canal. It serves to show a dilemma that faces all engineers, as where piling stops back erosion is inevitable, whether behind 1930s concrete piles or 1980s steel.

In December 1972 a need arose for the butty (unpowered) boat B39 to be moved along the Worcester & Birmingham Canal and it is seen here between Blackpole and Tolladine. No motorboat or horse was available so on a wettish day we have this photograph of Alf Watton, bricklayer, steering and Ernie Dickinson, his mate, acting as horse.

not know what had happened to him at the time but thought he had fainted or something. However, we went out of the tunnel to try and revive him, which we eventually did, and it appeared there had been a thunder storm while we were in the tunnel and he had had an electric shock.'

Nowadays there are a number of skilled tradesmen whose job is often underrated. Among these are the electricians whose jobs are infinitely varied, re-wiring the loom of a dredger miles from anywhere, which for reasons unknown had decided to burn itself out, being one minor example. Another specialist trade is that of the fitter who may one day be rebuilding a Petter, Armstrong Siddeley or Lister diesel engine in a working craft and the next day take an emergency call-out to a pleasure craft in trouble with hydraulic failure. Later he may be tinkering with the bucket on a dragline and after that installing a new stove on a motorboat. Incredibly, most are good-natured.

Most of the lorry drivers employed by the British Waterways Board have many encounters and meet many hazards. Looking at a canal with the muddy tracks leading to old wharves, weary old bridges and barbed wire, it is little wonder that being mired in is 'just one of those things'. One wonders, though, how the driver of one Waterways' lorry felt when he collided on a narrow bridge with another Waterways' vehicle — that accident report to headquarters must have made interesting reading! It should be borne in mind, however, that they also manage to drive upwards of 200 miles a day, come rain, come ice, or sun.

Some other drivers employed with the BWB have, more or less, replaced boats' captains; for in all too many cases all traffic to or from warehouses is handled by road, and the trucks operate on a scheduled run — day in, day out.

Piling is nowadays often contracted out but until quite recently was normally a two-man job under the guidance and assistance of a ganger. Materials have varied from plain wooden piles driven in by hand to pneumatically driven interlocking convoluted steel models. A transitional phase incorporated concrete piles driven in by a heavy hammer operated from a boat by means of a winch. The basic uses of piles were always to prevent undermining of banks in cuttings, and bank-strengthening on embankments. Here the marked contradiction between the commercially viable waterways of the North of England and the moribund canals of the South and Midlands become most apparent. As one potters along the Aire & Calder, neat concrete coping and a firm bank are visible, while lengths of the Staffordshire & Worcestershire canal towpath looks like Old Man's Teeth, with gaps and broken pieces abounding. One ex-ganger,

there, mainly to speed up communications between the lock-keepers and the administration; but upon requesting and receiving an estimate a cold shudder ran down the spines of the powers-that-were and instead, until quite recently, they ran and maintained a private network. There were even hazards in this:

'The telephone wires used to be fixed under the tunnels at one time, I remember I was helping to keep a boat steady in a tunnel, while two men were repairing an insulator fastening, when one of these men suddenly fell on to the cabin-top, where they were standing to reach the work to be done, we did talking of piling, put his finger on the hub of the matter: 'You see, if you got piles, the banks don't fall in, and you don't need so much dredging.'

Canal painters have always been in existence, although often a man would double-up on two jobs, the carpenters, for instance, being quite capable of looking after the painting of their own work. In keeping with modern trends such painters as waterways have, appear to do little painting, most of it being put out to contract; instead the painters paste up more notices to become defaced. A fairly common grouse today from the older men is that: 'When I were young, you dain't need to be told about a job, you done it, there were no jobs we carsn't do', whereas the newcomers to waterways prefer to know exactly what they are expected to do and when they will be doing it. Demarcation, however, does not in any vast extent rear its head, but on the other hand the influence of the unions on waterways has been beneficial to the working man, and in 1971 a grading system was introduced which laid down the jobs a man could do within his rate of pay.

A labourer might be expected, over a period of a few weeks, to undertake hedge-laying or brushing, hole-digging and leak-stopping, boat-steering (eel-catching), off-loading bricks from a lorry on to the bank and, a few days later, loading them back on to another lorry, handling a pneumatic drill, oiling locks, pumping out sunken pleasure craft, general stoppage work, stringing up a new wire fence to replace a hedge maliciously burnt down, ditch-cleaning, dislodging any unwanted articles from culverts, burying dead, decomposing and/or liquefying carcasses of animals (at 50p per head), clearing overhanging growth or one of a dozen other jobs. Some jobs, lorry-driving or boat-steering for instance, require considerable intelligence, others not. The differential between the one and the other was 10p per week in 1972.

Of the men employed a fair percentage used to be over retirement age, content to scratch away in an obscure corner of the waterway, working conscientiously, if slowly, at some mind-numbing task that could be done in a twentieth of the time with a machine; others by virtue of their friendship with the foreman or other official, were to be found in yet another obscure corner of the waterway where they contemplated a space six inches in front of their noses. A number of men, age is immaterial, are enthusiastic about the job, but the older they are the more competently it is carried out. For example, a willingness to spend 12 hours a night checking the water levels in a reservoir in times of rain, to go out in a van at two o'clock in the morning with a motor pump in order to help a pleasure craft owner whose boat is in danger of foundering after hitting an underwater obstruction, or to abandon the television at half past nine on a summer's evening to ascertain and

It is difficult to know who should represent the canal person of today but in 1993 the lock-keeper at Hazelford Lock won an internal British Waterways competition. Nothing too amazing about that and although it would have been almost unknown forty years ago the fact that this person was a 51-year-old mother is almost irrelevant. What is an intriguing fact is that she is a successful novelist.

Jenny Reah left school at 15, married the lock-keeper (Don Williams) at Hazelford when she was 16, and had five children, all brought up in a cottage with only a footbridge for access. Her first Mills & Boon novel, really the epitome of romantic writing, was accepted in 1987. Sadly the following year Don died, but Jenny met with nothing but old-fashioned help from British Waterways who allowed her to continue as lock-keeper: 'I thought it very understanding of BW to offer me the job. Taking over from Don worked out well. I was already familiar with what I had to do and it meant I could stay here which saved me the extra trauma involved in moving house. I needed the job: it helped me through a very difficult time'. In August 1992 she re-married, having met Jim through a singles club and enjoyed the wedding of her dreams, but she has continued as lock-keeper for 'I'm happy with BW, they have provided me with many happy years and happy memories and I hope many more to come.' Jenny then added a sentence in which could be heard a ghostly echo of George Bate: 'Life is precious to me, I don't take anything for granted and I hope that I'll have the good health to enjoy it. Without that you have nothing.' Media Relations, British Waterways.

check the damage done to the parapet of a bridge by moronic vehicle drivers, is found amongst these men. They are the type of men who, when out cruising on their own boats — and some canal workers are, incredibly, able to enjoy a busman's holiday — will endeavour to rescue a pig which has fallen down the bank into the canal, or will spend their spare time writing a report on local birds for an ornithological society or upon canal life for a church magazine. This enthusiasm, rather strangely, is more apparent in the lower strata of maintenance men; too often, the man above has become blasé on the whole subject.

A class of men whose enthusiasm, or lack of it, can make an enormous difference to the work carried out, is that employed on dredging. Here there is no clearly defined approach to the work, some gangs working on normal rates of pay and plodding away, others on the same rate rely upon the 'tat' (brass, copper, wire) that is to be found in the bottom of the canal to boost their pay. Others may find a bonus scheme applicable, whereby over and above a certain tonnage an extra sum is put in the pay packet every week. Dredging, by governing the depth of water, represents the tonnage capacity of a waterway and since early times various technical advances have been made on the machines used to keep pace with the ever-increasing acumulation of materials hidden beneath the waters. Foremost of them is mud — mud brought down to the waterway from the sides of cuttings, from faulty drains and freshets or rivers. It is unfortunate that a canal is dependent upon these natural sources of supply to maintain its water-level and that the one must go hand in glove with the other. What are extraneous are the polythene bags, mattresses, bed frames, lamp standards, telephone cables, diesel and waste-oil drums, tyres, prams, suites of furniture, carpets and the like which are so carefully deposited in the canal, not only by individuals but quite often by concerns who should know better. Within a twelvemonth it has been recorded that Post Office employees disposed of some unwanted cable, a motorway contractor dumped ten cubic yards of rubble, a chemical firm mistakenly ran the wrong pump into an outlet, killing all the fish thereabouts, diddicoys pumped upwards of 50 gallons of waste-oil over the bank, and contractors for a local council disposed of broken paving stones over a canal bridge; this was all seen over a 20-mile stretch. Whether the strengthening of anti-pollution Acts has had any effect is doubtful and until these people and firms can be caught and used as examples it is unlikely that any Act of Parliament, however strong, can materially alter ingrained habits. A flat statement is that a boat drawing three feet of water can pass through a bridge on the outskirts of Birmingham one day and be stemmed up the next. A week later a dredger will clear the obstruction, but within 24 hours the position will be back to where it was.

Arthur Cross, boatman in charge of the narrowboat Achernar, throws some rubbish on board during a scavenging operation.

No definite date can be fixed for the introduction of any one type of machine used for dredging, but the grand-daddy of them all, and he is still alive today, is the bag and spoon — simply a leather or canvas bag having a circular ring of iron around its mouth, the ring being fastened to a long pole. One man in a barge guides the pole, another man drags the bag along the bottom of the channel by means of a chain at the bottom end of the pole, which is wound around a winch at the far end of the barge. The mud is scooped up in the bag, the bag raised, tipped out into the barge or hopper, dropped back down again and so on *ad infinitum*. An aqua mortrice is an improvement on this method, utilising an iron scoop in lieu of the bag, this iron pocket being wound up by a small motor. It was estimated in 1896 that 65 cubic yards of gravel could be raised within a working day of 12 hours with this machine and it was probably an ancestor of this that was in use on the River Severn in 1842:

'This town (Upton-upon-Severn) owes its chief importance to the river, which is here navigable for vessels of 110 tons, and is being much improved by the Worcester & Birmingham Canal Co, during the present summer, who have expended nearly £2,000 in procuring a dredging machine, worked by a steam-engine of 8 horse-power, which brings up from the bed of the river about 150 tons of gravel per day; and it is hoped, by thus moving the shoals and banks, to render the river completely navigable at all seasons. If the silt thus obtained from the shallow places be judiciously deposited on the low banks, where the river is widest, there is no doubt much permanent good may be done to the navigation by narrowing and deepening the channel, in the way the Clyde and other rivers have been improved.'

For use in the wider, deeper canals there came next a bucket-and-ladder dredger. An eyewitness report of the operation of one of these on a narrow waterway in the early 1900s gave the method of operation very clearly:

'The dredger was iron hulled, fitted with elevator chain of buckets, one mobile steam engine, this engine was lifted out of the dredger when the dredger was not in use, or if the engine was required for more urgent jobs such as power for a centrifugal pump, etc., the engine would be lowered on to its chassis to be towed away to wherever it was required. There was a special bed in the dredger that this engine was lowered on to, so that the steam pipe and water intake pipe would be connected in a short time. When steam was up to required strength the elevator chain of buckets would be lowered on to the bed of the canal or the silt to be moved, the driving belt fixed from the flywheel on the engine to the pulley shafting driving elevator, the buckets loaded with silt or mud would rise up from the canal bed with the elevator in motion, the buckets would deposit the silt or mud on to a point. (The dredger would load a boat either side of her, whichever side was suitable to load.) As they went over to return to the canal bed again, this silt would slide down the point and into the iron container that was in the boat alongside the dredger. There were four of these iron container tanks in these boats, they would hold five to six tons of silt. Donkeys were needed to tow the loaded boats to the tip and bring empty boats back to the dredger to be loaded again. The procedure at the tip — the steam crane worked on iron rails similar to railway lines, the rails being laid down on timber planking, and trestles where required. The steam crane worked along these rails under her own power, when loaded boat came alongside the tip the crane would move up to the side of the boat and the lifting chain would be fastened to the lugs on the sides of the container tanks and lifted out of the boat and taken by the crane to the end of the tip, a stop lever being knocked out of its closed position, causing the tank to turn, depositing its load into the tip, the tank being righted again was taken back by the crane to the boat. This procedure went on day after day from dredger to tip. Many tons of silt and mud would be taken out of the canal every day, depending on the distance from dredger to the tip. A forty-foot long boat was used to stable the donkeys at night, the punt was required to take chains ashore to fasten the dredger to mooring stakes, otherwise she would crawl her way along when working. This was called the chain punt and this punt would also be used to fetch coal from a convenient place where coal had been placed for the dredger. There were four men required to work this dredging plant.'

The above refers to the dredging of a new winding hole, to enable the narrow carrying craft to be turned more easily. Unfortunately due to a lack of communication, or inattention on the part of the local lock-keeper, on a night of heavy rains excessive water was run off, causing the dredger to tilt over. As she rolled, the water ran over the low sides and she sank, though square on the bottom. In the process of trying to lift her one of the chains broke and she fell on her side in the middle of the fairway. To get her out a dam was driven across the canal and that immediate length of waterway was drained; although she was eventually righted and taken to the workshops she was never used again. When, during World War One, she was broken up, she was still in good condition, many of the plates still having the red lead paint on the bottom where the ballast had been laid. Although always regarded as being before her time, she had, rather

These photographs at Norbury Junction on the Shropshire Union Canal were taken by an iced-in boatman during the long winter of 1969-70. During this time domestic coal was being lorried into the wharf at Norbury but this nip came suddenly and the boats were trapped a mile or so away from this junction. J.J.Wright

In 1974 this gang were at work on the Stratford-on-Avon Canal, Northern Section, which has always been prone to silting from the number of streamlets which feed into it. In this particular case a new length of piling has been driven in to restore the towpath along a particularly weak embankment. The dredger is discharging mud while the tug-driver has abandoned his craft on the left to see what 'tat' is coming up.

incredibly, to be bow-hauled by men wherever she went. The mobile engine, however, ended up functioning in a saw mill, supplying power to the circular saw used in lock-gate making, and was not scrapped until 1924.

The principle of a dipper bucket dredger, a near relative of the bag and spoon, served both for drag lining and stray dredging. Essentially it is a large cylindrical steel bucket with a projecting lip fastened to a crane, job or boom, which is lowered into the canal and, by means of chains, drags itself into the mud, the jib raising it above water level. The bucket itself can either be bottom-opening or capable of being tilted to deposit the material. A grab-bucket dredger is the type most commonly in use now. The principle is that the grab is suspended from the jib of a crane and is lowered with its jaws open to the bottom of the channel, penetrating the surface by impact and its own weight. The jaws are then closed trapping a mouthful of whatever the grab has

An interesting example of dredging practice, involving the most modern of machinery with a mini-excavator, and tractor and tipper-trailer for use as the excavators motive power and for carrying away the mud. The hopper, which seemed to be used for waste metal, bears a strong resemblance to a nineteenth-century tub-boat. Neath Canal 1989.

The photographer caught this example of Japanese machinery at work at Canal Head, Pocklington Canal, 1991. There is always something vaguely menacing about the appearance of diggers like this; the fact that its teeth were dribbling does nothing to dispel this!

motion, or if the bottom be very hard it is not unknown merely to lift a grabful of water — or fish! Early models were worked by a steam engine with a boiler but problems have always been met with the rolling motion resulting from the movement of the crane jib. The vibration and rolling necessitated the monthly docking of early wooden craft and the inherent instability has caused a number of such dredgers to roll over.

Around the turn of the century it was common practice on narrow waterways to use a seven-foot beam dredger, which was either held by wire ropes or chains to iron bars driven into the banks, or supported on each side by sealed pontoons, wherever the waterway width permitted this. By virtue of their design they were not normally self-propelled, but were punted around with a small steam tug. A large crew was needed, two boiler tenters, one crane driver, two men on the tug and various others operating the boats with the waste and the steam crane at the tip; their capacity was claimed to be

found; the whole is raised and swung until it is in alignment with the hopper or waste boat, the jaws opened and the muck deposited therein. Different types of jaws can be provided, ranging from smooth lips to heavy teeth. There is nothing more frustrating than to operate such a machine, lift, open and see one brick drop out! Alternatively, if a brick is caught in the jaws, the silt will wash out during the lifting and swinging

400 tons a day. Today's dredgers of this type are self-propelled, fitted with a diesel engine which also operates a hydraulic grab. Theoretically only requiring one man, two are found to be desirable if the driver is not to run backwards and forwards from the grab controls to the steering controls time and time again, although they can pull themselves along the bottom of channel by the action of the grab. The latest design is controllable from the cab, but at the insistence of the union an extra man is often carried for safety reasons. The problem of stability has been overcome in a most ingenious manner, which can be effectively described as four legs with large, flat feet positioned one in each corner. By means of hydraulic arms these are lowered to the bed of the canal under considerable pressure and are self-adjusting until the dredger is levelled. Accidents can still happen very easily; without the feet in position they are hopelessly unstable and have rolled over when the operator has omitted to lower them. If moored in a lock pound special care is paid to the level of the water, as they are incapable of floating themselves off the bottom. Large warning notices are distributed liberally over the structure and the actuating mechanisms have the legs painted a lurid colour, following an unfortunate accident when the son of a dredger-driver put his head between the hydraulic ram and the cross arm as the leg was being raised. The father subsequently left the employ of waterways.

A final type of dredger, which is worthy of mention here and is in use on some river navigations, is the suction or centrifugal model, of which a number of varieties are available. The silt is sucked into the innards of the machine, mud being thrown out one side and water the other. They are, however, incapable of digesting the detritus of our civilisation and for that reason are not likely to be extensively used on the smaller inland navigations.

The deposit of waste mud has, over the years, fallen into three distinct patterns. In the early days most farmers welcomed the slurry and rushes ('segs') pulled from the bottom of the waterway as a good fertiliser. The material was shovelled out of the hoppers into barrows and, using long planks could, by a judicious agreement 'twixt ganger and farmer, be taken quite a long distance to the required field. As artificial fertilisers became easily available, the material lifted contained increasing amounts of 'foreigners'. With pedigree herds of cattle roaming the land, farmers no longer wished for such treatment, and it became necessary for the various waterway concerns to find among their own bits and pieces of land, or to purchase, a

declivity wherein the muck could be dumped. In suitable positions a quarter of a million tons of slurry can be disposed of. Needless to say by its liquid nature this material can often run amok, but it is the proud boast of the crane operators responsible for the discharge of waste that they can turn the course of the tip with a matchstick or a twig. Certainly the odd railway sleeper applied at the opportune moment and in the right place can swing the course of the mud 100 yards to one side, thus giving earlier deposits a chance to drain and settle. An alternative but restricted method of disposal is to dump the material on banks to raise them, or to backfill new lengths of piling. The final approach to the problem, more practicable on river navigations, involved the use of bottom-opening hoppers which could be towed to an estuary or spit of land to be reclaimed, where the contents were dumped.

A typical modern operation on a Midlands canal will necessitate the use of a dredger, two tugs, a discharging crane, and six or eight waste boats and any number of men from a minimum of four to a maximum of eight, exclusive of supervisory staff. In theory two of these men should be plant operators, one existing full time on the dredger at the dredging site the other operating the crane at the tip. A further two men should be tug drivers and an additional two men are normally required, as a minimum, to steer the waste or mud boats. Still, in theory, we should have two craft being loaded at the dredger, two being discharged at the tip and two trains of a tug plus two boats operating up and down the stretch of waterway. Sometimes, obviously, when the spoil can be dumped locally, it is easier to omit the tugs and shaft the boats to their destination, however it will be understood that on a narrow waterway tugs cannot be turned at any convenient point, but most often have to run a mile or so at either or both ends for this purpose. Again, the tugs are rarely matching pairs and one finds combinations like a converted icebreaker of 1900 vintage running the upward leg and pulling two boats, while the downward leg is being pushed by a modern pusher tug. The dredger may be working in an awkward site or in poor conditions where it is incapable of loading the boats at the same speed as the crane at the top can discharge them. A high wind can make the marshalling of the boats difficult or the proximity of a pleasure-craft base may mean that they have to be moved about to a great extent, as the standard penalty for damage to a pleasure craft is three days suspension without pay for the crew concerned, irrespective of cause. Not the most enviable of jobs.

An Inspector Calls

THE CHAIN of command within waterway companies was fairly orthodox and remained intact well into nationalised days. Maintenance and engineering were a vital part of any canal structure, and provided an interesting path for two-way communication. Under one job title or another there would be a director of engineering who placed proposals before the board of directors and received back, usually via the finance director, a given amount of money to spend, either quarterly or annually. Under this director would be an engineer-in-charge, who in later days, would have overall responsibility for a number of waterways, each having themselves a divisional 'main man'. Locally, each canal would have one or more inspectors or superintendents. Under them would be foremen and under them, in turn, gangers.

Each player would fight his own corner, thus the foreman bricklayer regarded his walling as a primary interest, as opposed to the foreman carpenter who wanted to purchase as much timber as possible for seasoning ready for any eventuality involving the wooden fittings on a canal.

Each produced a budget which, at the lowest level, was calculated weekly, but presented to the inspector as a monthly requirement. He would 'dress this up' to look palatable to the divisional engineer, who would have the unenviable task of deciding where priorities lay. Examples of purely local budgeting would include leak-stopping, hedge trimming and lock painting, while major lock works, dredging and house maintenance were the responsibility of the division, albeit normally discussed with the inspector. Overall planning and proposals for new works or improvements were discussed at director level, often to a degree of minuteness that would surprise the 'wining dining' directors of 1950s industry.

Inevitably, though, there were drawbacks to a system of this kind and good lower level employees were adept at manoeuvring inside a tight budget. On one waterway in the 1960s by tacit agreement between the foreman and the inspector a reasonable sum was allocated for hedge laying between mileposts 1 and 4. Nominally a ganger, three men and a boat were involved on a semi-piece work basis, their wages, boat depreciation, personal and general tool allowances and subsistence payments were all involved, plus overheads, said to be at the time no less than 323% to cover the cost of not only the chain of command but the administration.

Lower down the canal between mileposts 22 and 25 there was a hedge that was grossly overgrown and which, by allowing the cattle to ramble on the towpath, caused the ganger considerable grief as, being the nearest man to have a cottage, he was called out to restore the beasts to their proper field. True the ganger received on-call pay but as an elderly, rather stately man he had no desire to have his Sundays disturbed to go 'a-hasslin' and 'a-wallopin' on the towpath. So, he pushed for this hedge to be properly layered, pointing out, quite ingeniously, that (with the work being done in winter) the men could be used to clean the culverts and brooks on this length as they could dry out their clothing — and themselves! — at his house. The foreman pushed the scheme to the inspector, but unfortunately this particular canal was divided into North and South portions, with virtually all the toll-paying traffic moving over the Northern end which had budget balance of roughly 3:1 per mile in its favour.

All non-essential work on the Southern end was defined as just that, and the hedge laying project was deferred in favour of the proposed work between mileposts 1 and 4. What the gaffers were thought not to know (although maybe they turned a blind eye) was that there were no hedges in that area, just factory walls and brickwork.

On a larger scale it is generally accepted that the only way the Brecon & Abergavenny canal was kept open as a usable boating channel was by the then section inspector juggling his budget to allow for some dredging and local lock repairs; this canal together with many railway owned waterways having held the unenviable position of poor relation vis-à-vis the 'pure' railways. The Great Western Railway in the 1920s had long ceased to pay the magnificent dividends of earlier days and the last boats to carry freight on the canal (to any serious extent) ended their trading during World War One, leaving the engineer with the unenviable task of trying to extract money from a management who, however sympathetic, had a primary duty to support the paying parts of their business.

A third example of indirect use of funds was to be found on a Welsh canal which, although long since derelict, served as a water supply feeder to a batch of factories. A far sighted man, the manager foresaw the days when tourism and hence boats would become a vital part of Wales' economy and although his meagre budget allowed no slack whatsoever for anything more than basic water channel maintenance, he paid out of his own pocket for surveying, estimating and dredging to be carried out, albeit on Sundays and with minuscule amounts of mud being removed. Alas, he died just before 'proper' restoration work funded by the local Councils could begin.

In the case of the older 'heavy duty' waterways, by virtue of the long lines of communication and a firm desire on everyone's part to protect their backs, vast quantities of paperwork were (and still are) generated, all of which has to be filed and retained for a reasonable time; 'reasonable' seemingly being in excess of 30 years.

Unfortunately the vast bulk of this paperwork has long been destroyed, and there is not, and never has been, the market for canal orientated ephemera that exists in the field of omnibus and railway transport. It is no exaggeration to state that relatively recently four skip loads of documents were destroyed as not being required from one section office, while the great library of canal-orientated material held at British Rail's one time headquarters in London has been sold off and dispersed, much of it now (1994) retailing at £1 per page, with extra for drawings.

However, from time to time over the years bits and pieces of correspondence and the like have been 'liberated', and around 20 years ago a parcel arrived from a one-time boatman, with a verbal message to the effect that it could be used to enhance a book, but better keep it until there was no risk to his pension and, despite temptation, in the following pages are printed documents that have not seen the light of day from their writing until this publication, the

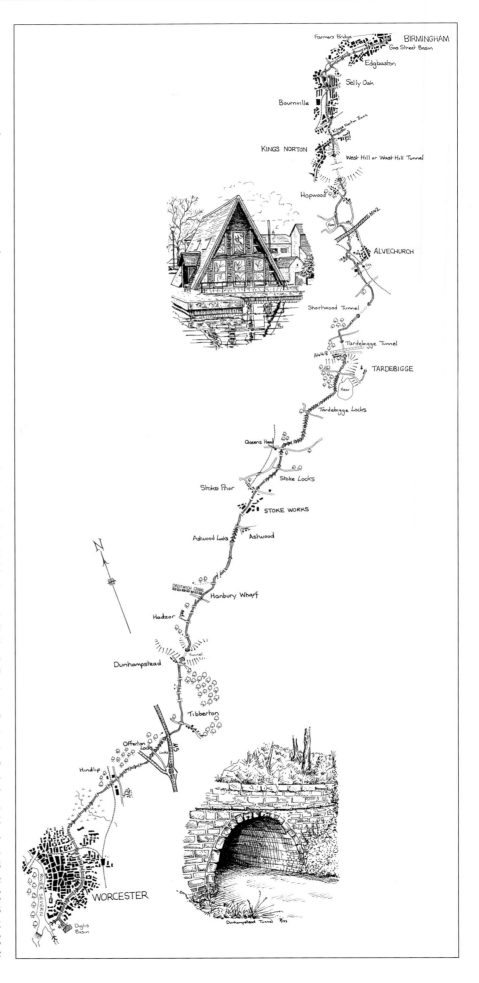

'finder' having moved off on his last great canal voyage.

Unfortunately, although most of the older letters have clearly originated within the Sharpness New Docks Company and are addressed to the superintendent at Tardebigge on the Worcester & Birmingham Canal, they are a curiously lop-sided selection with few replies retained; presumably these were filed in another bundle. But they cast a unique and quite fascinating light upon the minutiae of everyday canal life and the sheer complexity of matters expected to be dealt with by a relatively lowly placed official. In a number of cases minor alterations have been made to protect past and present employees' privacy.

It would seem that Tardebigge, or rather the inspector there, had considerable authority when it came to ordering materials. The usual technique at the time was to indent for an item from Head Office, have a discussion on this at the next monthly meeting and providing a good enough case could be made out, either requisition material from Head Office Stores or order from an external source. In nationalised days, all orders had to come via Stores, even though they might then order from the brick company down the road. Often (and I choose that word carefully) the order forms would come through weeks or months after the job was completed.

It is interesting to note that in all cases the suppliers whose letters are in the author's collection write to 'The Sharpness New Docks & Gloucester and Birmingham Navigation Company, Engineering Stores, Tardebigge, Bromsgrove, Worcs', hereafter, for brevity, referred to as 'SND'.

One typical batch of letters included orders to the Salt Union, who were to supply a (Black) Smith's hearth tuyere (the pipe through which air is pumped to the hearth) at £1.25; The Severn & Canal 3 x 16' (5m) lengths of second-hand Guard Iron; Joseph Wright was apologising for the delay in returning chains ('in the whole of February we had a good deal of sickness') but promising them within 10 days; John Wright could not meet Mr Spiers' requirements having only one tree 27' long 'but tapering to 16" or 17"', or if he really must have the wood 22" wide only a 22 footer could be had. Gloomily one should mention that Redditch (which was once to be connected to Tardebigge by a horse-tramway) no longer has a station yard, just a truncated single line and a massive car park.

Goodman & Co quoted for 30 tons of gravel (9/3d per ton) and 15 tons of sand (6/-) 'at our wharf' — in fact the ex-canal company's wharf then leased to Goodman.

A letter from Joseph Corbett & Son of Hartlebury, near Kidderminster, told Tardebigge: 'Although we had Elm Timber hauled from Hanbury Park into Hanbury Wharf unfortunately we cannot sell it as our customer at Great Bridge will not purchase as he says it is Elm diseased. As you know we have sent 8 of the large trees by boat and are hoping to send some more, but we cannot sell the small stuff. We were wondering if you would allow us to fetch the small stuff away so that we can cut it up at our Mere Hall sawmill. We have done our best to sell it but have been unsuccessful. Perhaps you will kindly drop us a line after the holiday and oblige.'

Was the Elm disease mentioned above the same one that eventually ravaged the countryside a decade or two ago?

A quite vital part of a canal inspector's job was keeping a close eye on reservoir levels and monitoring water flows. In the case of the Worcester & Birmingham canal, this juggling act was made more difficult by the necessity to maintain high water levels where (as at Bittell) the reservoir was built to compensate mill-owners for the water diverted to the canal. The following are a few of the weekly returns made by the inspector to Gloucester.

Worcester & Birmingham Canal
Reservoir & Canal Water Levels

18 August 1934
Upper Bittall Reservoir — 23'5" below weir level — a fall of 1'4" since 11 August.
Tardebigge Reservoir — 28'7" below top water level — a fall of 2'11" since 11 August
Canal level between Tardebigge and Birmingham — 7" below weir level
'The new centrifugal pump at Diglis, now being installed will probably be running for the first time next Wednesday. The present level of the canal generally is the same as for the previous three weeks. Rainfall has been negligible during the past week.'
25 August 1934 shows a continuing an worrying loss although 'The centrifugal pump at Diglis has been running since Wednesday 22 August and Diglis Basin is now full.'
By 8 September supplies to the 'main line' were seriously affected: Upper Bittall Reservoir — 34'0 below weir level — supply stopped. Tardebigge Reservoir — 34'8 below top water level — fall 1'9". Canal level between Tardebigge and Birmingham — 9" below weir level. 'Two inches less water than previous week. Rainfall for the week — very small.'
It was not until 17 November 1934 that Spiers could relax to any extent, but the reservoir levels still remained low:
Upper Bittall Reservoir — 33'1 below weir level
Tardebigge Reservoir — 28'8 below top water level
Canal levels — Tardebigge to Birmingham — 3" below weir
Five Mile Pound — 6" below weir

Lowesmoor — 6" below weir

'The canal water levels are now almost normal, the top level being in best possible working condition as far as water level is concerned. Lowesmoor and the Five Mile Pounds are about 3" below best possible condition but the installation of the new centrifugal pumps at the Blockhouse and Kings Head should be completed in about 10 days and these ponds can then be filled.'

At the other end of the canal we have a handful of pumping records for Diglis, Kings Head and Blockhouse pumps, all by 1935 electric but still requiring some attention by the lock-keepers to the intake grills and water courses. Two weeks are tabulated below, together with the inspector's notes; on occasion the pumping made no apparent change to the figures, this is explained by downhill boats taking water with them. Rarely in the days of commercial boats could water levels be kept 'on the weir', but 6" below weir level cut 6" from the depth of water available and affected the tonnage that could be carried.

Diglis, Kings Head and Blockhouse pumps operation w/e 14 September 1935 and w/e 26 October 1935.

Location	Date	Hours Pumping	Water Before Pumping	Levels After Pumping	Total Hours Pumping
	9 Sep	10	6 "	3"	27 ½ for the week
	11 Sep	12	7½"	2"	
	12 Sep	3	4 "	3"	
Diglis Basins	14 Oct	8	8 "	5"	28
	16 Oct	6	7	5½"	
	17 Oct	7	8½"	5"	
	18 Oct	7	6½"	4"	
	21 Oct	11	7½"	3½"	20
	23 Oct	9	5 "	2"	
Kings Head (or Sidbury) Lock No.3	9 Sep	11	3 "	3"	27½
	10 Sep	8½	3 "	1"	
	12 Sep	8	1 "	1"	
	17 Oct	9½	1 "	1"	
Blockhouse Lock No.4	9 Sep	11	3 "	1¼"	27½
	10 Sep	8½	2 "	2"	
	12 Sep	8	3 "	2"	
	17 Oct	9½	2½"	1"	

To metricate 1" = 2.54cm, thus 6" below weir level = approx. 15.24cm, 8½" = 21.57cm, etc.
The Five Mile Pound which acts as a linear reservoir between locks 17 and 16 was 1½" under weir level on 14 September, full on 19 October, but 1" under again by 26 October.

Although dated 16 January 1935, a handwritten answer by Mr Spiers to the Engineer clearly related to 1935 boat movements and contains unusual statistical evidence on the number of boats (all trading craft) that were passing along the waterway. There was very little shorthaul traffic by then.

'Estimate of water used in locking through Tardebigge top lock during the period 10 September to 22 December 1935. Number of uphill boats 493. Number of downhill boats 469. 26 Boats returned via Stourport. Total number of boats passing Tardebigge top lock — 962. Actual number of locks used would be approximately 812. This latter figure was arrived at by comparing figures taken during the years 1918 and 1919 when records were taken of the locks of water used and traffic was of similar proportions to that of 1934. Tardebigge top lock measures 78'0" long and 7'4" average width and must be filled to a depth of 8'0" assuming that the side pond is used in the most efficient way. The total weight of water used per lockage is 130 tons. The total weight of water used during above period = 105,000 tons. Assuming Battery Co's pump delivery 25,000 galls per hour for 2450 hours the water pumped was 61,250,000 gall or 273,000 tons.'

Water was a canal's life-blood, and there is no doubt Mr Spiers had to rely upon his staff to a very great extent for readings and information as his time was, all too often, diverted to running after Gloucester's problems.

All the general correspondence was filed in date order and it is rather unfortunate that the first legible letter is a rather vitriolic complaint from a Mr E.Mansell of 98 Wharf Road, King's Norton: "I understand that the Canal which runs from Birmingham through King's Norton to Hopwood, etc., belongs to your goodselves, this being so I regret that it should be necessary to communicate with you regarding the insulting behaviour of one of your workmen, William Leach, respecting the feeder which passes through my allotment. On the 8th instant this individual, acting on your behalf, wrongly accused me of depositing rubbish in the feeder and interfering with its course, using the most obscene language, and in earshot of several neighbours. I can say without the slightest hesitation that there is not the least grounds for such an accusation, and even if it were so, I feel sure that your Company would not uphold my being blackguarded by a workman in such an offensive manner."

Gloucester, while passing on the letter and asking for a report, added: "I hope his (Leach's) zeal for the Company's interests has not led him to act in a manner which is not becoming to one of the Company's staff."

The following letters are quite fascinating insofar as one wonders quite what Miss Carr was up to and where her trade would come from, as although the building was adjacent to the Evesham/Redditch/Birmingham road (now A441) as well as the canal, the whole population of Hopwood at the time was only 200.

On 21 January 1935, the SND manager and Engineer, Cullis (or, rather, one of his staff) wrote to Spiers regarding 'Premises adjoining Hopwood Bridge' ' . . .we shall have no objection to the proposed grant of tenancy being made to Miss Carr, to whom I am writing today. I note you state the water supply has been laid on, and take it the arrangements have been made by you for this following our telephonic conversation.' By 25 March the atmosphere had changed: 'I am duly in receipt of your letter of the 21st instant, enclosing one from a Mrs Moss, complaining as to the nature of the business carried on at the building adjoining Hopwood Bridge. We certainly cannot allow the premises to be used for the sale of fried fish, and I enclose you a copy of letters I have to-day written to Miss Carr and Mrs Moss on the matter. Miss Carr has paid no rent, and when you see her you had better intimate our Solicitors will be instructed if payment is not forthcoming at an early date.'

The letter to Mrs M.M.Moss of St Brelades, Hopwood, is both an acknowledgement of her letter and a promise that steps will be taken. The third letter of the 25th (actually from Cullis himself) is addressed to Miss F.M.Carr at No.10 Hopwood and while reiterating that the sale of fried fish is strictly forbidden refers still to 'a proposed grant of tenancy for the sale of sweets, cigarettes and light refreshments' but adds 'In view of the position, I do not propose to complete any arrangement for tenancy, and have asked our Mr Spiers to see you as to an early vacation of the premises.' That flurry of letters apparently crossed with one from Miss Carr although she may have dated her letter the 25th to avoid any difficulties: 'Regret I shall be unable to carry on at the above premises, as it will be too much for me with other business, so I vacate as from to-day. I think you will find I only owe Rent as from 25 December, because the Hut was closed down, that will be one quarter.' On the 26th Gloucester wrote again to Spiers and after referring to previous correspondence continued: 'You will note she (Miss Carr) proposed to vacate the premises yesterday, but even if they were closed down as stated, rent is due from Michaelmas Quarter Day, and payment of further rent could no doubt be enforced in lieu of notice. The rent was first fixed at £10 per annum, but we were prepared to install a water supply and bear the subsequent water rates provisionally on the rent being increased to ten guineas (£10.50) per annum.'

Single-handed working on canals has always been frowned on, primarily as the method of working used to pass through locks is rather rough and ready. It is quite possible to work perfectly safely, especially on 'narrow' canals, by using a long shaft, and judicious applications of engine power, but undesirable with a horse-drawn boat. Today such activity is disapproved of by our 'nanny' (British Waterways) who worry about single-handed boat people having accidents or drowning.

During February 1935, there was quite a flurry of correspondence over this, the Severn & Canal Carrying Company stating: "We feel that this is an isolated instance, and that instructions which have been given from this Office will ensure that it shall not recur, and we are somewhat alarmed at the statement that there is a growing tendency to work boats single-handed."

We do not know whether Mr Spiers had made any enemies but a letter sent by Mr S.W.Smith of Gloucester on 8 April 1935 has all the sound of a large ticking bomb, but hopefully and presumably it all turned out to be a red herring: "Information has been received at this office that the stabling conditions on the Worcester & Birmingham Canal are not all to be desired. The following has been mentioned: Blackpole — insufficient bedding; Stoke — Dirty and insufficient bedding, King's Norton — likewise. Will you please be good enough to look into this matter and see to it that nothing of this kind shall occur in the future. If you have comments to make upon this complaint, I shall be glad to have them"

The next two letters in the file cover, impart one of the small tragedies that are played out along the banks of any canal. It is worth noting that Kings Norton did not become a part of the City of Birmingham until 1911. The first letter is, as ever, from Gloucester to Tardebigge and is headed 'Occupation of canal bank near Kings Norton by a bungalow', and continues 'Referring to your letter of the 19 January last, I am enclosing copy of one received from Mr Dwyer, and shall be glad to hear whether the Company received any communication from the Birmingham Corporation at all on the matter.' and the second from Mr Dwyer to Gloucester. It read: "Please find enclosed P.O. and stamps value £1 6s 3d. I thank you for all the kindness shown by the Company and your servants. I have left the ground to my own regret. I was made to pull the bungalow down by the Birmingham Council, Being a disabled ex-serviceman having my leg amputated, it was very hard to leave after paying £100 for it and getting nothing back at all. Thanking you again for your kindness." The £1 6s 3d (£1.31) was presumably ground rent.

Generally speaking the Sharpness Company were quite unwilling to let outside concerns use their facilities unless they paid, but occasionally Spiers or other managers would recommend (perhaps for diplomatic or social reasons) that an exception could be made.

On 30 September the Company wrote to Spiers regarding the Kings Norton Hockey Club using 'our road adjoining Kings Norton Tunnel for the purpose of access to their playing field, as to which I shall be glad to have your observations' but added 'I might say that some years ago we had an application from the Football Club for permission to park cars on this road, but decided, in view of possible damage to the road, which was a cinder one, and also to the margins, that we could not allow it.' Spiers must have taken a different view for on 11 October the engineer writes again 'and note you see no objection to the use of our road as an approach to the Kings Norton Hockey Club's playing field, also that no cars would be allowed to park thereon.' By contrast on 25 July that year (1935) we had quite a liverish letter arrive: 'Wicket Gate — Coopers Hill. Referring to your letter of 13 July, the company consider openings in their boundary fences very objectionable. Whatever restrictions or provisions are made, they become neglected in time, and in this case, I consider the reasons advanced for the gateway do not justify granting the request which has been made by Mrs Morris and Miss Furber.'

The typist at Gloucester must have been busy as all letters from outside had to be labouriously copied, for no photocopiers or fax machines were available. One letter from Hussey, Egan & Pickmore read: "We should be glad if you would make arrangements to remove a telegraph pole carrying, we believe, your inter-lock wires within the next few days. We should be glad to see your local representative at the above site concerning this. We should be glad also if you would let us know your price for the hire of a barge or other large boat for the period of one week. We are proposing to drive a coffer dam at St George Bridge and to use the same boat to carrying the frame and driving gear."

The 'inter-lock wires' carried the local canal-use only telephone installation introduced on the Worcester & Birmingham canal before the national system had reached Tardebigge.

Next in the collection came a true rarity; the kind of ephemeral material that is all too often

List of Hours Water running between Offerton & Diglis

Date 1935						
					9	5
Nov	15	11	Hrs		10	4
	17 Sunday	16			20	10
	19	5			24	4
	20	9½			27	4
	21	5			29	6
	30	4		Feb	1	10½
Dec	1 Sunday	4			18	8
	25 Xmas Day	5			19	8
	26 Boxing Day	5			22	11
	27	13			23 Sunday	4
	28	11			25	4
	29	5		Mar	1 Sunday	4
	1936				9	4
Jan	9	6			Total	186 Hours

zexcepting Sundays & Xmas time over 50% of the above was done at night time between 7pm & 5am.

'binned' but which shows the conditions men worked under in the 1930s. The man concerned was one of a family who worked in the canal, the last of whom retired as foreman bricklayer in the 1970s.

During summer time the Worcester & Birmingham canal, like many, suffered from water shortages, but in winter the levels could rise very quickly indeed, and of course, there were boat movements all year round. The worst time for any foreman was when the ice thawed, as not only had this to melt but all the penned boats were freed to move through the locks.

Very few early timesheets have survived. One in the possession of the author shows an oddity in its commencement on a Wednesday. Pay day was, presumably, Saturday and it remained one of the foreman's duties even into the 1980s to collect the necessary cash from the bank, make up the weekly wages and then deliver them, although it was, of course, no coincidence that the men were normally working near a road bridge or pub!

Another less than usual document relating to wages is unusual insofar as the date confirms New Year's Day was normally worked, but we may infer both Christmas and Boxing Days were paid. Presumably if the icebreaker was about, Christmas 1935 was a cold and white one.

In part the letter, dated 1 January 1936, read: 'Also shall be glad to know what time was worked on icebreaking last week. You will remember having to send in the time sheet in advance and thereby not being able to fill them in quite accurately. The reason I am asking this is because I notice a few of the men having expenses for icebreaking this week omitted from the previous week.'

Around Christmas and New Year time few, if any, boatmen were more sober than their finances allowed them to be, but one wonders what lay behind the following letter. The date of the occurrence is in itself suspicious, as both locks 33 and 36 have (or had) footpath access to pubs. However, one must also say that Lock 34 can not be seen from 33 owing to the tight curve. Was it six of one and half-a-dozen of the other?

It read: 'MB No 4 Boat "Hempstead". On Tuesday last, December 31st 1935, about 4 p.m., we were working down the canal from Birmingham, and when locking down at No 35, No 34 was made ready for use. F.Silvey, with the boat "Hempstead", was working No 33 and his mate walked up and drew the water off No 34. As it is the rule that boats with the lock may claim preference, I would not give way either. At 5.30 a.m. the following morning, Silvey decided to give way and pulled his boat out of the lock and made it ready for downhill traffic. We then locked our boat down. Signed, W.A.Helm.'

It would seem that the relationship between the Sharpness Company and the City of

Worcester was not the most harmonious with, usually, the City pecking at either Spiers direct or via Gloucester. Here the Canal Company have brought up their heavy artillery and, incidentally, a very smart letter heading. The letter concerned the 'Reconstruction of Rainbow Hill, George Street and Park Street Bridges, Worcester' with particular reference to the first two named.

The letter continued: 'I have received several complaints with regard to the depth of the water near these bridges, and on investigation it has been found that this has been caused by the quantity of bricks and brick rubble which has been deposited there.

'This appears to be largely due to the fact that this material has been left on the canal side and has been thrown in by children, etc.,

'I shall be glad if you will instruct your contractors to clear away the accumulation of debris left on the canal side, and especially at George Street, where the surface of the towing path should be properly restored.'

'At the latter bridge there is a leakage of water from the canal at the south side of the west abutment. The water is apparently discharging into a drain near the adjoining house.

'This leakage has been kept under observation and definitely appears to be increasing. At the moment it is not serious, but unless early attention is given, I am apprehensive that it may develop to dangerous dimensions....'

For a long time it was understood by railway and canal employees alike that the Factories Acts only applied to the fixed workshops and that the mobile units were exempted. Thus in the 1970s an application for a mobile toilet at a lock stoppage involving 20 or more men was laughed out, and only recently have railwaymen working on the track been provided with Portaloos.

One sympathises with the complainant in the next letter and were one asked to guess the cause of the problem a fair suggestion would be anglers and until a couple of years ago (before the hedge was re-laid) the farmer who now owns the field could have written an almost identical letter.

It was from H.J.Mason of Woodlands, Alvechurch, and read: 'I am the owner of a small field between the Railway and Canal Bridges, close to Alvechurch Station (O.S. No 1270 and Pt 1269).

'I put Cattle to graze on this field, but I am having a great deal of trouble from trippers and others who break through your boundary hedge adjoining the tow-path.

'Week after week my man finds big gaps made in this hedge which he, himself, stops with thorns in order to prevent cattle from straying in to your tow-path.

'I am wondering if you could assist me by giving your men special instruction to try and catch some of those causing the damage with a view to a prosecution, which seems to me the only way way of ending the trouble which appears to occur mostly at weekends.

'I might mention that in addition to the foregoing I had the two locked Padlocks removed from my small gate upon two occasions.

'I have also had two Cattle Watering Troughs stolen from the site.'

Gloucester, incidentally, suggested 'putting a man on for a week or so.'

The next letter has clearly been carefully constructed and, in the original, was written in a fair hand on good quality albeit lined paper watermarked 'The Oscott, H.R.T., Birmingham.' The writing, the ink, and the paper remain as clear as when the letter was first written in 1936.

'Dear sir, I am writing on behalf of several persons who are jointly affected in my road, in reference to your Brook or Stream which runs adjacent to Masshouse Lane and the back of our gardens, owing to flooding caused by the recent heavy rains it has caused a quantity of earth to slide, and am afraid that a further fall may occur when the bad weather sets in, which may cause a partial or complete blockage of your brook, to avoid this and to repair the damage already done, we propose sloping the earth to a larger angle than it has at the moment, I am informed that you are shortly anticipating diverting the brook's course from its present position, and you will appreciate, if we had not your brook to cope with it would mean a far simpler job for us, and wondered if you were thinking of diverting it, whether you could give us the date you propose carrying out this work, or if we could persuade you in your generosity to have the work effectuated at an early date. Thanking you in anticipation that you will give this matter your kind and careful consideration. I remain, your faithfully, C.A.Lovegrove.'

In early September there was another little flurry of rent problems, Breedon Cross Wharf being let to A.R.Thompson 'for the purpose of erecting a carpenter's workshop thereon' but with a codicil that facilities were to remain for 'the unloading of general traffic', while on the 7th the question of Dumhampstead Wharf arose which, unusually, was only leased to the Sharpness New Docks Company and was 'practically unused.' The rent was, however, only £2.10.0. (£2.50) per annum!

October 1936 was engineering month with, on the 3rd, Spiers being told that a water main was to be laid over Pritchatts Road Bridge ' I shall be glad if you will see they do no damage to our structure' — a rather difficult assignment one would have thought. On the 20th, another letter arrived from Gloucester with the usual enclosure: 'At a meeting of Salwarpe Parish Council held last Thursday night, the dangerous state of the iron fence by the side of the Canal was considered, and

I was instructed to draw your attention to it. The railing in question is near the School playground, and unless it is repaired there is danger of the children falling into the Canal.'

'I assume' says the anonymous writer from Gloucester, 'these railings belong to us, and I shall be glad if you will look into the matter and do what is necessary if they are our property.' Still in October another part of Breedon Cross Wharf was let but an application was received from a Mr F.Waldron of 75 Lanchester Road, Kings Norton, to rent a small area of land near Masshouse Lane Bridge. The engineer thought ten shillings (50p) an adequate rent but Spiers wrote back asking what Mr Waldron wanted it for. The reply was quite clear 'I propose using it for a little gardening' wrote Mr Waldron, 'also for keeping the youths from the bottom of our garden for using bad language and being a nuisance.' We know in this case agreement was reached.

The saga of Stoke Wharf seems to have been a long-running saw; here one does not envy the luck of Mr Spiers, having to act as a bailiff. Initially, on 30 September 1935, A.C.Lisle, the secretary of the company wrote to Mr Spiers pointing out the tenant of the wharf owed £27 back rent, and steps should be taken to collect this. Although Spiers was partially successful on 5 May 1936 the letter styling is much more terse. Exhorting Spiers to again collect the arrears, Lisle states 'writing to him (*the tenant*) is fruitless, and the only way to get his account settled seems to be by means of a personal call.'

MONTHLY STATEMENT

PORT OF GLOUCESTER   DOCKS GLOUCESTER
                                        May 4th 1936
… Dr to the …
SHARPNESS NEW DOCKS AND GLOUCESTER AND BIRMINGHAM NAVIGATION COMPANY.
AS UNDER:

Date	To:	Inv No.	Amounts	
1935	A/c. rendered (bal of Sept Rent)		4	10
Dec 25	Rent		7	10
1936				
Mar 25	"		7	10
			£19	10

Whether or not Hopwood Wharf (siding) was leased out the following letter do not tell us but subsequently it underwent many vicissitudes, being used for trip boats in the 1950s and as a pleasure-boat moorings and sales office in the 1970s. The land is now (1994) used basically as a Calor gas store, the wharf is semi-derelict.

Gloucester to Tardebigge, 5 November 1936: 'I give you below a copy of a letter received from a Mr Hartill as to renting the land adjoining Hopwood Bridge for use as a coal wharf [presumably waterborne coal], and shall be glad to have particulars as to the available area, also your observations on the proposal.

'Is it likely the wharf will be required for general traffic?'

The letter in question was from N.F.Hartill of Cofton Lane, West Heath, Northfield, Birmingham and read: 'Dear Sir, Should like to know if you would lease or rent a siding you have at Hopwood Bridge for the conveyance of coal?'

Gloucester to Tardebigge, 8 February 1937: 'A.Clissett. Repeated applications have been made to the above mentioned tenant of Stoke Pound, Nr Bromsgrove, but no payment has been received from him for some time and he now owes rent for two years, totalling £1.

As he disregards these repeated applications, I should be obliged if you would call on him personally and endeavour to obtain the money from him.'

C.Wedgbrow was the local employee who collected the rents. He writes: 'Dear Sir, I have seen Mr Clissett (re letter). The Property was sold about 3 years ago to Mr or Mrs Holyoake (Solicitor). But I believe they have since died as I remember there was a notice in the 'Messenger' offering it for Quick Sale, but I could not say if there was any transaction done. I reported at the time when Mr Clissett sold the Property, and I have not heard of anything regarding the easement since.'

C.Wedgbrow then added a postscript: 'I forgot to mention there was a gateway put through into the garden for the Coal Trade beside the one used for the road and the shop, but the shop is not carried on now.'

Fisher, Holyoake, now trading as Morton Fisher, are still a well known firm of solicitors in Bromsgrove, Worcs.

Some of the Sharpness New Docks tenants seem to have been really long-suffering, while others write more in sorrow than anger. One or two must really have been the cause of grief to Spiers, including Mr Archie B.Solomon of D & M Davies, dealers in antiques, jewellery and silver etc., of 3 Livery Street, Birmingham. One does feel, looking at the last of those printed here, that he should have made some allowances for there being a war on.

On 6 February 1939, Mr Solomon complained: 'It has been reported to me that a window has been broken at our premises, No 46 Gas Street. A boatman pushed a boat hook through the window as he was passing. Should esteem it a favour if you would have it attended to.'

On 23 October 1939, he complained again: 'With reference to 46 Gas Street, re the outside door of basement, door jams are coming loose and require fixing. Should esteem it a favour if you would have same attended to immediately, as it not done now, they may cause great inconvenience and if done at the present moment, it would be a very small cost.'

On 13 April 1940, Mr Solomon was still more concerned with events much closer to home than the battlefront. He told Spiers: I have this morning received a letter from my tenant, Mr C.R.Howes, 46 Gas Street, stating that he would be much obliged if we could expedite the delivery of the Range promised <u>before</u> Christmas. He tells me that a gentleman called in and took measurements about the first week in <u>January</u> and said "we could expect same in about <u>three weeks time.</u>" Would you be good enough to look into this matter. I certainly should not like my tenants to leave, owing to this trouble.'

Coincidentally, we know the answer to the third letter as we have a pencilled note from Mr Spiers to Mr.G.A.Bevan, Moseley, Birmingham 13, in which, economically, he covers three requests. 'No.46 Gas Street. The grate for the basement of these premises has now been delivered. Do you think you will be able to fix it for us? Mr Davies house. While you are in the neighbourhood (assuming you can do the above work) could you examine the furnace in Mr Davies kitchen and let me know if you could remove it so that a gas stove can be fixed in its place. Bar Lock Stable Manure Pit. We have to provide a covering for this pit under corporation orders and I should like to have your advice. If you can spare time I will meet you on the site at your convenience. Any morning next week would suit me.'

Obviously, by this time, call-up for military service had heavily depleted the staff available for the work to be done by 'The Company' and Spiers appears to doubt whether Mr Bevan will be willing to undertake these relatively small jobs. Mr Bevan had obviously worked for the Docks Company before, as (again coincidentally) we have an earlier letter from him to Mr Spiers which is well worth reproducing below. Would that all builders had such clear handwriting in this day of the ball-pen, as the original is quite magnificent.

It reads: 'Regarding the work at Mr Powis, Selly Oak, I went there last Tuesday week and put in all cords that were necessary and eased some of the sashes that had been closed some time. Mrs Powis drew my attention to the damp on back wall. I got up on roof at side and I could see that the spout on the back overlooking the hospital ground is broken in several places which will no doubt require new spout. Also, I noticed a joint in the iron spout over entrance door canal side and a few brackets to support the present spout. I mentioned the troubles to Mr Dance and he said it would be best for me to write to you on the matter.'

The Warner family were quite heavily involved with the Worcester & Birmingham canal, many of the menfolk working on the length, the last widow still lived in a canal cottage remote from civilisation in the 1970s; she used to say her husband died from drink. Apparently he fell down the cottage stairs while somewhat 'peart'.

27 April 1937 from Gloucester to Tardebigge. 'Herewith copy of a letter to-day received, and we

shall be glad if you will make enquiries and let us have your observations in regard thereto' The rather sad note accompanying this is from L.Leek of 36 Almshouses, Holloway, Droitwich: 'Your man Warner at Droitwich is always insulting me as soon as he can see me. It seems to me that he is walking the streets most of his time. I have had a stroke and his sayings upset me. I can hardly get about. If you would kindly stop him doing so I would be very thankful to you.' This must have blown over, for the next letter is accompanied by a note from E.Perry of Gloucester asking, 'Can you arrange for Warner to cut these reeds down as soon as possible please?'

The SND had had a letter from the Borough Surveyor, Droitwich: 'During the last two or three years it has been your custom to cut down the reeds in the canal in Droitwich and I feel sure that this step has enabled both yourselves and ourselves to combat mosquito nuisance. I notice that nothing has been done in this respect this year and I would suggest that you give instructions for the reeds to be cut down at an early date at any rate in the vicinity of the town.'

A look over the bridge in March 1994 showed the reeds to be still there, albeit the canal was, to all intents and purposes, disused.

One cannot help giving a wry smile at the rather overbearing attitude of Lisle, the secretary, towards Spiers who had, as we see, quite a responsible job; from the viewpoint of an employee working on the length, Lisle was only a quill-pusher seen once a year when the Inspection Boat (always spelled with a capital letters!) passed by, whereas Mr Spiers was a real man, a Gaffer. Still, giving a cash float to Tardebigge was a concession and may have shown some degree of trust. The first intimation of this all important change of working came in a letter from A.J.Cullis ('manager & engineer') to H.E.Spiers Esq ('Dear sir') on 12 April 1937. 'Will you please note that the total of payments to be deducted by you on your March statement would amount to £4 7s 1d and not £4 8s 1d as taken, namely: Sundry payments £2 4s 2½d, Expenses, self £1 19s 5d, postages 3s5½d, total £4 7s 1d. This leaves a balance due from you of 1/-s, which kindly adjust in your next settlement.

'With regard to the various payments made by you, as these sometimes exceed the amount of cash due from the Tardebigge Toll Office, I propose to let you have £5 petty cash, which we will draw for at our next meeting, you forwarding vouchers from time to time as necessary so that we may remit the amount spent.'

This was followed three days later by Lisle's letter: 'Dear Spiers, It is noted that your payments for petty cash are made out of the amounts collected by you at the Tardebigge Toll Office, and as this practice somewhat complicates the books, it has been decided that you should have an amount of £5 to be used solely for petty cash payments. Accordingly, a cheque for £5 is enclosed herewith, and at the end of each month, you will be required to send a statement of your petty cash payments, and the balance can be made up to £5 each month, so that in future there will be no necessity for you to deduct anything from the amounts collected as tolls, rents etc., the statement for which should be rendered to this office in full.'

[Note: 1/-s — 5p]

The following letter is a remarkable example of just how varied the minutiae of day to day running of a waterway could be, and bearing in mind the date (before computers and electronic aide-memoire) proof of either a very retentive mind of the part of Mr Parry or an excellent filing system. Bittell and Tardebigge refer to the old steam pumping plant, what is left of the engine house at Tardebigge is now a night club.

"Upper Bittell Reservoir
We have accepted Messrs T.W.Ward & Co's price of £155 for the old Boilers and Beam Engine at Upper Bittell, and they say they propose to start breaking at an early date.

Chimneys
We have also accepted Messrs W.J.Furse & Co's tender for demolishing the chimneys at Tardebigge and Upper Bittell.

Spraying Machines
You will remember that when you sprayed the Droitwich canal with oil I sent up a spraying machine, I think this has not been returned, and as we want it for use at Sharpness, I shall be glad if you will arrange to send it back as soon as you can.

Whitsuntide Stoppage
I have arranged to send the concrete mixer to Lock 12 by the Severn & Canal Carrying Co's boat, and it should be there by Saturday."

All section offices mislaid anything loaned to them as they adjudged their need to be greater than that of Head Office; but the saga of the concrete mixer appears, to judge by a letter dated 25 November, to have dragged on: 'I have ordered the 'Winget' Concrete Mixer which you suggested was the most useful for your purpose, and have asked them to deliver it to you at Tardebigge as early as possible. In the meantime will you return the Gloucester concrete mixer which you have been using at R. & J.Hunt's'. A handwritten postscript rather dolefully adds that 'It is rather badly needed down here.'

Gary A.Footman, whose house at Hanbury Wharf still stands today, wrote a plaintive letter to Mr Spiers on 6 June 1937: 'Is it possible to have our floor done. it is now nine months since it started to give way and there are a few more places nearly giving way. It is not very nice when one draws their chair up to the table and find it a race to see which will get in the hole first oneself or the chair. We want to do our cleaning, it is useless until that is done. Will you please have it done as soon as possible and oblige.'

On the 9th a rather alarmed Gloucester wrote to Tardebigge concerning a Mrs Coleman, adding, 'I shall be glad to have all the information you can give me.'

Mrs Coleman's letter read: 'I would like to know very much, if we get another house could Mr Coleman keep his job. I couldn't stay here much longer — it's about time we had a change. Please let me know as soon as you can.'

Nearly sixty years later one wonders was contretemps caused Mrs Coleman's despair.

A vast variety of matters had to be attended to by a local inspector as, for example, on 28 September 1937 the Kings Norton Paper Mills Ltd expressed their unhappiness: 'We are requiring the services of your Dredger. Some of the tugs that have passed have swept the silt up so much in front of where we unload that we now find it impossible to get our boats alongside. We should be glad, therefore, if you could arrange for this to be done as quickly as possible, and we presume that the terms will be the same as last time.' 27 October 1937 Gloucester advised him: 'Will you please note that we have given the L.M.S.Railway Company permission to take approximately 600 gallons of water from the Worcester & Birmingham Canal for repairs in connection with the railway bridge at Lifford.' 2 May 1938: 'Under the requirements of the above Act, tenants have to be notified of the provisions of certain Sections of the Housing Act 1935, also the 'permitted number of persons' allowed in respect of the premises occupied by them. In the ordinary way, this information would be inserted in the Rent Book, but as such books are only used in a few cases, I am enclosing herewith Forms which I will ask you to kindly arrange to have delivered to the various tenants shewn theron.' And never short of an excuse to make a shilling or two, 16 February 1937: 'When passing Messrs Frank Ashby & Sons' premises at Stirchley recently, I noticed a window overlooking our property in respect of which no acknowledgment rent is, however, paid, but I have in mind some correspondence has passed with them as to alteration work, and shall be obliged if you will ascertain and let me know approximately when the window was put in, so that we may look up the matter.'

Would today's managers be so keen to look after their Company's interests? I think not.

In 1938 Mr. Cullis, of Gloucester, wrote to Mrs J.Hulton, Tardebigge Locks, 'I regret to hear from Mr Spires [sic] of the death of your husband, and understand you would like the tenancy of the above house transferred to you. To this we are quite agreeable, and I have made the necessary record in our books.'

But no matter how loyal the Company may have felt towards some of their staff, on occasion they could, and did, crack the whip. Quite how the Health Department got involved in dealing with the Wharf House at Lowesmoor is not known, maybe the Coroner had words to say, or just that there had been complaints.

The letter from the Chief Sanitary Inspector of Worcester read: The interior of this house is in a very bad state of repair and walls are very damp and will have to be thoroughly redecorated before being again occupied. The present w.c. is in a very insanitary condition and there is an old ashpit in the rear of the w.c. which should be cleaned out and demolished. There is no bath to the house and, as there is a box room which could be converted into a bath house and w.c. at little cost, I think it desirable that a w.c. should be provided inside the house rather than repair the existing w.c. I should like, if possible, to meet you at the property if you would let me know when it would be convenient for you to do so.'

Inspector Spiers wrote back by return: 'I think it only just to remark that the interior repair work was ordered last September but postponed, at the request of Mrs Reeves, owing to the illness and subsequent death of her husband . . .there is no need for the ash pit, as an ash bin was provided but has been lost . . .Mrs Reeves has been charged no rent . . .' At the same time he had the thoroughly distasteful task of writing to Mrs

Reeves: 'I should be glad if you would do you utmost to move from Lowesmoor . . .in the next week or two. We are handicapped by not having possession of the house . . .I understand the delay is not entirely due to you, but hope you will do your best to find other accommodation.'

In 1935 there was only a very small state pension and most transport companies were, in general, rather slow in extending the benefits of a company pension scheme to their hourly paid employees. Conversely from time to time most canal operators could prove to be quite generous in their concessions to loyal workmen; today it would be regarded as patronage but was, in reality, a boon for these people.

On 18 October, Mr Cullis, the SND manager (and, incidentally, a director) wrote an unusually informal letter to Spiers stating 'the Committee have agreed to the retirement of M.J.Bishop, and to the proposal that he should be granted the tenancy of the house at Stoke Wharf free of rent, as a pension.'

As can be seen from the page reproduced here, this was the beginning of a relatively generous pension scheme albeit split into two parts, the 'A' for which the employee paid, and 'B', the contribution from the Company.

A booklet was issued to contributors from which various pertinent facts can be garnered. First, men retired at 67, women at 60, although any member who was 'permitted' to stay on after those ages would not pay any further contributions but instead the cash value of the policies would be enhanced by 2 per cent per annum compound. Retirement through ill-health (commonplace among waterway employees) meant that although a pension was payable it would not be paid until the normal retirement age and then at a reduced rate. Conversely (and one wonders how many semi-literate employees were aware of this) the policies could be surrendered and the proceeds used to secure an immediate pension.

Three groups of employees were covered. Male staff paid subscriptions on a sliding scale based on their earnings, the lowest group who received £75 yearly paid £1.50 per annum (i.e. 2%), the highest 'exceeding £975' paid £26 (3.75%) and so-on pro-rata. Female employees were quickly summed up 'Each member of this group will contribute one shilling (5p) each week' (£2.60 per annum.)

However any member of staff

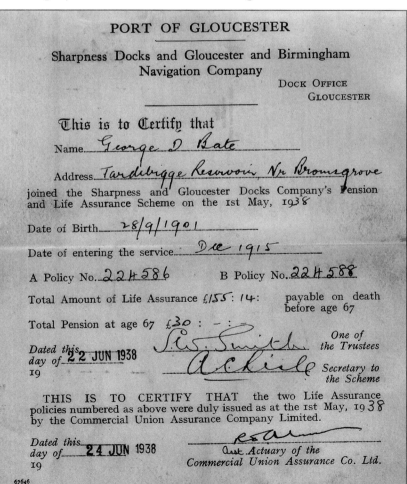

When George Bate completed 50 years on the canals a gentle and pleasant ceremony was held at the Bridge Inn, Tibberton, where George was presented with a pewter tankard by another George, the section inspector George Colledge. The hostess of the pub, Mrs F.A.Meigh made and presented him with a decorated and iced cake, both ceremonies that George would happily tell his friends about long after his eventual retirement.

(male or female) who had completed ten years' service could make an extra payment to enhance their pension, although 'it was not to exceed 5% of his (or, presumably, her) salary', the Company matching this.

Workmen paid exactly the same contributions as females but had no option to increase this. Payments for all groups were, for the time, generous at £1 per annum for each completed year of contributory service. One must add that the Company tried not to penalise older employees for 'every employee for whom less than 20 complete years of contributory service is now possible (i.e. those now aged 48 next birthday or more) shall receive a uniform pension of £19 10s 0d per annum'.

George Bate, BEM, foreman carpenter and a magnificent canalman, retired in 1968, receiving £36.55 per year from his Sharpness (Company) pension and an ex-gratia allowance of £15.45 from the British Waterways Board, i.e. a total of £52 per year for 52 years service.

As with most canal-side dwellings, many of the cottages along the Worcester & Birmingham Canal were (and are) inaccessible to motor vehicles. When one elderly gentleman was taken ill during 1976 it was a mile walk to the nearest

telephone and rather further for the ambulance men to carry him from his house.

The arrangement for fuel was that all employees working 'unsocial' hours, whether lock-keeping, water running or as stablehands were entitled to a given weight of free coal, generally one ton but sometimes more, which was delivered by boat. Oddly enough this canal company did not appear to have any specific mechanism for recovering the cost of coal supplied over and above the basic ration. Thus on 19 May 1938 Gloucester wrote to Spiers: 'We have been looking into the question of employees' coal supplies for this season, and on referring to our ledger, we find that certain individuals have not yet paid for their additional supplies last season.' He was required to chase them for the cash.

An entirely different matter was the supply of fuel to private individuals. They were required to pay as soon as the bill was received but even then there were recidivists who offended by regularly not paying. 'With regard to J.Hutton' Gloucester continued, 'this man is not an employee of the Company, and it must be made clear to him that only as an act of grace do we allow him to have any coal . . .We certainly shall not let him have any this time unless last year's account is paid forthwith.' The letter to Hutton, who lived at Halfway Lock Cottage, sent at the same time was, within the limits of 1930s business, quite remarkably sharp.

'We regret to find that the account for coal supplied to you last summer is still unpaid, the amount of which is £2 17s 6d. We are very surprised at this because we look upon it as a distinct favour that we supply you with coal. We must ask you, therefore, to please settle this account forthwith, otherwise we shall have to consider withdrawing further supplies.'

A quite one-sided correspondence matter concerns the Eagle & Sun Public House, at Hanbury. From time to time they made approaches to Spiers for odd bits and bobs of jobs to be done, dredging and tree trimming for example, but in May 1939 came the heavy stuff, when agents wrote: 'Our clients, Messrs Radcliff & Co of Cross Brewery, Kidderminster, own a freehold licensed property known as the Eagle & Sun, Hanbury Wharf and on the banks of the canal which we believe is the Worcester-Birmingham Canal. They are at present carrying out extensive alteration and they have asked us to approach you to ascertain if there is any possibility of negotiating for the sale of an old storage shed and site which you own on the opposite bank.'

Unfortunately, we do not know the answer but the Eagle & Sun still flourishes albeit seemingly as a roadhouse for company car drivers and their partners.

One of the vital tasks carried out by Mr Spiers was that of producing a weekly return of work carried out to submit to Gloucester. Then and until recently this could be a little flexible as any wise foreman 'banked' a few days work to cover the unexpected.

This particular weekly return is reproduced simply because there are a couple of details which show how the imminence of war was affecting work. In 1939 it was fully expected that the Luftwaffe would be bombing cities the same night war was declared, whereas there is no doubt that the British declaration of war caught the Germans quite unprepared and it was not until 1940 they were able to muster the men and machines to start serious bombing of Britain.

The gates at Diglis are self-explanatory but the work at Selly Oak was to fettle and re-furbish the stop-gates which when swung divided the canal into watertight sections. Freed of their retaining chains any bomb damage below their level would cause a sharp draw and pull them too, then being in effect a pair of lock top gates. Bearing in mind that the same canal level is maintained from the locks at Tipton right through to Tardebigge flooding would have had horrific if not catastrophic result on local industry.

1st September 1939. 'The following work is in hand on the W & B Canal: Diglis — the erection of the 3 pairs of double gates — at the wharf entrance, across the roadway between Bagott's & Bevan's premises and between Bagott's premises and the S & CC Co's stables. Two pairs are in position. This work has been put in hand at the request of the authorities guarding the petrol stores nearby. Diglis Basin — dredging here will be commenced on Tuesday next. Stoke Prior — dredging at Mula Co's premises. Three boat loads have been dredged here (two only discharged). Another two loads will probably be sufficient for boats to be loaded here until more can be dredged on either end of the loading wharf. Kings Norton — a trench 15 yards long has been excavated at the back of the wall immediately above the large culvert under the canal. Several large stones have been found in the puddle about 3'6" down. Thee have been removed and piles driven in the 15 yards length. The leak is slightly less and the trench is being extended southwards in the direction of the Paper Mills. Stop Gates at Selly Oak the planks and handrails required to form bridges across the canal to facilitate the closing of the gates is well advanced and will be completed tomorrow (Saturday). The fixing will be carried out early next week.'

While attempts at penny pinching might seem quite laudable, they can lead to a certain degree of ill-feeling, Gloucester to Spiers 26 September 1939: 'We have let the Old Grist Mill, Diglis, to Messrs Ratcliffe & Tysoe and they are to carry out any internal repairs during their tenancy. They say the skylights are leaking slightly and that there are a few holes in the floor which require patching. It is reasonable these repairs should be done before they take over, but I must leave it to you to see that no more is done than is absolutely necessary.' Presumably the absolute minimum was done for on 4 December, Gloucester are at Spiers' throat again: 'Referring to my letter of 26 September as to repairs to the above premises, Messrs Ratcliffe & Tysoe write stating that the roof lights still leak rather badly. They point out that dampness is fatal in their class of work, and I shall be obliged if you will look into the matter at your earliest opportunity.' But it doesn't end there...

On 3 July 1940, Ratcliffe & Tysoe wrote again: 'The contractors have now completed the roof of the south side of the building, so we should be glad if you would kindly give instructions for the south wall to be put in order as soon as possible, and oblige.'

One rather interesting letter was sent from 'The Austin' (as it was known locally) to Gloucester and forwarded to Spiers for his comments.

It read: 'A number of our apprentices are anxious to obtain swimming facilities in the district, and I have been asked to approach you to see if you could possibly grant a concession and permit a limited number of our boys to obtain these facilities at your Bittall Reservoir, Barnt Green. We would be prepared to see that they did not abuse any privileges extended to them, and if the question of a fee arises we shall be pleased to consider the matter. I trust you will pardon the liberty we have taken in communicating with you, and we shall await your decision with interest.'

'As you are aware (adds Gloucester) the banks of the Upper Reservoir are let to Barnt Green Waters Ltd (for fishing purposes) and those of the Lower to Water Inspector Mills...'.

Presumably some sort of agreement was reached as Gloucester wrote on 21 June commenting on this; but the apprentices did not have long to enjoy the facility before war broke out.

A letter dated 10 November 1939 from Gloucester contains the following: 'The Bournville Athletic Club are desirous of removing the hut at Tardebigge Reservoir belonging to their Angling Section, and erecting instead a smaller one on a site nearer to Warner's house which will enable closer supervision to be made than is at present possible.' This seems to relate to an earlier notice, which the author found in a somewhat decayed state in a pile of rubbish during 1979.

It told members of the Angling Section that complaints had been received from the steward at Tardebigge Reservoir and asked them to note that it was 'entirely contrary to regulations and the spirit of angling to kill fish with a ball gun', that it was a condition of the lease that 'no open fires are lit in the neighbourhood of the reservoir' and that it was 'a breach of regulations to cycle along the towpath of the canal without the necessary licence to do so, and even when the necessary licence is obtained, all cycling along the towpath should be done with care and discrimination'.

Members were warned that if the notice was not sufficient to put an end to the practices, action would be taken against offenders. In the cases of killing fish with a ball gun, the offenders would be 'severely dealt with'.

A note on wages is worth making here. Generally, canal wages have always been depressed, and although employees were liable to instant dismissal if they had a second employer, like the railways canal companies turned a blind eye to those who helped out during the various harvests (not only hay and corn, but potato, sprouts and beet) or who made items reflecting their skills. One writer's wife's proudest possession is a magnificent jewellery box made from part of a lockgate by a canal carpenter, another foreman has a beautiful serpentine walled walk in his garden reflecting the skill of a waterway bricklayer. Unlike railway property, though, few canal houses had much of a garden but locksides were often planted; on the offside of four consecutive locks locally may be found even today massive blackberries, together with raspberries, plum, apple and cherry trees, although the lockhouse was demolished in the 1960s. In 1943 the Worcester & Birmingham

canal seems to have had 27 hourly paid employees, although half-a-dozen or so were in the armed forces. Some overtime extra increment existed but in general a foreman carpenter or bricklayer received £4 11s 3d (£4.56) a man in a responsible position — the toll collector for example, about five shillings (25p) less, while a bricklayer's mate only had £3 8s 2d (£3.41). In early 1944 an average of £80.81 was paid out per week between the 22 remaining men although £1 16s 6d (£1.825) was collected in rents, these varying between 3/- (15p) and 5/- (25p) for property that in 1993 was let for £80 per week. Another deduction was towards the Hospitals Fund, this varying between 1p and 2p per week, the same scheme in 1993 (albeit improved) cost £3.20. The superintendent was, of course, responsible for making up the wage packets after collecting the money from the bank. A typical apportionment shows the detail required:

£1 notes: £67.00
ten shilling notes: £5 10s 0d (i.e. £5.50 in 50p coins today)
mixed silver: £5 4s 0d (£5.20)
coppers: 4s 7d (23p)
This was a total of £77 18s 7d (£77.93) between those 27 men.

Although we do not know how this was collected on the Worcester & Birmingham Canal, elsewhere the inspector went by horse and, on the Peak Forest, by cycle!

Time and time again modern commentators try to give the impression that the period of re-armament 1937-1940 meant paradise for all. It did not. It was a 'Golden Age' for a few, but a bitter hard one for others. The scene for this exchange of correspondence was Breedon Cross Wharf, located adjacent to the still extant Breedon Cross Public House on the A441 Redditch-Birmingham main road. Regrettably we only have some of the letters but the first is dated 30 January 1940 from Gloucester to Tardebigge. 'I understand from a Mr. H.Heard writing from the above Wharf as his address, that Mr Bates, who was our tenant of the Wharf, has died, and it would appear the Wharf has been sublet to Mr Heard who now desires to take over the tenancy. I find, however, that there are considerable arrears of rent outstanding against Mr Bates, and I shall, therefore, be obliged if you can ascertain the financial position as regards his estate, also as to the standing of Mr Heard.' On 2 February, Gloucester sent a supplementary letter stating that Mr Heard had forwarded his rent book to them, this showing regular payments, the last dated December.

Notwithstanding the exigencies and difficulties of wartime Spiers managed to reply on the 14th. Two sheds, one of which was used by Mr Bates for his upholstery business were unused and alongside was a sunken motorboat

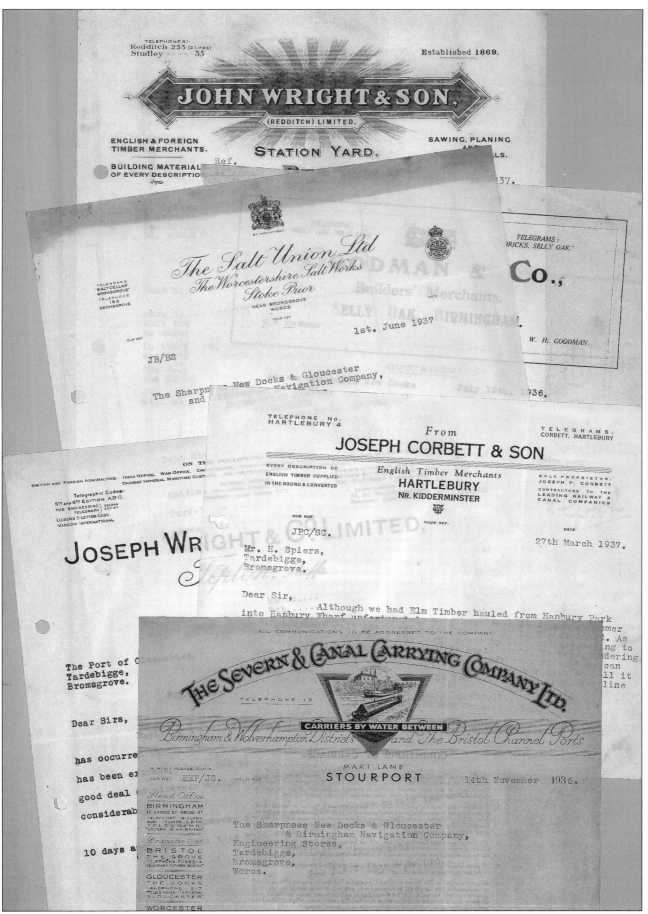

Just some of the correspondence referred to in this chapter.

belonging to either Mr Bates or his son. Paragraph 2 is rather sad: 'I understand that Mr Bates' estate is greatly encumbered by debt and his wife and his son are now living in rooms...I hope to have the address of his solicitor shortly . . .'. Spiers continued with the information that Mr Heard was carrying on his business as a scrap-iron dealer albeit 'in a small way' and wanted to rent the wharf from the Company but added the codicil 'that he does not appear to be in a flourishing condition, and it may be advisable to collect the rent monthly should you decide to have him as a tenant.' The letterhead from Mr Heard shows his variety of trades but accidently omits his telephone number, although in view of Spiers letter perhaps it wasn't so accidental!

Elsewhere in this correspondence file we find Gloucester writing to Tardebigge over the (horse) manure pit as Gas Street. One can well imagine that without a lid it was both dangerous and noisome but in 1940 one feels a little less 'Hitlerism' from the Public Health Department might have been better. G.Parry of Gloucester writes: 'You will remember that I sent you a notice some while ago from the Birmingham Corporation about the manure pit at Gas Street. We have now received the enclosed notice which as you see threatens legal proceedings. I have written saying the work shall be put in hand as early as possible and I shall be glad if you will get it done even if it means putting on an outside contractor. The notice required a cover over the pit if I remember rightly'. The document was obviously a standard one, but unpleasant enough for a rather stiff-necked company like the Sharpness New Docks, including as it did, a blunt threat.

'It has been reported to me that you have not complied with the notice served on you on 18th June 1940 requiring the compliance with the City bye laws, at your stables, canal side adjoining Gas Street. I have to request your attention to the matter forthwith, otherwise the Public Health Committee will have no alternative but to take the necessary legal proceedings to enforce the notice.' Private contractors were, in fact, called in.

However Mr Parry's letter also contained another short paragraph relating to attempts by both men and company to obtain exemption from military service: 'With regard to Watton (A) he should register as a 'Canal Attendant (Wharfinger)". But as many men were already Territorials and hence called-up the shortage of manpower was to become serious.

All bills had to be itemised and for most jobs a fixed rate was payable; thus tunnel work added two shillings (10p) to a man's daily wage, fishing a human or animal corpse out of the water and disposing of it was worth five shillings (25p) and so on. Two examples show similar oddments of unorthodox work. A.Watton, Blockhouse Lock 9/5/1938 'Expense for taking Horse from Worcester to Offerton, 3 May 1/- (5p)' and

G.Davies, Tolladine Lockhouse 9/5/1938 'Expense for taking Horse from Offerton to Stoke, 3 May 1/-'. Both were initialled AB, presumably the ganger.

Horse items do seem to have taken up a lot of Spiers time. On 5 June 1940, Gloucester wrote that 'To enable us to fill up a Return received from the Ministry of Agriculture and Fisheries, I shall be glad if you will let me know what acreage, if any, of our grazing land at Stoke, will be mown this year (including sub-let).' In return Spiers wrote on the 8th to the effect that 3½ acres of 'our' Stoke Meadows were to be put down to hay in 1940.

A letter is then missing but on 13 June, Spiers again wrote, confirming that a strip 70 yards (64m) long and 15 yards (13½m) wide should be reserved for dredging waste. He then continued 'The two remaining meadows we shall find useful, firstly, because of the additional stabling in the larger meadow, secondly we can still turn out one of our horses to graze in an emergency. Our stable on the wharf has three standings only, which are insufficient during icebreaking times. The meadows are of service at such times as when a horse, after bringing a boat to Tardebigge is not required for a few days and it is inadvisable to keep it at Tardebigge or return it to Worcester. For example, Ballinger has been on dock at Tardebigge recently for two weeks and his horse was kept at Stoke instead of being stabled at Tardebigge or sent back to Worcester.'

This is an interesting commentary on the traction used on the Worcester & Birmingham and contrasts with the motor boats commonly found on the Grand Union.

It is, perhaps, rather unfortunate to end this section on a less than cheerful note but the fact was in 1940, militarily, Great Britain appeared to be facing a hiding and no government propaganda could conceal this. Bomb ruins and most people having relatives who were called up, missing or dead precluded this. But everyday life on the Worcester & Birmingham Canal continued willy-nilly albeit with changed emphasis.

On the 20 July 1940 the ever diligent Mr Spiers wrote to Gloucester, telling them that 'Messrs Bagott & Co, Diglis, have begun the construction of air raid shelters in the bank along Diglis Road, Worcester, on the site shown roughly on sketch plan. Mr Bagott appears to have the impression that this land belongs to the owners of the houses in Bath Row, whose gardens reach down to the wall running along the top of the bank. I should be glad to have your observations on this point as we are under the impression that this is Company's land.'

Letters from Gloucester at this time had changed not only in the (relative) terseness of the replies, but the typing style was simplified and less even, so perhaps the regular girls had become WAAFS or WRENS and young replacements were doing the work? Mr Cullis, engineer and manager, advised Mr Spiers on the 22 July that although the land was company owned it was included in a short-term lease granted three or four years previously, 'but' he added, 'we were willing to grant permission for the erection of the Shelter, subject to no objection being raised by the Corporation, whose consent I understand has been obtained.' We do not know exactly what correspondence occurred after that as there are no written documents. Perhaps the telephone was used, but on 4 August we find Spiers writing to the Hartlebury Brick & Tile Co, Hartlebury, Kidderminster, as follows: 'We understand you are supplying bricks for work now in hand at the premises of Messrs H.Bagott & Co . . .Can you supply us with 4,000 similar bricks for work we have in progress on the opposite side of the canal at Diglis?' These, too, were for air raid shelters.

In among the very serious matter of running a complicated canal system just occasionally a true human touch can occur. In general these documents have been edited to reduce the humdrum and emphasise the variety of matters attended to and to some extent this must mean these notes are only an unbalanced record. But no one could leave out the following from Mr Spiers, written on 14 January 1941: 'Dear Mr Hemming, many thanks for your letter of 13 January and for the kindly thought which prompted the sending of it. We are fairly busy dealing with small problems set us by the weather clerks or bosses and the mad dogs of Europe. I have a suspicion that Old Nick is at the bottom of the trouble, for just when we are arranging to fly our kites or let the balloons up in pure joy at having accomplished something, he comes along cuts the string and we are as we were. Well! all the best for the remaining 50 weeks of 1941 and again thanking you.'

Those of the men on the canals who were not

called up (and many, being Territorials, were the first to go to France) joined the Local Defence Volunteers, later the Home Guard — the 'Dad's Army' of TV fame. Realistically how much use they would have been against the Panzers we shall never know and it might well have been decided by how seasick the invading armies were, for the German equivalent, the Landsturm, hardly altered the course of the invasion of Germany in 1944-5.

The war dragged on, affecting the staff of the Worcester & Birmingham Canal as much as any of the population and when at last peace was in sight one wonders what they hoped for. Since then change has been continuous with, today, a scenario that Cullis, Spiers, Walton and the rest of them would only have recognised by the unashamed declared intention to make money and reduce costs. Staff are cut to a skeleton, workshops are closed and even Mr Spiers' office is no longer in use other than as a place for men to report for duty. Repairs in the 1930s were almost always carried out manually, with men working off a boat, whereas today the towpaths are being rebuilt so that vehicular access can and will be used wherever possible to the exclusion of canal craft. Men learn to use machines or are employed because of their knowledge of machinery, foremen use computers and do all the required costing for jobs to be carried out. And one other difference exists. In the 1930s and later workmen with no, or very little pension, worked on until they were 70 if they could. Today they seek voluntary redundancy at 60 or less.

Whether working life on canals is truly better now I cannot presume to judge, but I will bet that despite facsimile machines and the telephone, someone somewhere will be writing to the local manager, 'Dear Sir, It has come to my attention . . . .'

Outside Influences

'That the inland waterways are to have a board of their own is good news, though it comes long after it was due. The independence now being given to the canals must be genuine, however. That implies that they must be admitted to have a strong claim to a share in the money that the Exchequer is going to devote over the next five years towards trying to straighten out the nation's chaotic transport system. So far the waterways have been the poor relation of the transport system. They deserve enough assistance to ensure that the results of administrative as well as physical neglect are overcome, for they still have a very important part to play in relieving traffic on the roads.

Birmingham Post, 21 December 1960

CANALS as a form of transport had a very brief heyday, probably not more than 50 years. Thereafter their very existence was, and still is, subject to the whims and wants of external demands. Briefly, the railways bought some, closed many, but those they retained were worked hard. Of the independents some — for example the Wey & Arun just died, others fought on. When World War One came the canals and their men did their bit, but some never really recovered from the lack of maintenance necessitated by shortage of manpower. Those left within the railway scope were run on with less and less enthusiasm, both the GWR before World War Two and the LMS during that war quietly getting rid of the bits and pieces that 'didn't pay'. Then with nationalisation came the last chance for commercial waterways to become a viable proposition. Instead it is on record that one well-known member of the D & IWE when told that canals were a part of his problem exclaimed, 'Oh Lord! do we have to have those as well?' This attitude, sadly, had not, according to the *Birmingham Post*, changed in 1958:

'Third time pays for all but Mr Job Clarke, a canal waterman who took the last narrow boat out of Stourbridge Basin yesterday. He has done this kind of thing before; he took the last boat along the Wolverhampton Canal, and the last one from the old Brierley Hill Basin. Each time he managed to find himself a berth on another section of the Midland network of waterways. But this time it looks as though he has finished with the canals for good, as he is being found a job as a railway porter. This after a lifetime on the water. Mr Clarke, who is 61, comes from a family which has worked on the canals for over 150 years, and he was born in a boat alongside a canal wharf in Birmingham. The section of the Stourbridge Canal which runs to the Richard Thomas & Baldwin Works at Swindon, was, until quite recently, carrying about 150 tons a week. Now British Waterways has found it 'uneconomic' and the job will be done by lorries. Three other boatmen will also be found other work by British Railways.

In 1963 docks and waterways were made independent of railway (British Transport Commission) control — a move bitterly regretted now — and the emphasis was, and is, in so far as southern and midland canals are concerned, solely on pleasure craft.

Fundamental causes of the decline of the waterways are not difficult to discover. In some ways most never recovered financially from the loss of confidence by shareholders when presented with what was, on the face of it, a far more efficient and economic form of transport, the 'Rail Road'. This loss of confidence led in due course to a parsimonious attitude to improvements, or indeed to any maintenance work.

Canals, as cannot be stressed too often, are dependent upon heavy goods for their livelihood. Such ephemeral items as market boats, packet boats and lightweight goods boats, whilst providing a welcome dollop of sauce, could not provide the meat, or revenue, for shareholders. Where one or two projected canals were concerned a cold douche of realism was necessary.

In 1825 the opposition to the proposed Romford Canal asked:

'Is it to carry agricultural produce from a large extent of country, *where there is no market?* No: for Grain often fetches as good a price at Romford, as at Mark-lane. Are there any manufactories of a *staple commodity,* at or near Romford, saleable in London, or elsewhere, and admitting of a profitable export trade, any spinning and weaving of cotton and wool as at Manchester, and in certain towns of Yorkshire? No. Are there any collieries, or mines, as in some other counties? Neither one, nor the other.

It is said in the Prospectus of this Canal,

A spectacular aerial view of a Birmingham suburb. The close relationship between the Worcester & Birmingham Canal and the railway (now electrified) are clearly seen, while the factory, making cartons, nestles cheek-by-jowl with the housing built to serve the area. The semi-circular buildings to the right are a part of Birmingham University, as is the monolith, left background. Boxfoldia Ltd

that manure and coals would be more readily and cheaply conveyed by water: but no man can *reasonably* expect that the freight of these things would ever pay common interest to Subscribers for the sum required in this undertaking.

If an example be required, take Croydon, which is at about an equal distance from London, *also in an agricultural district,* where coals, lime and manure are required: but this had the advantage of transit of goods to and from the extensive bleaching grounds in the neighbourhood. The £100 shares sell for £4 10s. They have paid no interest for many years...

The same at Basingstoke and at Ashby de la Zouch. The Thames and Medway Canal has *four* loans; but the *original Share-holders* receive no annual dividends.

Let any one ask at *Salisbury* about the Canal, and he will be told, that all the Installments upon the £100 shares were paid up, and the money expended; that a call of £50 more was made upon each share-holder, that some of them submitted to the first loss,

whilst others advanced this additional sum, *which was applied to liquidate arrears,* and the work was abandoned, about six or seven years ago; yet there must have been plausible arguments employed by the Proposers of all these undertakings, and prospects of great advantage held out, to induce people to invest money in them.

Independently of such considerations as arise from the mere hazard to Proprietors of land, or probably loss to Subscribers, there are a great many persons, unconnected with land-holders in the marshes, who object to a Canal, because it would *inevitably* lead to the augmentation of Rates, increase the number of parish settlements, by those employed in digging the Canal, and working barges upon it, (Excavators and Navigators) and...in fact, the only persons likely to derive any advantage, would be those, who were connected with the executive part of the enterprise, *as long as the money might last: but the Injury would be permanent.'*

That which was relevant to Essex was just as relevant to the rest of the country. Disregarding

It has been claimed that the Merry Hill Centre at Brierley Hill in the Black Country is the largest of its kind in Europe. Whatever the truth of this the fact is that the promotors have converted the area from a wasteland to a showpiece. And the canal locally has benefited with, however, a rather piquant contrast between the modern amenity waterway and almost literally around the corner, the dereliction of the vandalised Round Oak Rail Ltd's works. The pleasure boatperson appears oblivious of the fact that here was once pulsing, living canal-fed industry.

Merry Hill.

the apparent deliberate policy to run down the waterways, agricultural traffic could not have maintained the canals even in 1800 and much less so now.

So-called 'smokeless zones' have meant a changeover, for even if solid fuel is still used it is that from the Welsh pits, anthracite, and not coal from the pits in the Midlands. Possibly even this loss of traffic might have been overcome had coke still been processed from old-fashioned gas-works where it was a by-product; but natural gas supplies have ended this and large numbers of private dwellings and factories have changed from solid fuel to oil. This could to a certain extent have proved advantageous to canals for, certainly in the larger sizes, no road-tanker can ever compete with a waterborne tank-boat; but pipe-lines, the chosen alternative, while paying a wayleave for permission to pass along the towpaths, do not help to keep the channel clear.

When the canals were first built warehouses and factories sprang up all along their banks, now these factories are often scheduled for demolition and their replacements are being built elsewhere, often on good food-producing ground — the demolition sites remaining an eye-sore until someone can offer to buy them from the developers.

The last and final straw is the growth of motorways. Canals have been closed, the top end of the Lancaster Canal is a good example, because it was more convenient for the motorway to pass over a culvert than to build a decent bridge.

Other canals have, by the artificial restriction placed upon them by the supporting piers of the motorway, had their dimensions fixed for life at the old narrow gauge. The Birmingham Canal at Oldbury whose line was altered to accommodate the motorway, is a good example. It would take some vastly expensive operation to widen it to a 100-ton capacity, let alone 350 tons, the minimum which our partners in the European Common Market find to be desirable, and so commercially it is finished.

Another development, much praised, has been that at Farmers Bridge, where in exchange for the loss of a few wharves, lengths of canal and general loading and unloading facilities, a pretty public house has been built for the use of pleasure craft owners.

Similarly the building of the Merry Hill Shopping Centre has led to the canal being landscaped and it looks very attractively modern. But realistically such canal works do not make long-term employment for local people.

Now it will be understood that the British Waterways Board's maintenance engineers are overworked and suffering, in the lower echelons, from gross undermanning, so it would be unreasonable to expect the narrow canals to

Newport. Based on a contemporary postcard, this illustration shows the canal in the first decade of the twentieth century and is a most attractive scene. Shrewsbury Public Library.

receive anything other than vital works. Such trivia as weed-clearing and rubbish removal take place, if at all, as and when possible. The City of Worcester had a centenary celebration in 1971, and panics ensued when it was realised that the canal at Lowesmoor, through Blockhouse and down to Diglis was in a bad state, so men were drafted in to clear it up. Not, you will understand, to dredge out the city's refuse that had been carefully deposited in the channel, or even to paint up the locks, but to clear the weeds from the edges and cut the grass and bushes along the towpath. They even had to clear away the cider and methylated spirit bottles left by an itinerant gang of Irishmen who had frequented the towpath thereabouts. Did Worcester look any better for having its canal tarted up? — not it!

That said and done it has to be admitted that over the last decade the canal area in Worcester has changed immeasurably, as the city alters from a manufacturing centre to a dormitory town. A judicious mixture of warehouse conversions and newly-built flats and offices has greatly enhanced the Lowesmore-Blockhouse length.

The many causes of the moribund state of most waterways interlock, but certain threads can be extracted from the angled skein. It must have been a very uneasy time for the canal shareholder when railways, as opposed to tramways, were first mooted. Possibly they needed a schizophrenic mind to judge which way to jump. The average canal shareholder

The Newport Canal ran from Norbury on the Birmingham & Liverpool Junction Canal to Wappenshall on the Shrewsbury Canal and was opened 12 January 1835. The immediate result of this was to make trading on its line easier, although the canal's primary impact was to reduce the price of coal at Shrewsbury, after passing, as part of the Shropshire Union Railway & Canal Company's network, to railway control the arm closed from Wappenshall to Newport in 1939, the outer half being finally abandoned during the war, as trade was reduced to 100 tons a year, almost all from Newport.

Although taken at a different angle in the last decade of the twentieth century, the warehouse still remains, but the lock is 'cascaded' leaving a trickle of water to run down the concrete.

possessing a reasonable number of shares and a modicum of intelligence was already aware of the advantages of tramways. Even if, and it was rare, his own canal had no tramways, he would have seen them in use, feeding from a mine or to an iron mill. He would have noted that although it was not, in terms of bulk carriage, as efficient a form of transport as his waterway, nevertheless the early problems had been eliminated. Benjamin Outram or Josiah Jessop have been variously credited with taking the edge away from the earliest L-shaped rails and substituting instead a flange on the outside, or inside, of the cauldron's wheel. However, tramways were still not entirely cut and dried in their design, although the practical gradient for use by horse-drawn cauldrons, or wagons, was known and more or less fixed.

'On the edge-railway, the rims of the carriage-wheels are made broad, with a flanch on the side of the wheels to prevent the carriage from leaving the rails, which renders the carriage or *wagon* considerably heavier than the tram. On the other hand, the wheels of the tram are narrow in the rim, coming nearly to an edge; and there is a flanch on the inner side of the plate upon which they moved, to prevent the carriages or trams from running off the road.

Again, I completed a tramroad from the bottom of an inclined plane near Dowlais Works to the navigation house on the Glamorganshire Canal, a distance of upwards of nine miles, the fall on some parts of the road being upwards of one inch per yard, and on the remaining portion varying from two to six inches per chain. Upon this road, like the preceding, a single horse continued for some time to haul ten tons, and bring the empty trams back, travelling regularly a distance of nineteen miles per day. The horse here referred to, like those mentioned above, was greatly inferior to the horses generally used in the north.'

The animals used on such wagonways were overworked and it must be borne in mind that a canal horse could pull up to 50 tons without excess strain.

'As the horses belong to the waggon-men, whose occupation is not much more profitable than that of a common pit-man, it may be supposed they are not excellent cattle, nor in high order; yet such is the advantage of draft on these Rail-roads, that they usually convey a Newcastle chaldron [about 50 cwt] to the river side. If the coal-waggon be supposed to weight 10cwt no less than three ton is thus easily transported by one horse.'

The loading and discharging of such wagons was well organised, nowhere more so than in the area of the northern coal mines. 'When the waggon arrived at the Staiths, he lets down his Bottom-board, which is the bottom of the waggon, having Hinges on one side, and a hasp on the other; and the coals run down an opening in the waggon-way under the waggon, which has a box projecting off the dike of the Staith upon the water, under which the keels are placed which receive the coals ...'

Obviously, even accidents had reached a point where everyone was rather blasé over the matter.

Waggon-men, in going down very steep Runs, always take their horses from before, and fasten them behind their waggon; as they would inevitably be killed was the convoy to break (which frequently happens), or any other accident occasion their waggons to run amain; nor is this fatal consequence only attendant on the horses, but the drivers often receive broken bones, bruises, and frequently the most excruciating deaths. Indeed, in some place, a most humane custom is established, which is when any waggon-man loses his horse, the other waggon-men go a Gait (a journey to the Staith) for the poor sufferer, which is a little out of their profits, and purchase him another horse.'

In certain conditions rather unusual arrangements came into being whereby the goods would be carried part way by canal, part way by tram, again by canal, possibly even finishing their journey by tramway. Now shareholders in waterways were generally believed not altogether fallaciously, to be making a lot of money from the vast dividends accruing to them. Regrettably, quite a number were merely 'daddy's sons' — no longer the men who

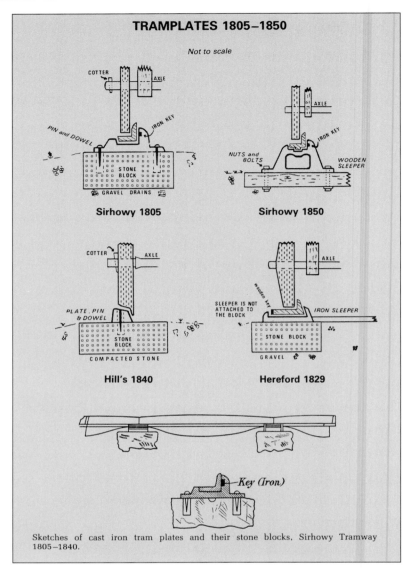

Sketches of cast iron tram plates and their stone blocks, Sirhowy Tramway 1805–1840.

had taken the risk of placing their money in the new-fangled canal in the first place. They were content to sit back, grab all they could and hang on to what they had got. If however, your father had not been one of those sagacious gentlemen, might it not seem reasonable to seek an

Although we do not know where exacly this photograph was taken nevertheless it typifies a horse-drawn tramway, c.1910. (E.C.C. Ltd).

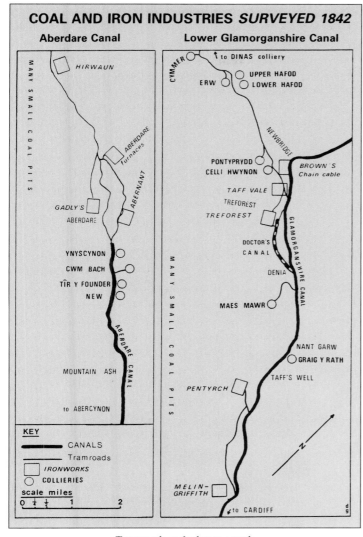

COAL AND IRON INDUSTRIES *SURVEYED 1842*

Aberdare Canal   Lower Glamorganshire Canal

HIRWAUN

MANY SMALL COAL PITS

ABERDARE furnaces

ABERNANT

GADLY'S
ABERDARE

YNYSCYNON
CWM BACH
TÎR Y FOUNDER
NEW

ABERDARE CANAL

MOUNTAIN ASH

to ABERCYNON

CYMMER
to DINAS colliery
UPPER HAFOD
ERW
LOWER HAFOD

NEWBRIDGE

PONTYPRYDD
CELLI HWYNON
BROWN'S
Chain cable

TAFF VALE
TREFOREST
TREFOREST

GLAMORGANSHIRE CANAL

DOCTOR'S
CANAL

DENIA

MANY SMALL COAL PITS

MAES MAWR

NANT GARW
GRAIG Y RATH

TAFF'S WELL

PENTYRCH

MELIN-
GRIFFITH

to CARDIFF

KEY

▬▬▬	CANALS
────	Tramroads
☐	IRONWORKS
○	COLLIERIES

scale miles
0   ½   1   2

Tramroads as feeders to canals.

alternative way of making money? Whatever the cause there was discontent and to overcome this plans were being mooted, initially for the extension of horse-drawn tramways and with increasing vigour for the use of the 'tea kettle'.

'In speaking of the intervention of seven miles of canal, my readers will wonder why a communication of the roads has not been effected, to avoid the tedious process of unloading the trams, loading into a boat, unloading to a wharf, and loading into the trams again. They will be still more surprised when I inform them, that these seven miles of canal do not in effect take us an iota nearer market; and that by making four miles of new tramroad, not only all superfluous expense would be avoided, with loss of breakage, delay, &c., but also (in addition to the saving of seven miles of canal) four miles of the present tramroad would be avoided, by cutting off that circuitous portion of it which extends from the canal to the point where the junction would be effected. The sum requisite to form and complete these four miles of new road would not exceed

£6,000...It will hardly be believed, that with all the energy which those fine and opulent counties possess, no attempt has yet been made to effect so desirable an object. The importance of the undertaking is felt and acknowledged; the sums requisite for its completion are at hand; and I hardly know whether I am justified in noticing the apprehensions which seem to prevail, that from a narrow-minded and selfish policy, the proprietors of the canal (who would thus suffer a partial diminution of their profits) would be induced to give such opposition to the measure, as would be fatal to a bill introduced into Parliament for that purpose.'

There we have an example of the tramway engineer boat owner and mining expert; then we have the canal engineer Josiah Jessop who recommended a tramway to connect the Cromford Canal with the Peak Forest Canal. In October 1810, John Rennie put forward a quotation for a roughly equivalent canal line which would cost £650,000. By 1824, when costs had risen, Jessop's figure greatly undercut this.

'Having completed the survey of the proposed Railway from Cromford to the Peak Forest Canal at Whaley, and prepared the Plans, necessary to enable you to proceed to Parliament in the next Session; I now submit to you the Estimate for a double line . . .£149,206 16 8. The comparatively small expense of forming Railways will be a cause of extending our resources and finding new channels for capital and industry, that would forever have been neglected, if there were only the more expensive modes of Roads or Canals to resort to; the first being expensive in the carriage — the latter in the execution.'

Then we have the dissatisfied customers. Dissatisfied in this particular instance with the Bridgewater Canal and the Mersey & Irwell Navigation, for a number of well-argued reasons. In this context it must be remembered that the Victorians abhorred anything that smacked of monopoly. These two navigations were both owned by the Trustees to the Duke of Bridgewater's Estates, whose secretary, Captain James Bradshaw, seems to have been a rather undiplomatic, heavy-handed, gentleman. Joseph Sandars represented a number of citizens who wanted to open a railroad between Liverpool and Manchester and in his 'letter' (actually a pamphlet) to the members of both houses of Parliament appealing for this, he firstly drew attention to the manner in which the rates were compiled for carriage on the Duke of

The awesome power of water is very easily overlooked when viewing a placid canal, but this shows the aftermath of the breach which occurred at Bollington (River Bollin aqueduct) on the Bridgewater Canal in August 1971. This length of the canal had an official depth of 4'4" (1.32m) and from this and the apparent height of the onlookers can be gauged the volume of ground actually moved. The retaining walls of the aqueduct still stand but the bank had been undermined. D.Valentine.

Bridgewater's Canal. In the authorising Act of Parliament for the waterway the flat canal toll rate was to be 2s 6d. (12½p), this to include warehousing for a reasonable period. After the digging of the Trent & Mersey Canal from Runcorn to Preston Brook, which the Duke of Bridgewater undertook on behalf of the Trent & Mersey Canal Company's shareholders. His Grace was to receive the tonnage dues of 6d (2½p) per ton on all goods which were destined to enter the Trent & Mersey Canal at Preston Brook after traversing his waterway. This was charged on *all* goods wherever they were bound, thus raising the tonnage duty between Liverpool and Manchester from 2s 6d to 3s (15p). His Grace then found it necessary to build a reservoir at Runcorn wherein craft would lie until they could pass the locks, which:

'he pretended to construct for the convenience and despatch of his own vessels; but he had had the kindness to permit those of other carriers, on the condition that they pay him 1s per ton for the privilege and this he collects on goods passing along his own Canal as well as on those destined for the Trent and Mersey. By this second device he raised his tonnage dues to 4s per ton . . .the

third and last device, for adding 1s 2d more to the tonnage dues, remains to be pointed out. At the time the Rochdale Canal Company obtained the Act for cutting a line from Rochdale to Manchester, His Grace obtained permission to make the Lock which now connects his Canal with the Rochdale; and for this he was empowered to levy 1s 2d on all goods which passed his Lock, for the avowed purpose of indemnifying himself from the loss which his warehouse property might sustain by the junction in question; but, in consideration of this, he was bound to find warehouse room, gratis, for a certain limited time. It will scarcely be believed, that instead of all this he exacts the 1s 2d per ton on all goods which are carried between Liverpool and Manchester, whether they pass the Junction Lock or not. Thus, you will observe, his Grace, by one manoeuvre or another, contrives to exact 5s 2d per ton on all goods that are navigated on his line, although it is perfectly clear that the Legislature never intended that he should have more than 2s 6d . . .There yet remains another exaction on the part of the Duke to be pointed out. All goods which pass up from Liverpool to

Runcorn, to enter the Trent and Mersey navigation, pay above twice the freight which they ought, owing to the Trustees of the Duke having monopolised nearly the whole of the land and warehouses at Runcorn. At the present moment, they charge 5s per ton on grain, while bye-carriers, in abundance, would be found to contract at 2s. But, if a bye-carrier arrive, the owner of the goods, who thought to save a few shillings a ton, finds that he had not only to pay the 2s but also the 5s; for say the Trustees, what will you do with the goods? Ours are the only warehouses, and your goods shall not be landed without your paying us as much as if we had carried them ourselves. Pay us the 5s and your goods shall be received and forwarded.'

Sandars then goes on to quote various examples of rates to prove his arguments. Perhaps these could have been overcome in the long term, but:

'the necessity depends on the fact, that the present means of conveying goods are not adequate to discharge the business of the port, and that another line of conveyance has become requisite. It is requisite to give due facility to trade, and without it there will never be any permanent reduction in the rates of carriage, and no security against future combinations to advance them. It is quite clear that, if another line of conveyance is to be adopted, it must be a Rail-road, for another Canal could not be formed, because the existing establishment have engrossed all the water.'

Here we have the appeal to the moral sentiments of the Victorians as well as a statement. Delays did occur, eight to ten days for the goods to travel from shipper to customer, eight to ten days to cover 50 miles. perhaps now we do not consider this unreasonable but in 1824 it was. Insurance premiums had crept up due to petty pilfering of goods *en route* and Sandars stresses the case of spinners and dealers who are obliged to cart cotton on the high road, paying four times the price they would be charged by the proposed rail-road. He was not, however, over-optimistic when he quoted that, 'A Rail-road will enable passengers to travel between Liverpool and Manchester at the rate of 10 to 12 miles an hour, at one-half the price they pay now. A Rail-road will prevent any future combination to raise freights, and it would make the Trustees of his Grace of Bridgewater as anxious to let and sell warehouses and land, as they have been to grasp and retain them.'

In 1934 a writer in 'John Bull' was worried about the speed of railroad travel:.

'Does anybody mean to say, that decent people, passengers who would use their own carriages, and are accustomed to their own comforts, would consent to be hurried along through the air upon a railroad, from which, had a lazy schoolboy left a marble, or a wicked one a stone, they would be pitched off their perilous track, into the valley beneath; or is it to be imagined that women, who may like the fun of being whirled away on a party of pleasure for an hour, to see a sight, would endure the fatigue, and misery, and danger, not only to themselves, but their children and families, of being dragged through the air at the rate of twenty miles an hour, all their lives being at the mercy of a tin pipe, or a copper boiler, or the accidental dropping of a pebble on the line of way?'

Then the writer passes to — oh, shades of a motorway! — the effect of railways upon the countryside:

'We, however, go farther, and denounce the mania as destructive of the country in a thousand particulars — the whole face of the kingdom is to be tattooed with these odious deformities; huge mounds are to intersect our beautiful valleys; the noise and stench of locomotive steam-engines are to disturb the quietude of the peasant, the farmer, and the gentleman; and the roaring of bullocks, the bleating of sheep, and the grunting of pigs are to keep up one continued uproar through the night, along the lines of these most dangerous and disfiguring abominations.'

It is at this point apposite to consider the history of one canal and the effects of the railway upon it. The Horncastle Canal, 11 miles long, extended from the junction of the Rivers Bain and Waring in Horncastle to the Whitham Navigation at Tattershall giving an outlet for this inland town to Lincoln and the port of Boston. The capital permitted under its act of 1792 was £15,000, with powers to borrow £10,000. A so-called 'mania' navigation, like many it ran out of money and was forced to obtain a further act in 1800 to raise a further £20,000, the rates on goods being adjusted. The work then proceeded very fast and the canal was opened on Friday, 17 September 1802, with the usual jubilations. Surprisingly, traffic flourished and the population of Horncastle doubled over the 50 years from 1801 to 1851, but after the completion of their main line in 1852 the Great Northern Railway sought additional sources of income. The Horncastle Railway Bill met with opposition from the navigation company, some landowners and tradesmen but was duly passed in 1854.

'Horncastle and Kirkstead Railway. We are informed that during the past week the levels of the proposed line of railway from this town to the Kirkstead station of the Great Northern Co have been taken. The line...will be contracted at a very moderate cost — less than £40,000 and it is believed it will obtain considerable traffic. Indeed, it is evident that if the present tedious and expensive means of transit, viz. the canal, can pay an average of 7 per cent on the capital out of the carriage of heavy goods alone, a railway deriving its revenue from passengers, heavy goods, light goods, cattle — etc. etc., must be an equally profitable undertaking. It is an important feature, that with the exception of a few of the canal shareholders, this project has the unanimous approval and support of the trading and agricultural interests.'

The railway was duly completed and opened a year later. The canal, however, did not go down without a fight, although they could not do very much. 'We hear that the dues on the navigation have been reduced very considerably in order to place them on a level with the charges of the railway, so that the public will reap the advantage of the competition. They were, one suspects, unlucky, when in December 1855: 'The late frost has completely suspended the traffic upon the Horncastle Navigation: if it had not been for the railway, the town and neighbourhood would have been in a deplorable state for coal, the stock in the merchant's yards being very low.' Although surely the coal traders, had they not had the railway to rely upon, would

have had the foresight to stock up with coals? The end came in 1871 when the navigation was finally closed. It is salutary to reflect however that the population of Horncastle has declined since 1851, for although the railways brought many conveniences they also brought cheap, factory-made goods and encouraged the depopulation of the countryside. Appositely enough the canal basin at Horncastle has almost disappeared and the dry dock is now the town's swimming pool!

It must not be thought that the coming of the Liverpool & Manchester Railroad in 1825 automatically ended the life of all canals, for even as late as 1833 *some* canal shares still maintained their high values.

Canal	Amount of share	Average cost per share	Price per share	Dividend p.a.
Barnsley	£160	£217	£290	£14
Trent & Mersey (¼ share)	£50	—	£640	£37.10
Coventry	£100	—	£600	£32
Erewash	£100	£750	£705	£47
Forth & Clyde	£100	£172.13.4	£290	£25
Grand Junction	£100	£224.10.0.	£245	£12
Staffs & Worcs	£140	£140	£610	£34
Leicester & Northampton	£100	£83.10.0.	£80	£4
Swansea	£100	£180	£220	£12
Ashby	£100	£113	£74	£4
Derby	£100	£110	£117	£6
Ivel & Ouse	£100	£100	£115.10.	£5
Portsmouth & Arundel	£50	£50	£10	—
Macclesfield	£100	£100	£50	—
Kensington	£100	£100	£10	—
Grand Western	£100	£100	£21	—
Basingstoke	£100	—	£5.5.0.	—

True, these figures were not as good as they had been. In 1821 a £200 share in the Trent & Mersey Canal cost, on the open market, £1,750 and by 1824, £2,250. The Coventry Canal, the shares in which were nominally of £100 value, stood at £970 in 1821 and £1,350 in 1824, but by 3 April 1840 the Coventry was declining, down to £218 buying price just as the Trent & Mersey had fallen to £597 10s 0d.

Ominously, as the railway companies grew in strength so some of the most vital connecting canals sold out to their competitors, including in 1846 the Trent and Mersey and the Birmingham Canal Navigations, in 1847 the Shropshire Union and the Stainforth & Keadby and in 1852 the Kennet & Avon Canal. By 1890 railway companies owned the following mileage of canals:

Company	Mileage owned
Great Western Railway	258
London & North Western	488
Midland Railway	50
Manchester, Sheffield & Lincolnshire	180½
North Staffs Railway	121
Caledonian Railway	60

In theory, it is true, tolls were tied but as we have shown drawbacks represented an essential factor if canals were to remain vital arteries of trade over long distances. For example, from London to Liverpool there were three possible routes:

Route 1	via	Braunston Birmingham Autherley Eastham	244 miles 252 locks
Route 2	via	Braunston Hawkesbury Fazeley Preston Brook	256 miles 191 locks
Route 3	via	Braunston Napton Heywood Runcorn	267 miles 283 locks

Each one of these routes had a portion which was owned by a railway company who were not obliged to give drawbacks, although it is true they could and would, if it gave them a chance to snaffle traffics from under the eyes of rival railway companies! And again, it was illogical for railways, unless they could hope to be totally rid of the canal with its concomitant maintenance costs — an almost impossible proceeding — to eliminate all the traffic. But, in turn, they were unlikely to want to encourage traffic on a canal if it meant their relatively expensive locomotives and wagons lying idle.

By 1841 to send one ton from Liverpool or Manchester to London, meant tolls and carriers' charges which worked out at disproportionate rates:

Canal	Miles	Toll £	s.	d.	
Duke of Bridgewaters	25		1	0	(5p)
Trent & Mersey	67		2	9½	(14p)
Coventry (Fradley)	5½			2¾	(1p)
Birmingham (Fazeley)	5½			5½	(2p)
Coventry	21¼			11	(4½p)
Oxford	23⅝		2	11	(14½p)
Grand Junction	101		4	2½	(21p)
Total	248⅞		12.	6¼	(62½p)
Carriers' Charges		£2	2.	5½	(£2.12)

In 1947, immediately prior to nationalisation, the discrepancies in the rates became even more interesting.

Canal	Mileage	Rate per ton s	d	Owner
Ashton	15	11	1	Railway
Derby	14½	10	0	Private
Grand Union (Brentford-Braunston)	93	£2 0	0	Private
Kennet & Avon	86½	£5 16	8	Railway
Leeds & Liverpool (inc. locks)	127	£2 1	0	Private
Oxford (Oxford-Hawkesbury)	77	£2 10	8	Private
plus locks		5	8*	Private
Stratford	25½	£1 17	4	Railway
Worcester & Birmingham	30	£1 12	0	Private
plus towage through tunnels		5	0	

*minimum.

We have already shown the basic reasons why coal traffic has declined on waterways. The direct effect on a waterway is shown in the gradual dwindling of the number of canal carriers. The old Grand Union Canal Carrying Company carried many thousands of tons to various factories in the London area, including Nash Paper Mills, John Dickinson & Sons, Colne Valley Sewage Works. These traffics were later carried by the British Transport Waterways in declining quantities until 1963. There were then some attempts by private carriers to keep coal moving, latterly greatly aided by the Ashby Canal Preservation Society, especially the traffic to Dickinson's Paper Mill at Croxley. It took, we understand, one ton of coal to make one ton of

Few people realise today that only 30 years ago in terms of tonnage handled Manchester was the third largest port in Britain.
Now the port lies almost disused, partly as Manchester no longer has the demand for 'heavy' imports or exports and to some extent as trade
has moved to more accessible entry ports than Liverpool. With the coming of the Channel Tunnel and the apparent intention of all political
parties (save those on the extreme left and right wings) to put all trade on the roads it is difficult to see any real recovery coming, but equally
the MSC 'the greatest waterway constructed in Britain' cannot really be filled in. In 1950 L.A.Edwards in the canal users bible, his Inland
Waterways of Great Britain could state 'The Canal is used by large Ocean-going vessels up to 15,000 tons deadweight. It is purely a
commercial waterway from Eastham Locks, junction with the River Mesey throughout its 36 mile (60 km) run to Manchester Docks. The
greater locks measure 600' (183m) x 65' (19.8m) although Eastham where there are three locks, craft of 80' (24.4m) beam can pass. A
draught of 28' (8.5m) is normal although of course the Mersey is tidal. The bridges either swing or at high level allow clear air of 70' (21.3m)
minimum.

But these are just figures for the whole story of the canal is one of typically British endeavour, from its pugnacious engineer Mr (later Sir) E.Leader Williams to the contractors having to invent machines to do the job. The first sod was cut by the Earl of Tatton on 11 November 1887 and Her Majesty Queen Victoria formally opened the works on 21 May 1894.
The trade in the years between then and 1914 was, to put it mildly, mixed, imports alone included cotton, cattle, sheep, poultry, butter, cheese, oats, maize, wheat, hay, wood pulp, oatmeal, eggs, lard (in tierces!), starch, sugar, deals, hardwoods, doors, glass, oil, spirituous liquor and many other items. Outward went coal, cotton and woollen goods and almost anything that could be made from iron and steel.
Most of all one must emphasise the engineering, whether Handyside's bridges or Cullins Patent Culverts. To make a mistake in the gradients on a motorway is really only an inconvenience, but to contain and handle the waters of a canal like this without error exemplifies the best we used to do.

Rogerstone, Monmouthshire Canal, 1989. These locks, built under the guidance of that great engineer Thomas Dadford, junior, are, even in decay, quite magnificent. Unusually they are a staircase pair, the upper lock feeding directly into the lower without an intermediate pound. Taking boats measuring 64'9"(19.73m) x 9'2" (2.79m) they were completed in 1799, and became disused in the 1930s.

paper and like all factories of any size Dickinson did not require fast delivery but a consistent flow, which circumstances are, of course, ideal for waterways. Sadly, the various carriers that were engaged in this trade were bedevilled by a number of small, niggling, occurrences — mechanical trouble with boats, the conveyor being out of action, difficulties with arranging a loading wharf and, indeed, obtaining the supplies of coal which had to be brought by road from the collieries to this wharf. With the lack of dredging loads had to be restricted and profits, without a suitable back-load, became very near non-existent. The final runs were carried by a consortium of 'number ones' (owner-steerers), who mostly carried in their spare time.

The Ovaltine Company had a fleet of immaculately turned-out boats carrying to their works at Kings Langley but the craft were sold when the works changed over to oil-firing. S.E.Barlow, coal contractors of Tamworth, sold their fleet more or less contemporaneously, then

Harvey-Taylor of Aylesbury followed by another coal carrier, Gilbert Bros. of Bedworth, operating as the Warwickshire Coal Carrying Company. These were only a few of the number who were doomed to die in the early 1950s. The last independent company to and from the coalfields was Samuel Barlow of Braunston, some of whose boats were bought by Blue Line Canal Carriers, Ltd, and operated quietly up and down the Coventry, Oxford and Grand Union canals, albeit with only three pairs, until 1970 — operating from Atherstone, or thereabouts, according to loading facilities, to the 'Jam 'ole' at Southall. It was a rather sad coincidence that a matter of months before the cessation of this traffic, Michael Street, the then owner of the Blue Line Canal Carrying Company had just obtained a number of relatively new craft to replace some the life of which had expired. Almost simultaneously, Captain Ward took the last pair of Willow Wren Canal Transport Services boats 'dahn the smoke', thus to all intents and purposes ending commercial carrying of coal in any quantity from Birmingham to London.

A wide-boat canal, in so far as the locks could take barges measuring 66 feet by 15 feet was the Barnsley. The principal objects were 'to open a navigation from Sheffield and Rotherham to the other numerous and important towns of Yorkshire and Lancashire, and to bring into use the coal of Barnsley, Silkstone, and the neighbourhood'. Receiving its authorising Act in 1793, the company was permitted to raise some £72,000 plus £200,000 by mortgage, but this did not suffice and a further sum of £43,200 was called for in 1808. This canal was, without question, of great advantage, both in so far as it paid good dividends to the shareholders and 'its execution has had the effect of introducing the coal worked in the latter place [Silk-stone], into the London Market, where it holds a distinguished place among the Yorkshire Coals. The making of this canal has also been of incalculable advantage to the agriculturists in its vicinity, by the facility it gives to the introduction of Knottingley Lime.' The canal proved to be very successful from the very beginning, and even the railway period which commenced in the 1840s did little to deter traffic. In fact the canal was financially attractive to the Undertakers (the title of the authorising body) of the Aire & Calder Navigation, who leased it in 1855, eventually purchasing it outright on 30 November 1875 at a cost of £48,800. In 1893 the section of the canal from the bottom of Barugh locks to the terminal at Barnby Basin was authorised to be abandoned, for the Silkstone pits were worked out. Despite this the coal traffic continued to prosper with the opening of new collieries between Barnsley and Wakefield.

During the 1940s the canal suffered three major stoppages. The first, for three weeks, from 27 October to 16 November 1942, the second of four months' duration, from 16 June to 18 October 1945 and the final and most disastrous stoppage, directly caused by a breach of the bank which occurred on 27 November 1946 to 1 May 1947. The obvious result of these stoppages was the breaking of contracts, and the resulting loss of trade and loss of livelihood to the bargees. Many barges, mainly of timber construction, were abandoned and left to rot. Most of the Rogerson's fleet, who were regular by-traders on the Barnsley Canal, were abandoned. After the re-opening of the canal, now under the authority of the British Transport Commission, there was little hope of succeeding in keeping it open, especially as officialdom had declared that the Barnsley had no future, so it was only a few years before the official abandonment in 1953.

It has already been shown that when waterways came on the scene Britain was still predominantly agricultural, both physically and mentally. Canals, and the quick transport they offered, invited the building of factories on their banks.

'The village of Etruria is wholly of the late Mr Wedgwood's creation. It is locally situate within the township of Shelton, upon the turnpike-road from Newcastle to Leek (two miles distant from Newcastle) and consists of the mansion called Etruria Hall, now occupied by Mr Francis Wedgwood, a partner in the firm of Josiah Wedgwood and Sons; the large manufactory, which occupied the western bank of the canal, two branches from which are carried into the manufactory itself, and a continuous street of about 120 workmen's dwellings adjacent, with an inn, and some houses of a better class, for farmers, clerks, and others.'

To serve these new factories people — men, women and children — were necessary and when Josiah Wedgwood was called before a Select Committee of the House of Commons in 1816 he no longer showed the interest in the pleasant things of life the family enjoyed during the building of the Trent & Mersey Canal. Instead by his own words and those of the Inspector, he exposed the true Victorian businessman's nature.

'Extensive manufactory in potteries, employs 387 persons, of whom 13 are under ten years and 103 between ten and eighteen. Irregular buildings, much scattered. Work-people now crowded, doors generally open, casements in windows which work-people may open. Work generally unhealthy but that part connected with applying the glaze is composed in part of white lead and if workmen careless in their method of living and dirty, very subject to disease, depends much upon care men take of themselves. Dippers work from 8 or 9 to about 5 in the afternoon with interval of half-hour for breakfast and 1 hour for dinner. Hours of work for other persons from half past six to six in the evening, with half hour for breakfast and an hour for dinner. The hours are shortened when they cannot see without candles except from 11the November until 3rd February in which period candles are burnt and they work from half past seven to six. Children work same time, the younger children employed in attending the men, assisting them in carrying their moulds. Wages of children paid to parents. Much too often these additional wages are employed by the parents not in giving the children improved clothing and food but in procuring spirituous liquor for themselves.'

'Then the Committee is to understand from you, that although you think that the curtailment of labour to children would be extremely beneficial, you object to an Act of Parliament, not for containing these clauses which would be beneficial, but you object to any legislative interference with the manufactories?'

'I have a strong opinion that, from all I know at present of manufactories in general, and certainly from all I know of my own, we had better be left alone...'

But what of the conditions elsewhere? Josiah Wedgwood was, within his own lights, a humane man. Thomas Gibson and George Bryan were witnesses before this same Select Committee during the investigation into the Duke of Bridgewater's coal mines at Worsley.
Both worked in coal mines since boys.
'What had you to do then?'
'Thrutching the basket and drawing. It is done by little boys; one draws the basket and the other pushes it behind. Very hard labour. Worked nearly nine hours a day regularly, sometimes twelve, have worked above

Brick carrying, at least on the Oxford Canal, was always called 'bally-bagging work'; not as a term of endearment. While the bricks could be loaded reasonably easily (even in the 1950s by girls) they had to be thrown out one by one on site; always preferably a job for some other idiot. Amblecote Works, Stourbridge Canal, 1930s. Price Pearson Refractories Ltd.

thirteen. We used to go in at six in the morning, and took a bit of bread and cheese in our pocket and stopped two or three minutes; and some days nothing to eat at all — we were overburdened, I had only a mother, and she had nothing to give me, I was sometimes half starved. They still have only a bit of bread and cheese sometimes can't eat it all owing to the dust and damp and badness of air; sometimes as hot as an oven, have seen it so hot as to melt a candle.' A boy of eight got *3d* or *4d* a day. A man's wages divided into 8, at eight years gets one-eighth, at eleven two-eighths, at thirteen three-eighths, at fifteen four-eighths, at twenty man's wages, about 15s in full employment, often not more than 10*s*. Out of this he has to get his tools and candles. Consumes four candles in nine hours work, in some places six, 6d per pound and 24 candles to the pound. Beaten a score of times, both purs [a local term for a kick from a clog] and kicks and thumps. Many girls employed, do the same work as boys, till they reach 14 when they get wages of half a man, never get more, and continue at the same work for many years. Both boys and girls fight, sometimes they are very loving with one another...'

At Bilston, a witness, again before this Select Committee, which was very thorough, stated that:
'Besides my husband I have a boy who works on the band [breaking up the coal on the conveyor chain or belt] with my husband, a dirt carrier, at 2s a day. We have also an apprentice, but we don't know his age nor he himself except what we guessen. He came from Manchester; a boatman picked him up upon the canal side and brought him with him to drive his horse, and he could not find his way back. He was about 10 or 11 years old, named William Butler, and he used to lie about and get burnt at the coke hearths. A woman brought him to me and asked if I would have him; and I pieced [bought] a pair of trousers and waistcoat for him, and a pair of shoes that were too small for one of my wenches I had tipped and put on his feet. He bound himself apprentice.'
Boats had to be loaded at coal mines, not always as you might think, by crane; there were other methods.
'On the banks of the canals in Staffordshire are seen many girls engaged in loading the boats with coals. These girls are substantially, though coarsely clothed, and the head and neck more particularly protected from the cold. The work is laborious, but not beyond their strength. The clothing is obviously such that a girl cannot continue to wear it after going home. She therefore lays it aside, and washes herself, and puts on more agreeable clothing for the rest of the day...The returns

from Staffordshire show the wages of the girls to be as follows:

Age	Pay	
12 to 13	4s.	to 4s. 6d.
13 to 14	4s. 6d.	to 5s.
14 to 15	5s.	to 6s. 6d.
15 to 16	6s.	to 7s. 6d.
16 to 17	7s.	to 8s. 6d.
17 to 18	7s. 6d.	to 9s.

Sometimes, then as now, canals had other uses than those they were designed for, and perhaps the most horrific part of this report in 1852 is the casual acceptance by the victim of what was to happen.

'My father was a porter at the railway station; and he came home drunk when he got paid, one Friday night; and he took James and me, and he said he would take us to the canal and drown us. He told our step-mother to reach our shoes; she said "If you are going to drown them, you may as well leave their shoes for Johnny." He took us, and he threw me in; and I should have been drowned only for a boatman. There was two policemen on the bridge, with their lamps; they did not come to us then but they came to our house after we came home; and they said they came to see about those two children; it was not a proper time to be on the canal side that time in the morning (2 o'clock).'

In Victorian times England and Wales were booming countries, we had great markets throughout the empire and there was a drive to get things done whatever the circumstances and despite regulations put out by the House of Commons. Every man upon whom the breath of civilisation had touched possessed the drive to do better, the fact that to do better meant trampling on the shoulders of other people was irrelevant. To make money there was trade. Canals brought the coal to make the goods and took away the goods to 'mek t'brass'. Conditions were, without doubt, appalling both in housing and nourishment. In the main, men who came from the countryside did not easily adapt to city life in a hovel but equally because they lived in a hovel there was a drive to make matters better. There was no sick pay, apart from the subscription clubs, there was no National Health, you paid as you went, but there was no limit to how far a man could go in the manufacturing field.

'Wanted. A Person who is acquainted with the Manufactures of heavy Iron Goods, in various Forms, to Superintend a Work of that Kind, which is established at some Distance from Birmingham, very advantageously situated for Coal, Wood, and the Exportation of its Produce; or, in any sober and industrious Person, with a Capital of One or Two Thousand Pounds, more or less, who has been brought up to the Ironmongery Branches, and accustomed to ride Journeys for Orders, &c. should want an Establishment,

and incline to become a Partner for the chief Conduct thereof; he shall have a Share therein proportioned to any Capital which he may bring, besides an handsome Allowance from the Company for his Superintendance of the said Work.'

There is a saying in Essex, 'from muck to muck in three generations.' The dozen of little factories that sprang up in every industrial city, Leeds, Manchester, Birmingham, etc., during the eighteenth century are mainly doomed. A few have grown and enlarged themselves by swallowing up the small manufactories during trade recessions in the twentieth century, but too many of the remaining small factories are out-dated.

One car factory worker, talking to us on the canal bank about housing and working conditions expressed the opinion that these have not altered much although they have been updated. Instead of a hovel there is a flat, perched 20 storeys up in the air; instead of the hot, humid, closed-in atmosphere of a working steam-powered factory there is a clinical, soulless, electrically-operated machine. He explained that he had to leave his flat at five o'clock in the morning to clock-on at six and then produce 1,000 items by clocking-off time at two o'clock. Then he drove home and had his dinner and watched the telly and so on, almost *ad infinitum.* He came to the canal bank to fish and enjoy the peace, little realising that where he sat there was once an industrious factory producing machines to make machines to make cars.

Given a reasonably short haul (not in excess of 20 miles), level countryside and a reasonably good turnpike road, a road-carrier could compete on more or less equal terms with the canal, providing that his load did not exceed five tons. For this reason parcel boats were not, in the main, successful ventures unless they could generate heavier traffics. To give an example, immediately prior to World War One, Messrs Fellows, Morton & Clayton ran a scheduled boat from Ellesmere Port to Wolverhampton, its purpose being to pick up goods of a reasonably light weight which were to be transported to destinations *en route.* If the first boat became full a second boat was immediately pressed into service. It was widely known that if the boat's captain could pick up a 'parcel' from a factory not hitherto served by the company Messrs Fellows, Morton & Clayton, hoping this would lead to further traffics, were happy to pay the captain the, then, magnificent sum of £5 by the way of a bonus. The boat itself did not, and could not, pay but it was a service which they hoped would catch the interest of any of the factories which favoured road or rail transport. There was no reason why any responsible carrier, prepared to run his craft on a fixed timetable of departure should not run such a service as it was possible, even until the early 1900s, to make up a full load of two-five or ten-ton lots; but on some canals restrictions hindered such operations. The Act of Parliament authorising the building of the Newcastle-under-Lyme Canal penalised boatmen with small loads, or empty boats; showing under the tonnage rates 'if less than a ton in a boat 6d per mile,' the normal rate being 1½d per ton per mile. The River Ouse, Sussex, in its rates, showed 'No vessel of less than Ten Tons to be passed through the Locks, without leave of the Proprietors', while the Peak Forest Canal were determined to both have their cake and eat it, 'No Boat under Fifteen Tons Burthen, when the Water does not, or under Ten Tons when the Water does, flow over the Weirs of any of the Locks shall pass through any Lock . . . unless the Navigator of such Boat shall pay Tonnage equal to Fifteen Tons or Ten Tons respectively as aforesaid.'

Most waterways had a restriction of some sort. It was, of course, reasonable to the extent that they did not wish to lose water; most waived the charge for a boat working back empty, but should it pick up even one parcel the rate was firmly enforced. Let us not, however, be misled into believing that in nine cases out of ten the would-be consignor in the early nineteenth century had any choice between road and canal. 'Roads in general, very middling, they look forward to the completion of the canal [Hereford & Gloucester] for very great improvement of the roads, not only by easing them of much heavy carriage but, for the supply of good mending materials which are now, in many situations, scarce and distant.' From this extract it will be seen that the ill-fated Hereford & Gloucester Canal was regarded not only as a means of lowering the rates of transportation but, indeed, as a means of improving access to the interior of the country. Without the land drainage of today, aided in many places by the canals, there was little hope for the old-fashioned soft-surfaced roads when the winter rains came. If it rained, wagons, horses and men alike got mired down and if it was frosty a horse's leg might easily be

broken. Even in November many roads could be impassable, as they were in 1770:

'By the very heavy and continued Rains, the Roads in many parts of Staffordshire and in this Country are rendered extremely dangerous: We hear of many Accidents occasioned by the Floods in Derbyshire, &c . . . Our Mails have arrived several Hours later than usual; and our Accounts from the Counties of Worcester, Gloucester and Hereford are of a similar Tendency. Last Thursday as Mr Robert Willis of Tamworth, was passing the new Bridge at that Place, the Rapidity of the Flood carried away one of the Arches, by which Accident he was unfortunately drowned. At Wrighten, near Coventry, the Bridge has been broke down by the Floods, which detains a Number of Carriages and Passengers at that Place. Yesterday between Beacon's End and Tamworth, a Waggon was overturned, when two of the horses fell into a Pit and were drowned.'

These conditions were, if not accepted, at least tolerated, and it would seem difficult to visualise that matters could be otherwise.

'Though this useful set of Men, the Farmers, will undoubtedly reap a Proportion of Advantages from the Execution of this beneficial Scheme, they are far from being satisfied, and seem to reflect upon it with many Doubts and Fears. Custom, indeed, and Occupation in Life, cast a wonderful Influence on the Opinions of all Mankind; it is therefore by no means surprising that men, whose Forefathers, for Ages, have been inured to rugged and deep Roads, to wade after their Beasts of Burden up to the Knees in Mire, to see their loaded Waggons stick fast in Dirt; Men, who from their interior, inland Situation, are almost totally unacquainted with all Objects of Navigation, it is by no means strange that People, so unaccustomed, should consider an Attempt to introduce a navigable Canal up to the Town of Chesterfield, and within the Air of the Peak-Mountains, with alarming Ideas, with Suspicion and Amazement.'

As time went on various attempts were made to introduce steam transport on the new turnpikes. These turnpikes were, in the main, an excellent arrangement, for quite simply a section of road was improved by

Toll house and toll-gate, Llandaff, Cardiff, c.1880. (Welsh Folk Museum.).

having a good surface made; the right to levy tolls was given to the proprietors.

Very often a canal act granted the toll-free passage of road stone, thus aiding its competitor, the turnpike, for having only the carriers to pay, stone could be brought easily and economically to the nearest wharf.

The earlier steam-engines were more or less prohibited by the high charges placed upon them by the owners of the turnpikes, and even traction engines, with their enormous capacity, still presented a weight problem which often meant they had to be diverted many miles out of their direct route to get from one point to another — a diversion often caused by canal bridges! A Fowler Big Lion of 1890 could handle 40 tons but it weighed 16¾ tons; the Super Lion, derisively rated at 10 nominal hp, could pull 120 tons, but weighed 10½ tons without its load of coals and water.

An entirely different competitor was the coasting vessel, certainly for long-distance traffics, Liverpool to London, Hull to London and the like. As long as sailing craft were utilised, with their attendant long delays, a state of easy co-existence was reached between them and canal boats, but as the steam coaster became more reliable so it was axiomatic that it would draw traffic from the canals, the very traffic that canals were designed to cope with — bulk. All things considered, from Nottingham to London a 100-ton load would require four men, plus their wives or lads, four boats, four horses and five days on inland water; a steam coaster, to which 100 tons was only a part load, would require four men only and could probably complete the journey in 48 hours. The railway, of course, could outdo both in terms of speed, but could not undercut either until comparatively recent times.

Motorways can be regarded as a political pawn — Adolf Hitler used them in Germany and Benito Mussolini in Italy as a means of absorbing unemployment. In lieu of our present-day dole, the men employed on such works were fed, watered and housed and their families looked after by means of a grant, which could be encashed at certain stores which, at least, obviated the present trend of spending the dole, or the Family Allowance, at the public house. In Britain the cost of motorways is very high and following, as we usually do, the American pattern, there is very little doubt that extra charges will be made, if not tomorrow then the next day, for the use of them, although whether by tolls or a licence differential remains to be seen. Boats and barges have a minimum life of 15 years, they consume diesel fuel at the rate of approximately half a pint per horse power per hour. Twenty horse power is adequate to move a pair of laden (55 tons) narrow boats along the midlands canals and 120hp is adequate to move 450 tons along the wide canals of the north. A lorry capable of pulling its own weight and carrying 20 tons has an engine of

A magnificent action photograph showing a Pan or 'Tom Pudding' in the Cawood Hargreaves fleet loading at Kellingley Colliery near Knottingley on the Aire & Calder Navigation 1990. The environmental advantages of such canal workings should not need explanation. Media Relations, British Waterways.

about 120hp and consumes fuel at between four and eight miles per gallon. This lorry in first-class motorway-hammering trim has a life of about five years. The barge will use an occasional drop of lubricating oil, a small amount of rope for its fenders, coal for its stove and little else. A lorry requires tyres, anti-freeze, windscreen-wipers, repairs and maintenance. A boat's engine will have a life of five years, a lorry's two. By deliberately eliminating canal traffic and encouraging that on the roads, governments are, in their own way, reducing the likelihood of unemployment in the motor industry and ensuring a greater income by way of motor-taxes, insurances and fuel taxes than could be obtained from boats and barges. The fact that using canal transport could reduce the cost of living is, in the light of the above, entirely irrelevant.

Niggles have always abounded on canals. Niggles which have meant reduced payloads, canals going by the least direct route due to landowners' influence and niggles which on occasion, have stopped canals from even happening. The Blythe Navigation on the Fens relied upon the harbour at Southwold for its outlet and when, due in part to inefficiency, in part to personal antagonisms and in part to parsimony the harbour eventually silted up, the navigation was finished. The North Walsham & Dilham Canal in Norfolk was built under an Act of Parliament of 1812, there being nothing unusual at the time of building except that the rate 'for all passengers in Boats or Barges...1d, per mile each' was specified. In 1893, the general state of decay in the neighbourhood was noted by a pleasure craft hirer. 'They had the greatest difficulty in getting above Dilham; the river was nearly dry and they were told: 'There's only been one wherry up since Christmas. Are you going up to Antingham?...that's a long way. I shouldn't like it. Right, you go!'...signs of decaying trade — a deserted granary, a decaying landing stage...a ruined corn mill. It was half a century and more since Thomas Fowell Buxton, moving to his new home at Northrepps Hall, had his furniture from London by sea to this very quay.' The canal runs through very attractive countryside and the scene of dereliction at Horning Lock gives no real clue to its possibilities. For a dinghy there is water through delightful woods up to the next lock, and the scenery is quite enchanting as it is typical of the North Norfolk country which is hardly ever seen by the Broadland visitor.

Another form of niggle which has affected a number of navigations has been that occasioned by business rivalry, the most blatant being reported on the Glamorganshire Canal when, following a dispute between two local ironmasters in 1794, the offended one wrote: 'I understand that Mr Crawshay has broke the locks and let off all the water from under the boats loaded with our iron...' Not really cricket, that! Such a trend was felt in the very last days of independent carrying on narrow canals when a lock would be drawn off (emptied) in the face of an oncoming pair of boats, a proceeding which, apart from wasting water, contributed towards delays in traffic. Many were the brawls, even in the 1950s at bottlenecks on the canal system — Farmer's Bridge, Camp Hill and Tipton. Is it a curious hangover of this that, in the amenity age, three 20-feet boats will work a flight of locks, even the 'thirty' at Tardebigge, independently rather than together? The third in such a queue surely vows never to go cruising again.

In 1890 a not very enthusiastic writer on waterways stated categorically that:

'It would be the idlest of idle dreams to expect that the canal system of this or any other country, as originally constructed, can be resuscitated, or even temporarily galvanised into activity, in competition with railways. Canals as they were built a century ago have no longer any function to fulfil that is worthy of serious consideration. Their mission is ended; their use is an anachronism. They do not provide the means of cheaper transport, and they have no other advantage to offer to the trader that would be a sufficient equivalent for the tedium of the transport.'

And it it curious, but true, that even in World War One canals were worked to nothing like their capacity, so much so that in 1919 the Canal Control Committee of the Board of Trade made a rather desperate appeal for their greater use.

'The principal method of transporting goods in this country is by railway. The railways have already rendered a great service to the country during the War. The demands which have been made upon them have increased, while the staff which is available for their administration is reduced...There is a limit to the work which the railways can do for the Country, and, consequently, it is of the utmost importance that other methods of conveyance of heavy goods, and indeed, of all classes of commodities, should be utilised to the same extent during the War. Motor traffic is not available to the same extent as it was. Certain facilities, however, do exist for transporting goods by canals and inland waterways...It is desirable that senders of heavy goods, manufacturers, and traders throughout the Country should render every possible assistance to the Government in dealing with the difficulties which have arisen in the transport of goods. The necessity is becoming more urgent as the War proceeds, and it will, therefore, be a patriotic step on behalf of all who can do so, if they will use the inland waterways of the Country, when they are suitable for the transport of their commodities between one point and another.'

The same pattern arose during World War Two and the comments of Mr E.J.Woolley, when addressing the Grand Union Canal Company and presenting their Annual Report for the year 1939, make interesting reading.

'When we met here a year ago it was under the passing shadow of a great crisis. Unhappily to-day we meet under the black clouds of what may prove to be the most decisive war in the history of the Empire, and I feel certain that you will appreciate that my remarks must be tempered with everything which that implies...But I have no hesitation in saying that if war had not broken out the accounts would have presented an even better appearance, and the board would have probably recommended some payment being made to the Preference stockholders. As it is we still find it impossible to pay a dividend...It is a lamentable fact to have to relate that for the last four months of the year there was a decrease of no less than 131,515 tons compared with the same period last year, and the all in tonnage revenue amounted to £6,145, so that even if the trade had continued on the same level after the outbreak of war we should have still shown an improvement.

'As you are well aware, a considerable portion of our traffic arrived in London from overseas. the diversion of ships to other ports must therefore have a direct bearing on our results, not only as regards the traffic carried on our waterways, but also on our dock receipts, for we lose the dock dues and quay charges, and our stevedoring and wharfage company at the same time loses revenue.'

After giving the reasons for the decline in

Surely the all-time classical canal photograph. It is pre-war and taken for the Grand Union Canal Carrying Company whose boats included the butty No.345 'Roade'. The location is Regent's Canal Dock, which was designed for transhipment from sea-going vessels up to 350' (107m) x 60' (18.3m) to narrow boats and lighters. British Waterways.

tonnage — primarily the now non-existent four steamers per week that had previously operated out of German ports, coal no longer being brought by coast-wise steamers, and the drop in revenue from timber traffics, Mr Woolley went on to say:

'On the other side of the picture it is pleasing to be able to record that maintenance shows a fall of £2,620, although the company has been faced with heavy expenditure in connexion with IRA outrages earlier in the year, and our troubles have been further accentuated by a serious burst in the canal banks at Weedon on 18 October. This was due to the exceptionally heavy floods, which I am informed were the most serious in living memory, both by reason of the large area covered and the enormous volume of water rising in a very short space of time. This cost us £1,180 in repairs. But unfortunately it necessitated closing this part of the canal for 10 days, and in consequence some thousands of tons of traffic were lost. It is to be hoped that both these items may be considered as non-recurring expenditure.'

After covering the revenues from the estates,

stevedoring and wharfage divisions, he continued into a report of the difficulties found by the Grand Union Canal Carrying Company which:

'...has experienced a year of somewhat mixed fortunes; but in spite of the extremely difficult conditions under which it has operated the company had made a trading profit of £1,779, as against a loss of £3,349 in 1938. Once again throughout the year the company has suffered for the lack of skilled boatmen, which seriously handicapped its operations, and in consequence many thousands of tons of goods were lost. Although the actual traffic booked by the company amounted to 211,959 tons, an increase of 16,178 tons over last year, it was only able to carry 166,044 tons in its own boats, the balance of 45,915 tons being given to other carriers operating on our canal. The tolls on traffic booked by our carrying company amounted to £22,309, compared with £17,466 in 1938.'

As a result of the war some new traffics were generated on waterways, including milk powder from Brentford to the Ministry of Food Depot at

Single motor boat Kenelm, then the flagship of Sir John Knill's postwar fleet, Captain Tom Moxon, c.1948. Noticeably different is the 'liner' funnel. (Sir John Knill).

During World War Two a number of girls volunteered to work canal boats. Even prior to 1939 some traffics had been relinquished by the Grand Union Canal Carrying Company due to a shortage of crews and this was exacerbated by some young unmarried men volunteering to join the armed services, so a training scheme was set up for both women and men to be shown how to work the cut. The difficulty of itinerants getting rations from small village shops, the (relatively) overcrowded conditions, the brutally hard work and long hours (5am to 10pm in summer) plus, perhaps attitude problems, led to the scheme, particularly where women were concerned, being less than successful. Loading at Baddesley Collieries, Coventry, 1944. The Geographical Magazine, London.

Blaby and flour, again for a Ministry of Food Depot, from Brentford to Tring. A very popular traffic was sugar, again from Brentford and destined for the Ministry of food Depot at Marsworth — popular with boatmen for obvious reasons! But, overall the same picture arises of a run-down of the canals, maintenance decreasing and traffics with it; in effect the preparation for the *coup de grace* given by nationalisation.

At Your Leisure

THE FIRST edition of this book was produced in a totally different format, but the price was relatively high as the publishers did not feel there were enough people interested in canals to ensure very high sales. They were pleasantly surprised but in the equivalent of this chapter, after covering the history of 'amenity' use of waterways there followed a few paragraphs on hire-boating as seen by an employee of British Waterways who all too often had to pick up the pieces. After reviewing boat availability and their condition with outboard engines as the norm, requiring the hirer to hump a 4-gallon jerrycan of petrol along the towpath daily, Elsan chemical toilets in a primitive cubicle (or even requiring the awning to be erected before their use), plastic water-carriers, two-burners-plus-grill calor gas cookers, none the less the late Arthur Rice, the owner of one of the oldest hire-boat companies, the Kingfisher Line at Hoo Mill Lock, told us he had customers who came back to him every year for 20 or more years, often adjusting their holidays in order to get the craft they wanted. He explained that he only advertised in the *Daily Telegraph* and *The Times* in order to ensure that he had a select clientele who would look after his craft and for this reason could fit them out just that little bit better.

Other companies, aiming at a wider market found all sorts of odd things happening to them. Given a wet week it was not uncommon for people to abandon a cruiser, often miles from the nearest safe moorings, catch a bus or train back to the boatyard and sneak their car out in the hours of darkness. This treatment was normal if any damage had been done to the cruiser but in any case many preferred to forfeit their nominal deposit rather than struggle with rain, mud and fratching children. On one occasion a hire-boat operator, hearing nothing through the grapevine, traced his craft to the Welsh Canal and found it

A delightful study of an elderly lady and her boat, both in retirement sixty years ago. The Geographical Magazine, London.

Left: Wintertime on the canals has a certain charm, but to the lock-keeper meant chilblains, split fingers and a high risk of accident as hobnailed boots slid and slipped on the lock sides. For his dog there was (after the initial shock) almost unalloyed pleasure. Right: Described in the 1970s as 'one of our latest canal cruisers', this BWB craft has rather coyly had her name painted out but is noticeable for her fibre-glass construction, collapsible wheelhouse and twin lifebuoys, really the antithesis of working narrow boats. (British Waterways Board).

Shropshire Union, Welsh Canal, near Bridge 27, 1967. Although a Chester-built river craft, the 'Barbara Joan' was based at Llangollen.

there, stripped of everything saleable. Another boat was brought back to the yard at 2am with a hole in the side, the engine damaged from having been run with no cooling water, vomit all over the cabin and beer bottles tinkling musically in the bilges. Another fibreglass craft was taken out for a week, and on the Wednesday the hire-craft owner was asked to go out to the Birmingham Main Line as there was a hole in the hull. 'Not uncommon' he thought and picked up a fibreglass repair kit. On the main line at that time one was only permitted to use one of each pair of arches on the double bridges, as the other side was not dredged. The hirer had taken the wrong side and hit a piece of scaffolding pipe. He blithely explained to the owner that he had then reversed, saw what had happened and tried to go through again, inevitably making another hole. The owner was more resigned than angry.

Some lock-keepers live in mortal fear of hire-boat companies who have 70-feet converted ex-working boats. Generally they are well and sensibly crewed, sometimes however, the crew will be made up predominantly of schoolchildren with one or two adults (nominally) in charge. There can be little more horrifying to a lock-keeper plodding peacefully up the towpath than to see 13 tons of motor boat with the engine still going at full speed approach his lock gate without a steerer being visible. Called to attend to a boat once which was parked

on the top gate of a lock on the Grand Union Canal, with both gate paddles and the handrail broken, I ascertained that the steerer was an 11-year-old boy and the box he was standing on had collapsed at the wrong moment. He protested that 'it ain't got any brakes like a car'. The adult in charge just shrugged his shoulders and said 'Send the bill to the . . .Comprehensive School', obviously thinking it was only a matter of a few minutes' work to repair the lock.

Buying a boat in the 1950s and 1960s could be a problem. In 1956 a canal cruiser (converted pontoon) with a British Seagull outboard and battery lighting (and **that** needed recharging every 3 to 4 days!) was available for £99, but a snazzy converted narrowboat with Morris Navigator (petrol/paraffin) engine cost £1,200. Conversely a year later, Mr Hill of The New Inn, Prees, offered a 'small boat hiring business as going concern' with 'caravan type accommodation' available for £700 plus stock at valuation. However one did not rush off for this when in 1958 'converted narrowboats four and six berth with Diesel and Petrol self-starting engines' were available from £16 per week each (plus fuel), rising to £22 in the peak season. Not really a recipe for a fortune!

In 1959 an iron butty-boat was available for converting for £250, but also available in the same IWA Bulletin was a metal camping punt for £120 but including 'four bed-frames'. At the

Barnton, Trent & Mersey, 1967.

Edinburgh & Glasgow Union Canal, Scotland. The 'Thomas Telford" being launched. A product of one of the specialist canal pleasure boat builders, 1979. R.J.K.Murphy.

> *Canal tunnels have a curious attraction for the most blasé of canal users, even though some were once notorious for bats (Greywell on the Basingstoke being their last refuge), some soaking wet (Harecastle before repair), some crooked (Braunston, for example) and others quite welcoming (Shortwood). Passage of the longer ones can either mean the end or beginning of a voyage of exploration and once through Blisworth or Wast Hill there is a feeling of doors both closing and opening simultaneously. Unfortunately a degree of the mystery is being destroyed for safety's sake, as handrails are being fitted to help those who try to swim through and lighting being installed wherever possible.*

A filthy wet day but the steerer of this little craft showed true Northern grit by continuing on his cruise. Cooper Bridge Lock No.1 at the junction of the Huddersfield Broad and Calder & Hebble Navigations. August 1970. Peter L.Smith.

same time a full length Town class narrowboat was around £300 ex-engine and stripped to a bare hull and cabin. As late as 1962 the following appeared 'Paddle-boat 'Maybug', Jowett engine, twin stern wheels, self-starter, electric light, Elsan. Sleeps three. Beam 5'6". Overall length 23' Draught 18". Designed for navigating the weedy canals. Hull built 1955, overhauled June 1961. Has travelled hundreds of miles. Selling with reluctance 300 guineas.' And there was the problem. Canals which were still in use for trading purposes (and the boats grew less by the month) were still relatively deep, but elsewhere weed and mud were killing waterways. The Macclesfield then resembled a Sargasso Sea, on the Stourbridge we bowhauled to save our propeller from further damage, and on the Stratford begged a tractor driver to drag a 2'6" (76cm) draught boat out of a bridge-hole, this boat having its bows a foot higher than the stern where it was perched on brick rubble.

And the reason for this? In the *Daily Telegraph* of 10 August 1962 the Principal Traffic Officer and Deputy General Manager of British Waterways bluntly stated:

'It is interesting to note that Mr A.G.Allan admits that the choice of Stourbridge for a rally of boats had the deliberate aim of enforcing the retention of a canal whose future is now under consideration by the Government. We do not accept the view that pleasure craft can navigate the canals as of right nor that we are bound to maintain the canals for that purpose — and certainly the rally committee has no right whatever to attempt clearance work without our consent. As far as the so-called obligation of the British Transport Commission to maintain canals is concerned, Parliament has recently enacted provisions in the Transport Act which preclude this.

That was the official face of British Waterways but, in the March 1958 edition of *Waterways* 'Staff magazine of British Transport Waterways', the Editor wrote:

'The year 1957 will stand out later as the year in which we in British Waterways really began to awaken the public to the wonderful opportunities that our waterways offer as pleasure-cruising grounds. Mind you, we have some way still to go. But I feel in my bones that we're getting there. The reason? The public, in growing numbers, are making the discovery that in these days of rush and tear, strain and responsibility, a holiday on the Waterways has much to offer in the way of peaceful relaxation. From our point of view, this is a good thing. It means more people to meet or give a helping hand to, and more interest in the job we do. And while it will not mean greatly increased earnings in the kitty, and while our main efforts must always be directed towards getting commercial traffic, we like to feel that we are

An idyllic scene, typifying what the amenity use of waterways should be like, although a little more sunshine would be an enhancement! The original caption of 1971 reads: 'British Waterways hire cruiser 'Water Hyacinth' waiting in lock for water level to lower during holiday amid lovely scenery.' A period piece, of course, in those days girls really did wait for the boy to lift the paddles; and then they did the cooking. British Waterways.

Right: A goat poses for the camera, lockside, Worcester & Birmingham Canal, 1993.

Far right: Long Buckby, Grand Union Canal, 1989 and a smart pleasure boat emerges. It is, perhaps, a sign of the times that the girl, by contrast with working boat children, necessarily wears a life-jacket.

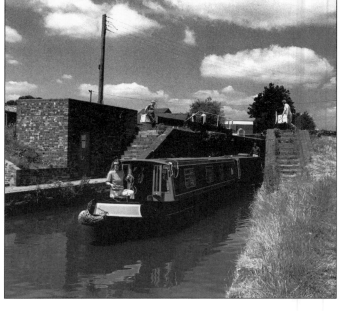

adding something to the health and happiness of our fellow men.'

That was five years previously. And in August/September 1967, *Waterways* again:

'The Government is committed to maintaining an amenity network of canals,' said Mr John Morris, Joint Parliamentary Secretary to the Ministry of Transport, when he re-opened the 'Sixteen Locks' on the Stourbridge Canal at the Spring Bank Holiday weekend. 'What is not always realised is that we are equally committed to encouraging the development of the waterways so that people using them have all the facilities they need. We shall be spelling out our plans in this direction before long."

After giving a résumé of the story behind this happy event, the magazine reported John Morris as saying:

'This is a very happy occasion because today we are restoring a piece of waterway to full use and that means that thousands of people are going to be able to use and enjoy this waterway when travelling between one part of the canal system and another. I say thousands of people — not because we have precise estimate of what the pleasure traffic on this waterway will be, but because we do know that waterway cruising is no longer a minority pleasure. Only fifteen or twenty years ago the case was very different. In those days the Inland Waterways Association and its allies were a band of dedicated enthusiasts — cranks some people would have said. Today they are an army — perhaps, looking at all these lovely craft here — I should say an armada. And a growing armada at that. Unlike so many of the enthusiasms which have developed in the last few decades, as people have found themselves with more money and more time for recreation, waterway cruising does not lead to over-

crowding of the recreational space and facilities we already have. There is a ready-made canal network for it. What we have to do now is to develop that network.'

These amenity waterways were to be called 'cruiseways' and in effect they were to remain open, although not improved — 'drowned in aspic' as one IWA member succinctly summed up the situation.

Since those days much has changed; in detail perhaps not always for the better insofar as the individuality of canal fittings is being destroyed as 'nanny' tries to make waterways 'bland' so that from appealing to the individual, the cranks Mr Morris referred to, they will appeal to repmobile drivers, those who like their hotels and their food the same whether in Bangkok or London; so the canal user of today and tomorrow will find the same equipment whether in Oldham or Devizes. Such individuality that will — must indeed — remain is in the hands of canal restoration groups. Some are trying to restore 'their' bit of a waterway, others the whole length. Each society faces a unique challenge, unique because each waterway was unique both in its inception and its building. There were in 1994 around 130 canal societies recorded with the Inland Waterways Association and others outside giving a probable total of about 200 'restoration' bodies each fighting their corner. Obviously no book of this type can give justice to them all and therefore the six examples that follow are chosen for the sheer variety of problems they face.

The Barnsley Canal

With the passing of an Act of Parliament in June 1793 the construction of the Barnsley Canal could begin. Under the guidance of William Jessop, the consulting engineer, a broad canal of sixteen miles in length was driven from the Aire and Calder Navigation at Heath near Wakefield

In late October 1993, a 'Gathering of Boats' was held near The Bonded Warehouse on the Stourbridge Canal. The atmosphere and the boats' appearance was superb, enhanced by a number of (pseudo) nineteenth-century boatmen who looked the part in big boots, collarless shirts, corduroys, neckties and flat hats, and were willing and able to answer the public's questions. A good example of modern canal public relations.

An item often overlooked on waterways are these apertures in bridge parapets, fitted (mainly during World War Two) to allow firemen to draw water when attending major conflagrations, caused by German bombs.

to Barugh and then on to Barnby Basin in Barnsley *(writes Roger Glister).*

Opened from Wakefield to Barugh in 1799 and to Barnby Basin in 1802 the canal was centred on the vast coalfield which it was built to serve. Engineering works were numerous and included twenty locks, lengthened in 1881 from their original dimension of 66 feet to 84 feet, an 11½ mile lock free pound with two spectacular cuttings and an impres--sive five arch aqueduct.

The Barnsley Canal suffered from an inadequate water supply from the start. The main source was via two reservoirs, Cold Hiendley and Wintersett, situated between Walton and Royston with the summit pound below Barnby Basin supplied by back pumping up the five Barugh locks.

The canal's trading peak was reached in 1837 when the company paid a dividend of 8½%. After some years of prosperity the down turn in fortune began in 1842 with the coming of the Great North of England Railway. This enabled coal from the Durham coalfields to be sold more cheaply to the customers formerly served by the canal. In

An early boat rally at Stewponey, Staffordshire & Worcestershire Canal, 1967. The first modern-type narrow boat based hulls appear.

Who said canals are rubbish? Newton Lock, Bridgwater, before restoration work started, April 1978 with the junk 12' or so (3.66m) deep.

an attempt to safeguard the future of the canal lengthy negotiations were entered into with various railway and canal companies. The conclusion was reached in 1854 when the Barnsley Canal was leased to the Aire and Calder Navigation Company until in 1871 the Barnsley Canal Transfer Act enabled the A&CN to buy the company outright.

Towards the end of the nineteenth century the canal became increasingly subject to subsidence as the coal measures beneath were systematically removed. As early as 1893 the five locks and two miles of canal above Barugh Wharf were abandoned. Two major breaches were suffered, in 1911 and 1946, both of which were repaired. However, the cost of this last catastrophe coupled with rapidly rising maintenance costs resulted in an abandonment warrant being issued in 1953.

Over the years more and more restrictions have been placed on the activities of volunteers. Only twenty years ago 'hard hats' as worn here on the Kennet & Avon Canal, Bull's Lock, in 1976,. would have been unthinkable and were virtually unknown on even British Waterways' official sites. Insurance companies first demanded these and then outlawed children or animals being near the working site. This meant — and means — that no longer can the worker take his or her partner and children, together with their pet, out for a Sunday dig. And that's a shame. R.G.Liddiard

Left: Canal volunteer up to his knees in Heaven only knows what, 1978.Right: A petrol barge unloads it cargo in the late 1920s at Barnsley Basin. This part of the waterway is almost totally obliterated, although the wharf where the clinker built barge is moored is now the boundary wall of a supermarket car park with the mooring rings still in place. Barnsley Canal Group.

Walton Hall Bridge.
A laden coal barge passes Walton Hall Bridge. This bridge is still intact and carries the entrance road to Walton Hall. Barnsley Canal Group.

For the next 31 years the canal languished in decline experiencing many acts of official vandalism as bridges were lowered and sections filled in. Even the magnificent aqueduct was demolished soon after closure because it was considered unsafe.

Then in 1983 a series of letters appeared in national waterway magazines and the local press criticising the lack of support for the canal and suggesting that interested persons should join forces to safeguard what was left of the waterway. Thus on 1 April 1984 an open meeting resulted

Redfern Glass.
Coal barges unloading at Redfern Glass c.1950. This is the original factory on Twibell Street, Barnsley. The loaded barges will have travelled only one hundred yards or so from Barnsley Basin. Barnsley Canal Group.

Royston Lift Bridge.
This electric lift bridge, provided by the West Riding County Council, in 1934, was of remarkable and probably unique construction. It had four brick pillars and the road deck with controller's cabin lifted vertically about two feet to give clearance for navigation. In 1943 some 856 craft passed through the bridge. Barnsley Canal Group.

River Dearne Aqueduct.
Demolished in the spring of 1954 due to being potentially unsafe. It proved so 'unsafe' that the contractors had to use dynamite to reduce this monument to the canal builder's art to the sad state it is in today. Barnsley Canal Group.

Aqueduct Breach.
This breach happened on 20 November 1911. One wing wall and part of the embankment gave way due to subsidence. The canal was closed until 10 July 1912. Roger Glister.

in the formation of the Barnsley Canal Group. Their first task was to survey the whole length of the canal which was done in a very competant manner giving the data for a report entitled 'The Barnsley Canal — a forgotten waterway?' This was published in July 1984, a great achievement in only four months. It makes out a very compelling case for restoration and proved so popular that a revised second edition was printed in May 1988.

The reaction to the report by the local councils involved was at first somewhat guarded. However, following various meetings agreement in principle was arrived at for the restoration of two lengths of canal from Royston to Barnsley and from Smithies Lane to Barugh. Nothing has yet come of these proposals. Although the councils have offered their support to the above schemes they still feel unable to make decrees giving protection to the lengths of canal still free from the clutches of the developers.

One major obstacle to the proposed restoration scheme was identified as the Redfern National Glass factory where part of the complex is built over some 600 yards of the main line. Alternative routes are being sought but as yet are inconclusive.

At the junction with the Aire and Calder Navigation the entrance lock and the first ¼ mile of the canal were destroyed by the building of a power station. This line, however, had been built in 1816 when the entrance to the waterway was moved westwards to overcome silting problems.

The original line, on Oakenshaw Beck, was allowed to revert to a stream and the 1988 proposal was to open up this line again. But in 1993 the power station had been demolished, the site cleared and overtures were being made to the developers to include a canal corridor on the 1816 line through the area.

The aqueduct over the river Dearne was the marvel of the canal — indeed, the company were so proud that they used an engraving of it on their toll tickets. When the superb stone structure was demolished in 1953 the piers and abutments were left which could once again be used to support a steel trough and restore navigation over the river.

In 1987 the group started to look at the Dearne and Dove Canal which is the other waterway to serve the coalfields of Barnsley and the Dearne valley. Running in a southerly direction from the Barnsley Canal to a junction with the Sheffield and South Yorkshire Navigation at Swinton it has two branches to Worsbrough and Elsecar. During October 1987 the second report entitled 'The Dearne and Dove Canal — the vital link' was published which is a fitting companion to the Barnsley work.

It is on the Elsecar Branch of this canal that the physical restoration work by the Barnsley Canal Group is concentrated. In 1989 Barnsley Council, who own the canal corridor, opened up a Greenway Project to help combat the dereliction left by the closure of the collieries in the area. An engineering survey was commissioned in 1990 and following recommendations arising from this volunteer work parties are active all year round.

The Barnsley Canal Group has a very enthusiastic membership and through their commitment and dedication the message is slowly getting through to the powers that be. The future of the Barnsley Canal is healthier now than at any time during the last fifty years.

Basingstoke Canal

The Basingstoke Canal reached the town of Basingstoke in Hampshire in 1794 since when it has had a checkered history of failure combined with little pockets of success such as the trade generated by the building of the London and Southampton Railway in the 1830s and the Aldershot Military Camp in the 1850s both of which helped the canal's survival into the twentieth century *(writes Alan Lucas)*.

In the early 1920s Mr A.J.Harmsworth, whose family had been connected with the canal since the mid-1800s, bought the canal from William Carter and ran what was possibly one of the most successful businesses in the canal's history over a period of some 24 years, until his death in 1947.

Although Mr Harmsworth's trade was mainly to Woking, only some three miles from the junction with the river Wey at Woodham, there was some boat movement to Ash Vale, where his boat building and repair yard was situated, a distance of 14 miles. Despite being only slightly more than a third of the original 37 miles which terminated at Basingstoke Wharf, it was nevertheless a vital life giving injection enabling the survival of the canal for many years.

The canal's survival continued and when in 1949 it was put up for auction it was purchased by a Mr S.E.Cook. Under his general manager, Mrs J.Marshall, considerable restoration took place, but disappointingly the bid to re-establish commercial carrying was a failure.

Having gone through many years of steady decline the once living and thriving canal seemed doomed to the grave by developers hungry for land. But rescue was again at hand, when a group of waterway enthusiasts got together to form The Surrey and Hampshire Canal Society in 1966. Their objective was to campaign for the full restoration of the canal albeit for amenity purposes. Their efforts were rewarded when, after negotiations, Hampshire County Council took possession of the Western side of the canal in 1973, followed by Surrey County Council's possession of the Eastern side of the canal three years later. Progress, with volunteers working only at the weekends was, obviously, slow but with the advent of the Job Creation Programme in 1975 things were to accelerate and successful negotiations resulted in schemes being implemented on various sections of the canal.

Not all canal restoration schemes carry with them the originators and differing views of how

and why canals should be restored can cause schisms in the most dedicated of committees — one has only to remember the Bridgwater and Taunton restoration group which began life in 1965 under the aegis of the Inland Waterways Association's South Western Branch. Their early leaflets stated the objectives of the IWA were to save, restore and develop the inland waterways, that restoration costs would be met in part by the local councils and part through 'interested bodies' by sponsorship but utilising volunteer labour wherever possible. Furthermore when asked whether they wanted commercial traffic on the canal part of the committee answered a definitive 'yes', adding 'pleasure and commercial boats can live side by side . . .each boat passing up the canal would take 50 tons from our overcrowded highways'.

Eventually the group was reformed with 'canoes' and 'towpath walking' being the priorities rather than through navigation; this had to wait nearly 30 years.

Similarly, the Basingstoke has had awful problems. In 1992 Dieter Jebens, Press Officer to the Surrey & Hampshire Canal Society wrote in their magazine, *Basingstoke Canal News,* that he remembered 'discovering the canal for the first time in 1964: there were no glossy leaflets interpreting it for you. It was simply a matter of searching for the canal on a one-inch Ordnance Survey map, picking an access point and anticipating what you might find. That sense of discovery has, unfortuantely, been lost forever in the relentless urbanisation of the canal's environment: green fields have disappeared under bricks and mortar, factory estates have erupted on open spaces, shopping malls have replaced market places and the roads seethe with traffic in a never ending rush hour.

The village cricket pitch at Colt Hill has long been reduced to a car park, and Odiham bypass is a permanent scar on the landscape. At the other end of the canal Goldsworth relief road had brought a traumatic change to the length of the canal running parallel. Next will come the Blackwater Valley relief road to wreck the environment of Ash Embankment.

Restoration of the canal has brought pressures too. Mountain bikers stream down the towpath 20 at a time, oblivious of their surroundings. Coach loads of fishermen arrive to sit along the banks, hunched over roach poles reaching to the opposite bank. Housing estates and any amount of infill building have been allowed to crowd on to the canal banks. Industrial estates have mushroomed likewise. And once the recession is over building will no doubt start in earnest again. Thank goodness for the large tracts of army land fending off development, although one imagines that such a valuable asset will be among the first to be sold in the military's reassessment of its training needs. Ironically the only pressure on the canal yet unrealised is that of boats!

Wharf Bridge, Aldershot. Construction of new by-pass bridge, 7 April 1959. Martyn Denney.

Left: Lock 18, 8/9 October 1977. Although the lock has been dewatered, the dreadful conditions accepted by the volunteers leave one with nothing but admiration. Alan Lucas. Centre: Lock 18, 8/9 October 1977. Symbolism is strong and without question the volunteers needed to be. Alan Lucas. Right: Lock 24 looking back to Lock 25. Beautiful autumnal scene of a restored waterway, December 1993. The lock tail bridge styling is unique to the Basingstoke Canal. Alan Lucas.

'Left: Deepcut Dig' 8/9 October 1977, Lock 16. The use of 'Decauville' railway track as a footbridge is, shall we say, interesting. 600 volunteer navvies were on site. Alan Lucas.

The Surrey and Hampshire Canal Society's traditional style canal narrow boat 'John Pinkerton' leaving Colt Hill, Odiham, Hampshire on the restored length of the Basingstoke Canal. Deiter Jebens.

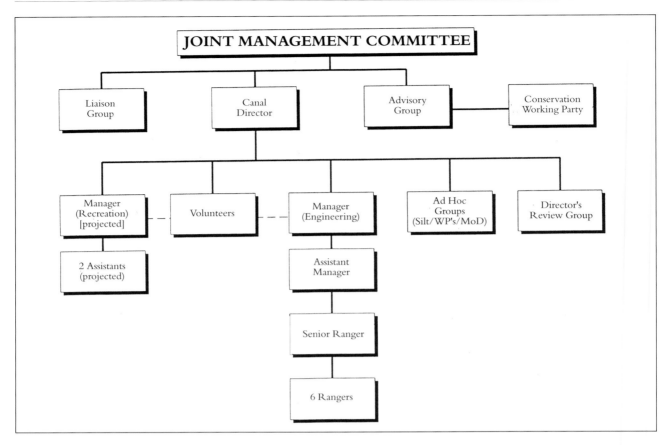

Considerable lengths of canal do live up to the dream of 25 years ago — but for how much longer?

The towpath in the 1950s required almost a 'hands and knees job' to pass along and can now be walked three abreast, water is far cleaner with the bottom visible (notwithstanding the rubbish dumped by thoughtless morons) locks are generally smart and well restored, and aquatic life has vastly increased, the movement of power boats aerating the water, while since the reopening as far as Greywell on 10 May 1991 there seems to be more of a feeling of purpose in the actual waterway.

One noticeably professional aspect of the Basingstoke lies in the use of a Joint Management Committee whose structure is shown below, reproduced from the September 1991 Society magazine.

The JMC has since March 1991, comprised eight county councillors, eight district/borough councillors, one Society representative and one from English Nature. First set up in 1981 to oversee the restoration of the canal, at one time the IWA, anglers, ramblers and two county wildlife trusts had representatives but these and others are not part of the 'Advisory Group' symbolic perhaps of were the financial strength really lies.

However, like all restored and hence publicised waterways vandalism is an evil canker. The trip boat John Pinkerton, a vital source of income for the Society, suffered their attentions. In 1993 'Unhappily . . .the boat was broken into at Odiham. The galley doors were wrenched off their hinges and all the drink and money stolen, as well as bins, towels, the cratch cover and seat cushion which presumably were used to pack the loot. We replaced and reinforced the doors, but the thieves struck again in July when the boat was at Winchfield. This time they used oxy-acetylene equipment to burn the locks off before driving the boat down to Dogmersfield in the middle of the night to unload it. It is said that the culprits are known but that the police cannot prove it.' Quite heart-breaking for everyone concerned.

The Bude Canal

Shelly sand from the beaches of Bude has been used from time immemorial to fertilise the heavy clay soil of the interior. One can still find signs of the 'sand paths' used by carts, packhorses, and mules to carry the sand from the beach to farms a mile or two inland *(writes Lawrence Wheatley)*.

The idea of a canal to take large loads of sand a greater distance inland was first mooted by John Edyvean in 1774. Several plans were considered and sources of capital explored but it was 23 July 1820 before a route designed by James Green was agreed and the first sods cut and the first stone of the breakwater laid by Earl Stanhope before some 12,000 spectators. Dancing began in two long sets and continued for several hours amid great gaiety enhanced, no doubt, by 10 hogsheads of cider and some thousands of cakes for the assembled populace.

On 21 April 1821 No.1 barge was taken out of

Bude Harbour & Canal Company's steam inspection launch, c.1860. (Museum of English Rural Life)

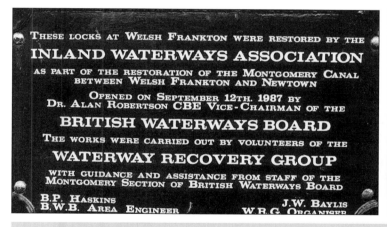

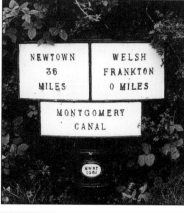

Left: The replica milepost seems to promise hope.

The story of the Ellesmere Canal's branch from Hurlesdon Junction to Carreghofa is one of success, apparent self-dereliction and now of a promising future. The canal was officially abandoned, together with many others, in 1944 by the London Midland & Scottish Railway. It had long since ceased to have any great value as a commercial navigation and at a time when the railway was itself under enormous material and financial strain it made sense for them to be rid of an incubus. The locality is Welsh Frankton, once a scene of bustle and hustle but now almost ignored by the majority of boats passing along the Welsh Canal, but it is a location full of interest and charm; albeit if not one of 'neglect and desolation' as a writer put it in 1980, still one of some sadness.

the sea lock, loaded with 24 tons of sand, taken back through the lock and towed up to the wharf at Helebridge some 2½ miles inland. This sea lock is the only manually operated lock in this country opening directly from a canal into the sea and still in use. There are two other locks, at Rodds Bridge and Whalesborough. All other changes of height were made by six inclined planes. The longest (935 feet) at Hobbacott Down was operated by two buckets 8 feet in diameter and using 15 tons of water in wells 225 feet deep. When the bucket reached the bottom of the well it hit a striker which operated a valve allowing

the water to run out through an adit or tunnel to the lower pound.

The others used overshot water wheels, that of Marhamchurch being 50 feet in diameter, lowering tub boats 60 feet down a plane 836 feet long. The other wheels were 25 feet in diameter. The tub boats were fitted with small wheels which ran in U-shaped rails fitted to the planes and were hooked on to a continuous chain running above the rails.

The canal was eventually some 25½ miles long with branches to Holsworthy and Druxton, near Launceston.

Left: The boat-builders house and forge, together with the adjacent dock lay derelict in 1993. Above: The strapping post has not felt a boat's line for many a year.

Left: Here the gates look ready for use and slightly bleached and dried by the sun. Centre: The date tells a story. Right: But the dewatered pound below tells another story. The low building on the left was once the company's stables, the cottage housed the lock-keeper, and on the right was the direct access from the waterway to the Canal Tavern and the Clerk's house. Following the line of the canal to its junction with the Llanmynech Branch there lies Lockgate Bridge.

Trucks running on 4 feet (later 2 feet) gauge rails brought the sand from the beach to the lower wharf where it was transferred to barges which were towed by horses as far as the wharf at the foot of the Marhamchurch incline where it was unloaded and distributed to farms thereabouts or loaded into tub boats 20 feet long, 5'6" wide, and 20 inches deep which were hauled singly up the plane and towed in trains of six or eight on the narrower canal. Only the leading boat had a pointed front, the others being rectangular. It was not long before it was realised that transferring the sand from the 24 ton barges to the 4 ton tub boats at Marhamchurch was an unnecessary labour and the sand was loaded directly into tub boats at the Bude Wharf.

When working well the planes were efficient, for example on 25 June 1827, 59 boats were taken over Hobbacott plane in seven hours, but breakdowns were frequent and most caused a stoppage as replacement parts were not easily obtained. The bucket chain broke at Hobbacott in December 1825, January and April 26 and both chains broke in May. Each time the bucket was broken or damaged as it fell down the well. The main chain broke twice in May, a boat running away on the first occasion, and twice more in June. In the autumn of 1830 the Clerk to the Company, John Honey, was in dire straits over the delay in delivering new iron wheels for the bucket machinery and at his wits' end to pay

taxes and his men's wages, and because the tolls were too high 'it appears to me that the Farmers who are the only support of this canal, have . . . totally set their face against it.' John Honey seems to have set his hand to repairs of many kinds to keep the canal working and eventually applied for the post of engineer. He was an earnest and hard-working man but consistently looked on the dark side and grumbled perpetually so that he probably got on the nerves of the chairman and was replaced by Joseph Cox, one of James Green's men, in March 1832.

Tolls were lowered in 1831 and trade gradually improved but tonnages never reached the 300,000 odd tons hoped for. In 1838, 59,620 tons were carried (54,016 being sand) and in 1848, 52,501 tons and this figure remained fairly constant throughout the canal's history. The revenue of between three and four thousand per year, less about two thousand for the running expenses, had to be applied to repaying the Exchequer Bill Loan Commissioners £21,037 for principal and interest. Only one dividend of one halfpenny in the pound was paid throughout the canal's operational life. Apart from sand to the hinterland ships came into the basin bringing coal, culm, salt, and miscellaneous cargoes and taking away grain and bark or leaving in ballast. This dropped sharply away when the railway opened to Bude in 1898 and it seems unlikely that there was any canal traffic after this year,

Left: Derby Canal bridge No.1 at Swarkestone, junction with the Trent & Mersey. Right: Sandiacre branch, Station Road bridge No.19 in Spondon. M.W.Hudson.

though a small transhipment trade from ships to rail developed. The feeder arm from the original reservoir, Lower Tamar Lake, was purchased for £8,000 by Stratton & Bude UDC in 1901 and used to supply water to the town and is known as 'The Bude Aqueduct'.

The Bude Canal Society was formed in February 1990 to preserve, promote, and maintain the line and works of the Bude Canal. To date the Society has cleared the towpath from Lower Tamar Lake to Dexbeer following on the work done by the MSC earlier, and exposed stonework around Rodds Bridge and Whalesborough locks; has engaged the Waterway Recovery Group to clear the wheelpit at Merrifield; the bottom of Hobbacott plane and the adit; and to strengthen with gabions, 100 yards of the canal bank where water was leaking into the wildlife preserve. Many walks have been led and illustrated talks have been given. A cruise boat, *Ruby*, lent by West Country Branch of IWA has been used for trips on Sunday afternoons in June, July, and August 1992 — despite being set on fire one Friday. In 1993 permission was given to run for four months but, sadly, the engine seized up in August and the repairs proved too costly. This was particularly frustrating, since the publicity was better and people were beginning to ask about trips. Our Secretary, Audrey Wheatley, was able to persuade *HMS Dasher*, a patrol boat, to make a three-day visit in our promotion week in 1992 and in 1993 we had a week's 'Waterways for Youth' event involving some hundred and twenty children from the ages of 9 to 14 in activities such as abseiling, canoeing, sand modelling, rowing, canal walks, and a quiz and treasure trail.

A trust is in the process of being formed to be administered by the Society for the maintenance of 'The Bude Aqueduct' as a five mile walk along the disused feeder arm from Lower Tamar Lake.

There is much still to do but the Society has generated much goodwill locally and looks to the future with confidence.

Restoration of the Derby Canal

The Derby canal ran from the Trent & Mersey Canal at Swarkestone (south of Derby), across the River Derwent near the centre of the town, and then east to the Erewash Canal at Sandiacre south-west of Nottingham *(writes M.W.Hudson)*. A branch from Derby ran to the north at Little Eaton, where it connected with a tramway bringing coal from collieries further to the north. Also in Derby, a very short arm after the river crossing gave access to the river itself, allowing navigation up river to mills at Darley Abbey. Originally, a short additional length of canal very near to the Swarkestone junction connected the Trent & Mersey to the River Trent. The whole route was open by the summer of 1796.

The cut between the Trent & Mersey and the River Trent was the first to close, at some time between 1817 and 1837, due to a combination of high tolls demanded by the Trent & Mersey in compensation for loss of traffic that would otherwise proceed along that canal to join the Trent down river at Derwent mouth, a general falling off of navigation on the upper Trent, and problems with the maintenance of the locks. In 1908 the tramway carried its last coal, due to railway competition, but the canal from the tramway terminus to Derby struggled on until 1935. The Canal Company sought to close the Sandiacre branch in 1937, and again in 1945.

Following the latter attempt, the company prevented commercial traffic from using the canal and finally, in late 1964, succeeded in obtaining a Warrant of Closure for the whole canal. This followed an unsuccessful last ditch restoration campaign, driven by the Midlands Branch of the Inland Waterways Association which formed a Derby Canal Restoration Committee.

In spite of the failure of this campaign, the enthusiasts have not given up. Support from the general public was high in the 1960s and has since increased. Of crucial importance to modern restoration attempts, however, is the new found interest on the part of the local authority. Refurbishment of what by then was for much of its length either a rubbish-filled ditch or a linear bog garden did not seem an attractive proposition to Derby Corporation in the 1960s. At that time, new always seemed better in the eyes of authority, and the wholesale destruction of well-loved area of our towns that occurred in the 1970s was already in the wind. Recent successful restoration of other canals, coupled with a growing realisation of the amenity value of a waterway to an increasingly pressurised public, now seems to be changing the bureaucratic mind. This is apparent in support for the project described below.

In early December 1993, the Derby and Sandiacre Canal Company was launched with the objective of restoring the canal from Swarkestone to Sandiacre as a navigable ring, and has produced a comprehensive report on which the comments on the work required to restore the canal, included in the following description, are largely based. Consideration of restoration can be neatly divided into three sections: Swarkestone to Derby, Sandiacre to Derby, and Derby itself.

Sandiacre branch, Station Road bridge no.19, in Spondon.

The Cuttle Aqueduct between Baltimore Bridge and Bridge 46, carrying the Swarkestone Branch over the Cuttle Brook.

Swarkestone to Derby

From the Trent & Mersey junction, where an original accommodation bridge would require some extensive remedial work, the route has been converted to a cycle path cum bridal/walkway as far as the inner city suburb of Wilmorton. The canal bed could therefore be re-excavated in a fairly straightforward manner.

Not far from the junction, a new movable accommodation bridge would be provided.

A little further on, the Department of Transport's planned Derby Southern Bypass threatens to strangle this stage of the new restoration initiative at birth, by crossing and blocking the canal route. It is believed that a presentation to the Public Enquiry has succeeded in persuading the Department to include a navigable culvert in the canal crossing.

Not far from Swarkestone, Cuttle Brook ran under the canal through a stone-built culvert. That culvert still exists, but the brook has been diverted through a cutting a short distance away. A new, larger, culvert would be installed, to cope with the flow which has increased since the original was built.

The next obstacle is formed by the infilled Baltimore Bridge, carrying Sinfin Moor Lane over the canal route. planned developments in the area would probably result in the removal of the bridge; naturally, the restoration case calls for its replacement instead.

The route now becomes suburban, passing a new housing estate. The stone work of Fullen's Lock can be seen here on either side of the walkway. To avoid a sewer, this would be rebuilt a little distance away.

After passing under a bridge carrying the Derby to Swarkestone road, by the Bridge Inn public house, the site of Shelton Lock, is reached. It is not proposed to restore that lock, but instead to lower the canal from Fullen's Lock by about five feet for just over one mile, in order to reduce or eliminate the raising of the levels of three subsequent roads (one of which is the Derby Inner Ring Road!) when reconstructing the bridges which have been removed. A new lock would be built just north of the ring road crossing.

From the ring road, the route is open until, after passing under the bridge carrying London Road, it enters the grounds of Wilmorton College. At this point, the canal swung around behind houses and passed beneath a railway line near Derby Station. As far as the railway embankment, no obstruction currently exists. However, a bridge would be needed to carry the access road to the college. The restored canal would either pass through the embankment at the spot where it once did, or could utilise an adjacent road bridge as the road itself may become disused when new access to the industrial site which it serves is provided from the other side of the site. Either way, the canal would then enter Pride Park, of which more later.

Sandiacre to Derby

At the junction with the Erewash Canal, the line of the Derby Canal is blocked under a bridge carrying Lock Lane: the bridge itself is in good condition, and would require minimal restoration. From the other side of that bridge a public walkway begins. Here, Sandiacre Bottom Lock would be reconstructed; the scale of that task depends on the (unknown) level of a sewer at the site. As it is proposed to lower the water level from the original, it is not intended to reconstruct Sandiacre Top Lock, the site of which is evident by the rise in the land, a little further along the line.

A bridge carrying a major road is reached next, and is in excellent, navigable, condition. The canal route, still a walkway, then turns sharply to the left to pass for a short distance between the major road and residential streets. It is likely that restoration in this area would be to a restricted width.

Two new bridges, in rapid succession, under a side street and a main road at the end of the walkway, are the next requirement, followed by the construction of a new lock.

A seemingly insuperable obstacle is now reached: the M1 motorway! Fortunately, a plan exists to widen the motorway in the near future; this gives a heaven-sent opportunity to build a canal crossing without boring through the motorway embankment.

On the west side of the motorway a new accommodation bridge is required and then, almost immediately, the line is blocked by a farm building; this problem would be circumvented by moving the route slightly towards the south.

The canal line now passes just to the north of the village of Breaston, through a series of linear fields used for horses. A movable accommodation bridge is proposed between those fields.

At the end of the horse fields, two blockages are encountered: a works car park, which would need resiting, and a fairly busy road. Due to the road level, a fixed bridge to modern standards is not possible unless the water level is dropped by dispensing with the new lock mentioned above, and instead building one to the west of this road. A movable bridge is unlikely to be permitted, due to the level of traffic. Re-routing of the canal to the north is another option. This would be necessary a little further on anyway, as a number of back gardens have been extended across the line.

Just before leaving Breaston, Golden Brook crosses the route and a new culvert would be provided. A little further on, another culvert is needed and, a little further still, accommodation access across the canal.

The imposing structure of the Derwent Valley Aqueduct is now reached, carrying water pipelines over the route. No work on the aqueduct is needed to enable the canal to pass under as before.

A country lane is then encountered. Again, this is busy and therefore a movable bridge would probably not be allowed. In this case, however, space exists to raise the level of the road whilst preserving acceptable gradients up to a new fixed bridge.

Still passing through fields, after crossing two farm tracks where movable bridges would be provided, the route next goes beneath a concrete main road bridge (the first sign of water, but only under the bridge, is at this point!) at the outskirts of Draycott. Luckily, the bridge itself needs no work to restore navigation beneath it.

The line of the canal continues to run through fields, necessitating two more movable bridges, and then passes through the site of a new sports ground development; it is hoped that a culvert for the canal would be provided by the developer.

Yet another culvert would then be needed, to replace the original at the crossing of the Ock

If a waterways' writer were feeling totally dejected he or she would say of the Anderton lift that it was brought into use in 1875, engineered by Sir E.Leader Williams, later engineer-in-charge, Manchester Ship Canal, using hydraulic pressure to assist the counterbalanced caissons, and that it was converted to electric power in 1907 with the caissons moving independently. Even then some electrolytic corrosion was noticed as the lift's feet were standing in a saline solution, but none the less L.A.Edwards in the 1972 edition of our bible Inland Waterways of Great Britain could say: '...the main attraction to the canal voyager in this area is the Anderton Lift, the only lift in Britain, which takes boats from the Trent and Mersey Canal over 50 feet down to the River Weaver ...the tanks are suspended from wire ropes which go round overhead pulleys to counterweights of 252 tons, little power, therefore, is needed to raise the boats in the tank or lower them as the case may be. The lift takes under 15 minutes to move a boat up or down and it costs £2 single or £3 return and a souvenir ticket is issued.'

In a more poetic mood the late Robert Aikman, poet, visionary and founder and vice-president of the Inland Waterways Association wrote in his superb Know Your Waterways that: 'It is fascinating to take up a quiet mooring near the top of the lift, and during the hours of darkness to look down at the factory, which works all night and gleams with strange bright colours and sudden flashes, far below. The fact that one seldom sees a worker adds to the illusion that one is looking — from a peaceful vantage-point and distance — into the future.' Our historian would then add that in 1983 the lift was declared unsafe and a year or so later that wondrous set of gears, wires and ironworks was dismantled, leaving just a mute skeleton. And that would be that. Except. Canal people do not easily let go of their heritage. It may be rubbed away by Nanny who frets and worries about perceived danger — in all seriousness one British Waterways spokesman stated that they (BW) heaved a sigh of relief when it (Anderton) closed as there was no way of making it safe for pleasure boaters. Twice now a 'Friends of Anderton' — type body has been set up and it may not be too long before scenes like those here can again be photographed. Anderton Lift is a Scheduled Ancient Monument and it is saddening that neglect has led to £2.8 million having to be spent to restore it. Or shall we lose one of the seven wonders of the Waterways? Remember them? Pont-y-Cysyllte Aqueduct, Bingley Five-Rise Locks, Standedge Tunnel, 29 locks of Devizes, Barton Swing Aqueduct, Burnley Embankment ...and Anderton.

Right: Sombre, Anderton waits for another boat in 1966.

Below: Narrow Boat Trust single motor 'Alton' at the bottom of the lift, September 1976, on a domestic coal run. Mike Black.

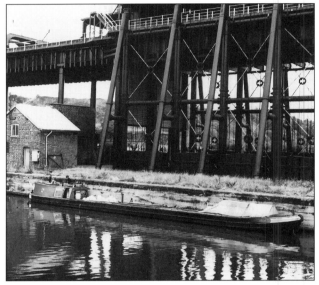

From within, towards the Weaver and the ICI works.

Brook. Shortly after this point, water reappears and the old canal becomes very obvious at last.

The small town of Borrowash is now reached, the route of the canal running to the south of it. Borrowash Bottom Lock is partially intact, and would be restored at the same site. A road next crosses the line; reduced water level here would allow the road to cross the new bridge with very little increase in gradient. After the road, where the line currently becomes a section of walkway again, Borrowash Top Lock would also be renewed.

Little work is required on the accommodation bridge arrived at next, although some strengthening and easing of access would be carried out to allow the farmer to use it, instead of the canal bed which he now crosses.

A little after passing over a stream, where the vanished culvert would be replaced, the route is completely blocked by a factory road. Because a railway line runs just to the south, the canal cannot be re-routed. Instead it is planned to move the road, for which ample space exists.

The bridge which used to carry the next road crossing would be replaced by a movable bridge, since little traffic uses it.

At the outer Derby suburb of Spondon, the road to the railway station passes over a bridge that needs no restoration. After this point, a complicated road junction is soon reached: another seemingly insurmountable obstacle. (Nearby waste ground to the south of the line would make a good site for a marina, useful as an interim measure as well as in its own right.)

Two alternative solutions to the above obstacle are suggested; boring through the road embankment, or utilising spare space which could be created under a nearby railway bridge by realigning the tracks.

From this point, the old route to the crossing of the River Derwent near the city centre (where the Sandiacre and Swarkestone branches met by locking down into the river) cannot be used: a dual carriageway occupies most of it, and the adjacent space has largely been developed. Similarly, development near the city centre prevents moving the line nearer to the northern bank of the river. Instead, it is proposed to follow the railway to the spot where it crosses the river, where an aqueduct would carry the canal (its water being supplied by pumping from the river at this spot) into Pride Park, the area mentioned at the end of the Swarkestone to Derby section.

Derby itself

Derby City was a successful applicant for redevelopment funds under the government's City Challenge program. Derby Pride Limited, the company charged with spending the money, has as one of its major projects a reclamation scheme covering a large area of waste ground between the River Derwent and the old Midland Railway Works (still in the railway business but now operated by ABB Engineering). This area, now designated Pride Park, will combine light industrial, retail and leisure facilities. The company has accepted the benefits of a restored canal running through the park, and close liaison between it and the restoration group continues in order that the exact route of the link between the Swarkestone and Sandiacre branches of the canal may best fit in with the planned building and road developments within the park.

Although the restored canal as described would fulfil the objective of providing a navigable ring (Trent & Mersey Canal — Derby Canal — Erewash Canal — River Trent — Trent & Mersey Canal), it is also considered desirable to provide for navigation some distance up the River Derwent.

After passing under the railway at Wilmorton, the original route of the canal's Swarkestone branch passed around the edge of the Midland Railway Works and then under the railway tracks north of Derby railway station, heading towards the river crossing. As implied earlier, an exact route within Pride Park remains undecided, but the intention is to route a branch from the main canal to utilise the same railway bridge. (It is currently used for road access to the railway works, but access elsewhere is already planned.)

The old canal then ran parallel to a millrace loop from the River Derwent, and passed over the millrace and a brook via a small aqueduct, before meeting the river. Since the canal bed along the millrace is now the site of Station approach, a wide busy road, and the aqueduct area lies under a large roundabout, some changes here are obviously necessary.

Both problems would be solved by moving the line to the north. The canal would cross the millrace on an aqueduct, pass through an existing small landscaped park, and then under a wide road via two new bridges before locking into the river just above a weir, as did the old canal. The towpath used to cross the river here on a wooden bridge: it is planned to replace that structure, to protect boats from the weir and to provide a peaceful river crossing for walkers and cyclists. A last barrier to craft passing up river, in the form of another, old and redundant, weir close by, would be removed.

Although, at first sight, it may seem that restoration of the Derby Canal poses several large and expensive problems, it does look like an idea whose time has finally come. The Inland Waterways Association has commented that the time taken by the restoration group, the Derby and Sandiacre Canal Company, to reach this stage is unprecedentedly short, and there is no doubt of local public support. The cost of fully restoring the canal is estimated at just over £17 million, however almost all of that is expected to come from European and Government funding. To put that sum into context, it should be born in mind that the original £100,000 building cost of the canal translates to almost £55 million in modern values!

An article in the *Derby Evening Telegraph* in the summer of 1954 when the canal was already derelict, ended thus: 'The near-ruinous canals, which wind disconsolately between allotment gardens, and pass darkly under crumbling hump-backed bridges, have, even now, in certain aspects of the light, a grey and melancholy beauty . . .With waters clean and fish-haunted again, what vistas might open before the eyes of the inland voyager!…It is a pleasant pipe-dream.' It is now much more than a dream.

Pocklington Canal

Only nine and a half miles long and entirely rural, Pocklington Canal was a late addition to the north-eastern fringe of Britain's canal system, separated from the main network by the then tidal River Derwent and the still tidal river Ouse *(writes Sheila Nix)*. So why the great fuss about rescuing it from threatened destruction in the nineteen-fifties when much of its length was already more or less derelict? And why was Pocklington Canal Amenity Society set up, determined to restore it in the early seventies? Was its isolated, rural location in fact one of the reasons? Certainly, despite its apparent unimportance, it had then, and still has, enthusiastic devotees not only in is own area but around the country and overseas as well.

Pocklington Canal occupies a curious niche in local history. For a start it never actually reached Pocklington, the small East Yorkshire town from which it takes its name and which it was designed to serve. George Lether (junior)

Looking from Top Lock on the Pocklington Canal towards Silburn Lock in 1992, during which time extensive rebuilding of the lock sides was underway. It is difficult to envisage laden barges passing in and out of these gates.

The original gearing at Walbut, together with derelict gates, August 1982. The use of scrap rail betrays the one-time railway ownership of the canal. Mrs S.Nix/PCAS.

produced plans for the route, starting from the River Derwent at East Cottingwith, up to the York to Hull turnpike road, at an estimated cost of £32,000. To extend the route a further mile into Pocklington town itself would, he said, be likely to cost an extra £8,257. The canal's financial backers decided to build the terminal basin beside the road, all goods to be off-loaded there and transported the rest of their ways by horse and cart.

Probably the last pleasure craft to pass up the Pocklington before restoration started, some of the Ripon Motor Boat Club boats are seen in Melbourne Basin, 1933. Mrs S.Nix/PCAS.

This stand was to weigh heavily against the canal's commercial prospects in time to come.

The promoters could scarcely have guessed just how soon that time would be. The canal was completed to its roadside terminus (beside the present A1079) in 1818. Less than thirty years later, in 1847, George Hudson's wonderful new railway linked Pocklington with York and Market Weighton, with a handsome station right in the centre of town. The extra labour and expense involved in off-loading barges at Canal Head soon resulted in traffic being lost from the canal to the much more convenient new trains. Discussions were already taking place with the railways and by 1848 the canal had been sold to George Hudson and his York and North Midland Railway Company.

Following their usual pattern, the railways did little or no maintenance on the canal and

nothing to encourage traffic. The upper pounds became too shallow for fully loaded craft. By the end of the century keels could navigate to Canal head only after transferring part of their cargo to flat wooden lighters provided for this purpose by the (then) North Eastern Railway. Few craft ventured above Bielby. Most stopped halfway up at the mooring basin in the growing village of Melbourne, where there were coal wharves and warehouses. World War One brought further neglect. The last keel was sold off in 1932 and, by 1934, most of the locks had become impassable. The canal was never formally abandoned. It just quietly mouldered. With nationalisation of the railways in 1948, ownership passed to the British Transport Commission and then, in 1963, to the British Waterways Board, now known as British Waterways, which is the present statutory authority for the canal.

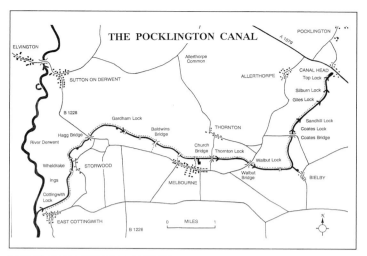

THE POCKLINGTON CANAL

During World War One (c.1915) Walter Hutchinson and his friends are seen swimming at Silburn Lock. Mrs S.Nix/PCAS.

would generate more traffic and consequent toll income for the promoters of the scheme. The Earl could bring up more of his South Yorkshire coal and roadstone and more farm produce could be taken down to Hull or the growing towns of the West Riding. In addition to the big landowners, however, many local townspeople, owners of small businesses, and local farmers and villagers, also became 'undertakers' with shares in the new Canal Company. They might only have contributed a sum of £10, but they had a fierce pride of ownership. This was their canal. In 1959 descendants of these 'undertakers' were still living locally (there are still some today.) They were not to be pushed around by any distant corporation, especially with such a disgraceful and dangerous proposal. The concerted campaign was successful and Sheffield's plans were brought to nought.

In the 1950s there was talk of eliminating or filling in the canal, but nothing came of it. Then, in 1959, Sheffield Corporation Waterworks came up with a proposal to use the canal as a tip for 'inoffensive sludge' from its water treatment plant at Elvington, not far away, beside the River Derwent. They planned to buy up sufficient land along the banks of the canal to enable them to fill it with slimy, chalky water, a potentially lethal, linear quicksand. There was outrage — amongst farmers with canal-side land, amongst local waterway enthusiasts, members of the Inland Waterways Association, fishermen and many, many others. They lobbied MPs, went to the House of Commons, secured extensive press coverage, and enlisted such indomitable allies in their cause as Mrs Bessie Bunker and the Inland Waterways Protection Society.

Not surprisingly, back in the early 1800s, when a canal to Pocklington was first proposed, the plan had come from local landowners, chiefly inspired by the Earl Fitzwilliam, who already owned the Derwent Navigation and levied tolls on the river traffic. A canal leading from the Derwent into the remote surrounding farmland

By this time derelict canals in other parts of Britain were beginning to be restored and some of the local campaigners began to think about the possibility of reviving the Pocklington Canal and making it navigable once again now it had been saved from such a terrible fate. But it was the Labour Government's 1968 Transport Act which finally enabled the Pocklington Canal Amenity Society to be set up and to make a start on restoring the canal.

Twenty-five years later, despite the canal's short length, the Society is still hard at it! The canal is currently navigable to Melbourne, approximately halfway up from the Derwent. The next two locks are virtually ready for use but cannot yet be reached by boats due to the need for dredging. Much other work has been carried out, including installation of six new swing bridges and one new fixed bridge, lock chambers repaired and provision of a picnic site, car park and information centre, now well established on one-time wasteland at Canal Head. Many other repairs and environmental improvements have also been carried out. New top gates should soon be installed at Top Lock and an unsightly temporary dam removed.

At the start of restoration, in 1969, the Canal Society was chiefly up against lack of money and lack of credibility. After all BWB North-East were used to large commercial waterways. Why would any sane person want to restore a tiny 'Remainderised' appendage on the outer edge of their patch? They must have been quite startled, indeed fearful! The Society's credibility was soon established, however, when they saw what could be achieved between us all. Money continued to be more difficult. The Local authorities were on our side and helped as much as possible. They still do but, in this sparsely populated area, have never had the funds which are sometimes available in other parts of the country for helping canals.

In the nineties it has seemed easier to raise money. As the restoration has progressed more and more people have visited the canal and, almost without exception they express their admiration and support for the Society's efforts. Many have donated most generously to Society appeals. There are few folk left now who worked on or for the canal in the old days, but a surprising number who have close connections with those who did. They are most enthusiastic and keen to see further progress with restoration.

On the other hand, at the same time as the canal was becoming better known, so the 'green' movement was growing too. The whole of the canal corridor has, for some years, been a Site of Special Scientific Interest and this has meant that English Nature (previously the Nature Conservancy) now places considerable restrictions on what it is prepared to allow the Society or British Waterways to do in the way of restoration or maintenance. English Nature is of the opinion that boat movements on the canal are detrimental to wildlife, most especially on the upper reaches which are currently unnavigable and which it would like to keep that way.

But the Canal Society too is firmly wedded to conserving wildlife; it is an amenity society. Equally it is convinced that use of the canal by limited number of boats (and several factors will always limit their numbers in any case) is the least damaging way to maintain an open channel, essential if the canal is not to become totally overgrown and dried up. The Society also believes that conservation of the built environment is important, hence its efforts to have locks, bridges and other structures restored to their original design and materials. It has sometimes been an uphill battle to persuade other organisations of the importance of this aspect of conservation and efforts have not always been successful. At least English Nature agrees that the canal structures do need to be restored and maintained.

We hope to persuade them, and the local Wildlife Trust which is also opposed to boats, of the need for access for people, some of whom would wish to travel by boat. Often access in a suitable boat is the least disturbing way to visit and observe the wildlife. The Society believes it can often be more rewarding and far less intrusive than access along the towpath by walking or cycling (which is officially encouraged). But there does seem to be a need for better understanding in many quarters of what is meant by suitable boats and of the fact that both topographical and geographical considerations will ensure that only certain craft will be able to make their way to this canal at any time, especially to its upper reaches.

So much for the problems and true Yorkshire determination to overcome them in the best way possible for all who enjoy the canal. Now a little more of why so many do enjoy and value it so much.

The country beside the lower reaches of the canal is flat and regularly floods in winter, but has always been noted for its thriving variety of wildfowl and other birdlife. In the tiny Georgian church in East Cottingwith, near the junction with the River Derwent, there is a memorial to Snowden Sleights, the famous early nineteenth-century wildfowler and punt-gunner. As the canal winds its way eastwards, and then north towards Pocklington, it brings views of the foothills of the Yorkshire Wolds. The land beside the banks becomes more fertile and the ings water meadows give way to small scale farmland, surrounded with hedges and many handsome trees. There is a profusion of birds, wild flowers and colourful insect life.

Four roads cross the canal during its nine-mile journey. But these are local roads and still cross by the original arched, brick bridges, which fit perfectly with the nearby countryside, both in their scale and design and in the local bricks used for building them. There are also eight swing bridges and nine locks along the course of the canal. There are few 'great houses', but many older farmhouses and cottages which, like the bridges, seem to fit comfortably and naturally into their surroundings. At Canal Head there is a (now well converted) warehouse and a small lock house, both originally built about the same time as the canal. The best of the four road bridges is of a design which, though basically simple, is handsome and thought to be unique. so, likewise, is the design of the original paddle gear on the locks. Specially made replicas have recently been installed on Walbut Lock. The towpath hedge on the upper reaches of the canal encloses a hidden world of locks and water and wildlife in perfect scale and harmony (most of the locks are on the upper section) — it also provides welcome protection from the sometimes bitter wind!

Perhaps all this goes some way to explain the compelling charm and attraction of the Pocklington Canal. Canals of this sort are rare in this part of the country, too. We have the large commercial navigations of South Yorkshire and the mixed river and canal systems of the Driffield Navigation and the River Hull. But, to many of its fans, the Pocklington Canal is unique, an isolated retreat from a noisy world and a continuing challenge to its restorers, who remember that only the devotion and persistence of its earlier protectors saved it for those who enjoy it today.

Whitchurch Arm of the Llangollen Canal

When this book was first published in 1973, the mile-long arm linking Whitchurch town centre to the Llangollen Canal had for some years been filled in and, in parts, built on. Legally abandoned under the 1944 act, it had no special circumstance by which it might have hoped to survive, in the way that the Llangollen Canal itself continued as an essential channel to 'transport' water between the Dee in North Wales

Top: The first was taken in 1992, but the field's appearance remained the same till the early summer of 1993. Adrian Cooper/Shropshire County Council.

Middle: The second shows the bed excavated and work being carried out on the towpath in September 1993. Adrian Cooper/Shropshire County Council.

Bottom: The third is the scene prior to the arrival of the crowd which gathered for the official opening on 10 October 1993. Adrian Cooper/Shropshire County Council.

and the waterboard reservoir near Nantwich *(writes John Ward).*

However, by the beginning of the 1980s, Whitchurch Town Council had recognised the potential that existed, to capitalise on the growing leisure use of the Llangollen Canal. This awareness coincided with a downturn in the town's manufacturing and service industries, a downturn which was to become progressively worse, year by year. This, in its own sad way, acted as a spur to restoration plans.

With the Llangollen Canal attracting over forty thousand visitors every year, the lack of a link to Whitchurch meant that substantial trade was being lost. The town was so close to the canal and yet not discernible from passing boats. The town council decided that something had to be done. It is noteworthy that it was the council which made the first move, rather than a canal society, a boat club or a developer. Any of these might have acted by now, but back in 1982 it was Whitchurch Town Council which, after some preliminary discussions and probings, commissioned a feasibility study from Liverpool Polytechnic.

Four routes were identified, for the restored waterway to negotiate the obstacles which had resulted from the abandonment. The first quarter mile, from the main line to Chemistry Bridge, had been used as a rubbish tip and then grassed over to form rough grazing. The next half-mile was built on, or incorporated into, neighbouring properties. The second bridge, at the foot of Sherrymill Hill, had been dropped and the final quarter mile used to bury main services. This last section had been incorporated into the town's Jubilee Park.

A route was chosen. It was decided to restore the first section to Chemistry Bridge, then take traffic down an inclined plane to a canalised section of Stag's Brook. This would be an attraction in itself, for water-borne visitors and car travellers alike, in that Whitchurch was home to the only working inclined plane in the country.

By now it was realised that a charitable trust could carry forward the scheme more readily than a town council, with greater access to grants and an ability to involve individuals and local and national organisations. An eon dragged by (or so it seemed to those closely involved), until the Whitchurch Waterway Trust was formally recognised by the Charity Commissioners.

The district and county councils supported the town's initiative, and protected the proposed line of the canal on the District Plan.

Eventually planning permission of phase one was obtained. In 1992, thanks to various grants and fundraising activities, the land for this phase was purchased from a sympathetic landowner. The project was gaining momentum and it was not long before the County Council successfully presented to the Department of the Environment the case for a derelict land grant, to help pay for the initial section of the restoration.

'On a courtesy visit to London before entering service between Rotterdam and the Humber, barge-aboard-catamaran mother ship 'BACAT' gives loading demonstrations in the Pool of London. Two 140-tonne BACM lighters wait to be lifted to the main deck on the ship's submersible elevator, while on the right is the stern-flow section which smoothes the ship's underwater profile when the larger LASH-type lighters are in transit between her twin hulls'. This was the British Waterways Board's press release in 1974, when what may well turn out to be Britain's last chance to have Euro-barges in service was tried out. The whole plan was really quite ingenious and to us the important part was that these lighters could traverse the Aire & Calder Navigation, giving through communication from Basle, or Dortmund, or Paris to Rotherham. The intransigence of certain trade unions who demanded the rate for a lighter the rate they would have got for a break-bulk (i.e. loose-handled) cargo killed this particular goose. One is reminded of just how powerful these unions were when it is recalled that before they would load a private-owner narrow boat in London Docks the boat captain's membership card had to be the first thing passed up to the crane driver. British Waterways Board

During the summer of 1993 the work was carried out. The top soil and the refuse used to infill were removed and the original puddled clay was found to be in excellent condition throughout most of the quarter mile — confirming the results of earlier test excavations. As well as making good the bed, a new winding hole was provided, plus path and a staircase (steps,

Evening tranquility as a lengthman plods home. Burscough, Leeds & Liverpool Canal, October 1989

that is, not locks!). All the major works were completed in time for the re-opening ceremony on 10 October, 1993.

The Trust then turned immediately to having brought up to date the feasibility study for the remainder of the waterway, with the costings and method of operation of the inclined plane a priority. Further on along the new line, a box culvert is in place already, to enable boats on the canalised section of the brook to pass under a service road to a new housing development. Eventually this second phase (thought to be the longest completely new canal constructed in Britain this century) will carry traffic on from Chemistry Bridge to near the bottom of Sherrymill Hill. Incidentally, this coincides with the length of the arm as it was when completed in 1808. It was because that 1808 basin was a poor site for the carrying boats that the extra few hundred yards were added in 1811.

When completed, it is proposed that the second section will end in a marina development with pontoon moorings and boat servicing facilities. Having brought boats 400 yards nearer

to the town already, and with Whitchurch clearly visible from the arm, the ultimate object is to have visitors mooring only a short distance from the town centre's facilities. With the diminuation of conventional passing trade, following on the completion of the Whitchurch by-pass in 1992, the town is keener than ever to bring the project to a speedy and successful fruition. Certainly, as the contractors worked away on the first stage in 1993, goodwill blossomed on very side — proving the old truism, 'nothing succeeds like success'.

The last text paragraph of the first edition of this book is as pertinent now as twenty years ago: It is my own opinion, and that of most of my colleagues, that canals must not be closed, but enlarged or superseded by modern navigations. We cannot, nay, must not lose this heritage of ours; for 200 years canals have moulded and assisted Britain towards her greatness; it is not fanciful to visualise that both country and canal will, if left to do so, decline together. Should they? Will they?

Epilogue

Sporadically, there have been attempts to organise groups of canal boat operators into cohesive bodies, primarily to reduce expensive and unnecessary competition but also to reduce overhead costs. Obviously it makes commercial sense to be able to offer ten or twenty boats all with the same rates and (hopefully) abilities. Before the war there were a number of such alliances, primarily linked up family ties, but, 'buttying', working four or six goats together, was practiced until well into the 1980s. The National Association of Inland Waterways Carriers acted more on behalf of the large carriers than the small but at a time when coincidentally the Cadbury canal traffics were in decline, George Cadbury (of chocolate fame) became President for a while, giving all the help he could. Postwar Sir John Knill tried to form a consortium of 'Number Ones' (owner-drivers) and small independent companies, Willow Wren eventually drifted into a curious system where the boatmen in effect hired the boats and equipment from the holding company; Barry Lycett had a pool of boats organised in the 1960s but was unable to lease a vital warehouse, while the Canal Transport Marketing Board, who were very alive to publicity and professional in their approach in obtaining some new traffics in the North East, suffered financially in the process. The Birmingham & Midland Canal Carrying Co started with much enthusiasm and still exist, although not entirely popular with some of their one-time sponsors but a new-ish group the Commercial Narrowboat Operators Association, have an entirely professional approach, marketing themselves vigorously but without false claims. Their literature is a curious blend of the matter-of-fact and sentiment: "There is, we believe, a widely held misconception that worthwhile commercial carrying by canal is dead. True, Canal Transport went through a bad period in the 60s, 70s and 80s, but today the canals are making a very determined and successful comeback as a not too slow but very reliable method of carrying your raw materials for recycling, building materials: And also for carrying delicate pottery and other fragile cargoes. Also those cargoes which must not get wet, let alone amp, carpets, salt, chemicals, sugar and chocolate crumb. Canal carriage is vibration free, virtually vandal proof, we can if you wish advertise your firm on the craft, and it is the environmentally acceptable way of transporting your goods, safe in the hands of one of our skilled boatmen . . . The CNOA can call on a fleet of over forty craft with a potential annual carrying capacity of over 40,000 tons . . . The canals are truly a sleeping giant now awakening to serve our country as they have served it in the past. We will get your precious and your humdrum cargoes to where they are wanted when they are wanted. By making use of England's 1500 miles of waterways you will be improving your green image and putting your brand or name before the public in a new and exciting way. Be seen as helping to conserve Britain's Historic Heritage." A new, bright future for narrow boat carrying can only enhance our waterways.

'Buckden' discharging stone for towpath surfacing work on the Coventry Canal.

Appendices

Appendix 1

Stoppage At Lock 25, Stoke Prior, Worcester & Birmingham Canal

Period of Stoppage:	11th-22nd October 1971
Reason for Stoppage:	Replacement of two bottom end gates, together with paddles, etc.
Craft Utilised:	Motorised flat No.B67. Butty boat *Leo* (ex-Grand Union Canal Carrying Company, No.300).
Mechanical Equipment Available:	One hired 3 in. pump. One hired digger/excavator. One BWB-owned gantry.
Personnel:	Two carpenters, one carpenters' mate, one bricklayer, one bricklayer's mate, three labourers (one of whom was also a driver), one foreman (part-time).

Prior to the actual stoppage a certain amount of work was involved, taking place mainly in the preceding week. On Monday and Tuesday the craft *Leo* and B67 were loaded at Tardebigge Yard and a baulk for use as a clap sill and part-assembled gates were brought from Bradley Workshops (Birmingham Canal Navigations) together with the gantry, by road. A number of men were employed on the unloading and subsequent reloading as they were available, while the carpenters prepared the new paddles, assembled new ironwork and cut wedges, packing pieces, etc. On Wednesday and Thursday the craft moved from Tardebigge to Lock 5, with seven men, three to handle the motor-boat and four bow-hauling (pulling by hand) the butty-boat through the 33 locks *en route.* On Friday two of the labourers proceeded to clean up the banks, hedges, etc., to allow free movement of men and materials up to and around the stoppage site. The bricklayers, carpenters and their mates moved the *Leo* into Lock 25, assembled the gantry and pulled it into position. The gantry ran on wooden baulks; wedges were laid down fore and aft of the gantry wheels to prevent unwanted movement.

Halfway Locks, 1989.

Monday 11 October. Prior to moving off from Whitford Bridge, one set of stop planks, used to retain water, was dropped off, together with a small amount of ashes for 'racking-up' purposes. At Lock 26 a further set of stop planks was dropped off and the craft proceeded to Lock 25, where it discharged the stop plank for use at the top of the lock; the boat was completely stripped of all the equipment lying in the hold. The clap sill, a piece of elm measuring 12 feet by 12 feet by 7 feet long, weighing 3 cwt, was lifted out manually — only the gates were left in the craft. In the meantime B67 had dumped a set of stop planks at Hammonds Wharf and had taken on board a mechanical pump. A rough inventory of the material now on site would show, apart from miscellaneous packing, etc., two full-length ladders for access to lock chamber, three double walking-planks for crossing over the lock when it is de-watered, iron posts and their attendant lines for placing around the lock, the clap sill, gantry and six baulks per side of the lock, two boat shafts, a dismantled anvil-cum-vice, normally carried by the carpenters on *Leo*, tool boxes, 'horses', sawing-bench and trestles, two new paddles and their attendant iron-work, ashes, clay, wedges, iron pots for fitting to the new gates, etc.

At eleven o'clock a number of men were sent out on water control. Two pounds, those between Locks 28 and 27 and 27 and 26 were lowered between 18 in and 24 in to provide reservoirs to absorb water spilling over the weirs from higher up the flight. Despite the issuing of Stoppage Notices it was still obligatory on the Board to warn persons who had craft near any locks liable to be affected that that was a danger of grounding. The foreman and one labourer were engaged in cutting teeth from the bucket of the hired digger in order that it might lift the slurry from the bottom of Lock Chamber 27. The machine had previously been brought across the fields, uprooting various trees, bushes, etc., en route so that its movement would not be obstructed on the lock-side. The trees and bushes then served as a dam to stop the slurry from washing down into the farmer's field.

One labourer was engaged at Lock 25 unbolting the old ironwork from the bottom gates in order to lighten them, while the carpenters' gang sawed the balance poles off the old gates and put the lifting chains ready. The balance poles had to be sawn off to allow the gates to lie lengthwise within the *Leo*. Walking-planks were placed across the lock, together with walking-platforms, to give safe access; handrails were not fitted.

Due to the very poor condition of the outside bottom gate, the lifting chains were not easy to place in a secure position, but were eventually located underneath the walking-board. By one o'clock the gate was manoeuvred into the bottom of *Leo*, the heel being dropped in ever so gently and by gradually lowering as the boat was moved out of the lock, the gate slid into its appropriate position.

During the afternoon two men manhandled the pump uphill from Lock 4 to Lock 25. By Monday evening both old gates were out, the chamber of Lock 26 cleansed of slurry, stop planks were in place at Whitford Bridge and Hammonds Wharf and the new balance poles taken out of the *Leo* ready for use at Lock 25.

Tuesday 12 October. Three labourers loaded a two inch pump for de-watering the lock plus safety helmets and other bits and pieces on to the flat at Hammonds Wharf, whilst the other men lifted both new gates out of the *Leo* and put them roughly in position.

By midday both balance beams had been moved and were in position on the gates, the procedure being that the tenon (pronounced tenant) was located in the mitre-post and wiggled into the hole, the mortice was lowered and any final adjustments were carried out with a sledge-hammer. All the labour force was by now assembled at Lock 25, but regrettably only five partook of the work involved in moving gates and balance beams. The foreman arrived mid-morning and all the material that had been carefully unloaded from the *Leo* had, due to inefficient planning, to be moved to new locations. The digger, after picking up the old sleepers and piles used to cross the lock, was escorted by the foreman and two labourers down the towpath, where it placed piles across the lock and assembled in its new position proceeded to excavate the chamber of Lock 25.

By two o'clock the pump had been positioned ready to pump out the immediate area. Stop planks were now in position above Lock 25, and the areas between Locks 27 and 26, 26 and 25 and 25 and 24 were de-watered. The *Leo* was left in the centre of the channel below Lock 25, the flat B69 being on the opposite (offside) point between Lock 24 and 23, the water-level of which was maintained because of the number of craft moored at the pleasure boat base.

Wednesday 13 October. The digger the previous afternoon had cleaned out only half of the chamber at Lock 5 and did not finish the job until 10am. Most of the men arrived a little late, but the vacuum pump was already running, having been set going by a labourer who lived at Hammonds Wharf. The first job was to clear out the chamber and apron at the bottom end, prior to fitting the gates. Most of the slurry was shovelled into the bucket of the excavator and lifted out that way; surplus water, etc., was scooped out with an instrument the name of which is pronounced 'scope'. In the meantime a pump had been set going to pump out any water which worked through the stop planks at the top end of the lock. This, and shepherding the digger when it moved off to Lock 24, was to be the sole work of two men for the day. By ten o'clock the lock chamber and general area were clear and the gates moved over by gantry to allow access to the rubble, etc., in the paddle holes. Two windlasses were found.

After the morning break work started in

preparation for the demolition of the old clap sills and the pivot boxes, which proved to be rotten where they were set into the main sill. The weather was bitterly cold at this point and work proceeded slowly. At eleven o'clock a foreman arrived and detached the labourer/driver for other duties. The digger made its way down the towpath to Lock 24, crossed over and commenced work clearing the lock chamber. The other workmen continued as planned, one carpenter cutting the clap sills to size and shape.

At twelve o'clock the rain which had been coming down quietly fell hard enough to drive the men undercover and, with one small exception, that was the end of the day's work. The exception was when the foreman and labourer/driver loaded a further set of stop planks and placed them in position above Whitford Bridge at Lock 26. The rain continued heavily and it was anticipated that there might be difficulties with excessive water.

Thursday 14 October. The weather continued cold and overcast, but all labour was on site with the exception of the labourer/driver who was posted elsewhere. Work continued with fitting the pins and boxes for the gates and the gates were then relifted with the gantry and lowered into place; the boxes, incidentally, are cut from elm and their replacement was necessary as the previous cups had worked loose and become oval - they were installed at the same time as the gates, 1917 and 1925. The new boxes were countersunk into the old main sill, caulked in with oakum and hot pitch and the cups inserted and treated in like manner (the old ones were discarded). Having finally got the gates into position they were prepared for the mitre cut. The majority of labour was involved on this. Using pumps at the head and tail of the lock, one labourer kept it clear of water. The bricklayer and his mate were engaged in minor repairs to the lock walls and various of the available men were detached at odd times to check the condition of the stop-planks, level of water in the pounds, etc. The hired excavator, together with one labourer, continued to clear out the lock chamber at No.26; the operator afterwards turned his attention to the intervening lock pound which he was unable to reach with any success, due to the relatively short reach of the machines' arm.

Friday, 15 October. The majority of the labour, with the exception of the pump-man and the labourer/driver, were involved in cutting the gate mitres. When the gates were first dropped into place the

7.45am at the stoppage site.

minimum amount possible to make a watertight seal was cut away from the mitre-posts. The gates arrive in a rough sawn condition and having cut one post to the right size with a two-man manual cross-cut saw, the second gate had its high points indicated by putting raddle (venetian red) on the face. The gates were then closed and the high points, indicated by the raddle being transferred, were adzed away. In the case of Lock 25, however, the cross-cut saw, operated by two carpenters, was used for both cuts, mainly due to the irregularity of the face. As the cross-cut saw is six feet long the gate was held in the open position and ladders placed against each face, firmly secured at the top and bottom, and each carpenter ascended his own side of the gate and was retained by a labourer holding him there. The adage 'one hand for the job and one for yourself' cannot, in these circumstances, apply. Having completed this, each carpenter cut his own half of the clap sill to size. Where the halves abutted to the quoin a notch was cut out, measuring approximately 4 in by 4 in by 8 in, which at a later stage had an insert made to fit the round nose of the quoin. These throwaway pieces should, in theory, if the joint is to be kept watertight, be replaced every five years. Only one lock of the 58 on the Tardebigge flight had a sharp-nosed quoin and it was often cursed by boatmen as it was easy to catch. The digger-driver completed the cleaning out of Lock 24, but inadvertently lifted away the mud plank kept at the tail of the lock to prevent mud, bottles, etc., coming between the gates and the clap sill when they are not in use. The balance of the afternoon was spent in moving everything possible from the site due to anticipated vandalism over the weekend.

Monday 18 October. Several men were late and it was about nine o'clock before work could start. Even then the local labourer had not had any morning overtime authorised and had not, therefore, activated the pumps, with the result that until about 9.45am the site was not ready for use, although some tools were brought out. While pumping-out operations began the labourer/driver and another labourer fetched a good paddle from the yard in lieu of one that was found to be damaged and unloaded piles.

In the meantime the carpenters had recovered a clap sill that local children had dropped into the bottom of the lock and it as also found that 35 out of 100 bricks had gone missing. Incredibly, little else was damaged. The carpenters then lowered both clap sills into position fitting them to one another, while a new paddle, a bag of cement and some bricks were brought up, plus a ladder for the use of the bricklayer and his mate who had to fill a hole in the lock wall, together with an extensive hole in the weir at the head of Lock 24. Another labourer spent most of the day with a hammer and chisel cutting away a rotten curb stone at the head of Lock 25.

The clap sills did not fit and it was not until about three o'clock that they could be persuaded to do so. The carpenters and foreman then took it in turns to bore four $1^1/_8$ inch holes in each sill, prior to inserting the gagg pins, a job which was completed the same day. At 3.30pm the threatened rain dropped but work continued until 4.30pm.

A party of schoolchildren with their teachers visited the site despite the rain, a rather dangerous proceeding as the children persistently ducked under the safety ropes.

Tuesday 19 October. The pump man having been paid his hour's overtime the site was ready for immediate occupation. Most of the men were involved in 'barring' the gates, which was done with an implement like a heavy crowbar with a hooked or oblique end; this is pressed into the brickwork at the bottom of the lock chamber and the gates are then levered forward. Next the 'bars' are set in position by means of two specially cut pieces of timber having a 'v' notch at one extremity. The idea was that the bars would hold the gates and the gates hold the clap sills in place. Unfortunately, the gagg pins were knocked in with sledge-hammers which moved them apart about $^3/_{16}$ of an inch and it was necessary for one carpenter to cut pieces of elm to this size while the other inserted oakum between the clap and main sills to make a watertight seal.

To pass the time one labourer was engaged in trundling barrowloads of ashes from a dump at Whitford Bridge to the various locks, as insufficient had been left previously.

At approximately eleven o'clock it began to rain but it was not until twelve o'clock, when all the men on the site were soaked, that the carpenter, who was acting-foreman, called a halt to the work. Everyone retreated to the cabin of the *Leo* and, led by the carpenter, groused about the rain until 2.30pm, when the men proceeded to make up a mortar mixture and cut out an extension to the area left in the clap sill to take the throwaway portion. There was no apparent reason why this was done on site apart from a slight miscalculation. The bricklayer then used the cement mix, which was lowered to him a bucketful at a time from the cement mixer standing above the tail of the lock, to make good the brick chamber and as a grouting or back-fill to the clap sills, incidentally screening the misjoin on the clap sills. Having put a very good finish on the surface of this, a number of attempts were made by one of the labourers to cut his initials in the surface of the cement, but due to the presence of both gravel and cement fondu (quick-hardening) he only succeeded in making a mess. Two halfpenny pieces were also inserted, rather pointlessly, as they were dated 1955 and 1960 respectively, and the bricklayer neatly cut his initials in (A.W.). One carpenter had cut his quoin fit (throwaway piece) and drilled and nailed this into place in the meantime, and proceeded, while the other men were clearing up, to assist the other carpenter. The quoin fits were made and put in place towards evening.

Wednesday 20 October. The weather was pleasantly warm and tempers became so when it was found that although the gates were a good fit to the clap sills and to one another the rubber inserts which make a watertight seal for the length of the gate against the quoin were not touching it. It was, therefore, necessary to lift the gates with the gantry (the inside gate also being rather less than satisfactory), dig out the pivots and relocate them approximately half an inch to one side, which involved cutting away the old elm around the pivots, moving them and re-packing. Minor complications were found in so far as the collars had to be slightly readjusted and the cotter pins holding the collars in place proved difficult to extract. Therefore the two carpenters and most other men at various times were engaged solely in this work, together with the fitting of one gate paddle and general fitting round of the gates. The resettlement of the gates meant, of course, that the mitre had to be recut once again. While the carpenters' gang were busy at this the bricklayer and a couple of other men were engaged in repairing the weir at Lock 26 and cutting out, ready to rework, some faulty brickwork at the tail of Lock 25. Two labourers had to take one paddle to the yard, because although it had been apparently cut to the correct size it did not fit. Four was found to be the absolute minimum number of men necessary to operate the power-saw in the yard.

On returning to Hammonds Wharf and having wheeled the paddle up to Lock 25, the two labourers were then dispatched again to the yard to collect three cwt of cement and two bags of building sand, and with instructions to fill the crew bus to the roof with loose sand and gravel. With a payload of one ton this was not possible, but 16 cwt was taken to Hammonds Wharf, where it was shovelled on board B67 which had been brought down by two labourers for this purpose.

In the afternoon the lock hangers were assembled. These comprise two baulks which are placed across the lock and have hanging from them by chains two further baulks which drop inside the lock and are wedged into position with planks placed across to make a good working platform. At this point it was found that one of the carpenters had gone partially deaf, and an accident was only averted by someone's quick thinking. The lock hangers were for the benefit of the bricklayer; unfortunately in order for him to get at the brickwork it was again necessary for him to lift the outside gate.

The rigid pump hoses were taken down from Lock 25 to Lock 24 by four labourers, ready for pumping out that lock chamber, but due to a change of plan they were then carried back up to Lock 25. Of the material brought in the van none was used this day. Fairly heavy rain had caused the two lock pounds above Lock 25 to rise dangerously and water was run off for about an hour by removing the top stop plank and lifting the second to give a gap of about two inches, the intention being to drop the level of both pounds by approximately 12 inches (this water would, of course, have to be pumped out by the pump-man on Thursday morning.)

Thursday 21 October. Weather overcast, all labour present although the driver made three trips to Tardebigge for materials. The first load comprised one cwt of cement, seven cwt of sand and gravel, three cwt builders' sand and bits and pieces; the second, another bag of cement and the third trip was for an old scrap door to be used as shuttering. In the meantime the carpenters, together with two labourers, were putting into place the new paddles for the gates, with paddle-rods, paddle-rod cramps, etc. This kept them busy for most of the morning, although at one stage all available labour was engaged in manhandling the three inch vacuum pump down the towpath to Lock 26, where it was set going after stop planks had been placed in the bottom end grooves. Due to that rather peculiar shape of these grooves some difficulty was experienced in getting the planks in place, the operation taking two hours in the afternoon and involving six men standing on them to drop them into place. Lock hangers were also put in. After the pump was moved the bricklayer and his mate completed the brickwork required at the weir at the head of Lock 26. After the pump had lowered the water from the bottom end chamber it was seen that there was a foot of mud, in which the carpenters flatly refused to work; however, one labourer occupied himself for an hour going around the bottom with a shovel seeing what he could find, ending up with one paddle key. Due to the conditions the site was vacated at approximately four o'clock.

Friday 22 October. The weather was warm and sunny. The bricklayer had been detached for duty as relief yacht-basin attendant at Diglis (normally the bricklayer's mate would do this.) The van driver was detached in the afternoon to dry-dock a boat at Tardebigge yard. In the morning, however, the pumps were running on arrival and the carpenters were engaged, while waiting for the water to drop sufficiently, in various odd bits of repair-work around Locks 25 and 26.

At Lock 25 one of the curb stones previously cut away was to be replaced by concrete. This was done by one of the labourers. The shuttering which had been brought out so urgently the day before was strutted into place and the hole filled. When the foreman arrived at midday he expected to see this dry, but the labourer who had done the job had not added enough cement fondu to the mix, fearing it would go hard before he could use it.

At 10.15am two labourers had begun shovelling the mud from the bottom and chamber of Lock 26, but all work stopped for 20 minutes at eleven o'clock to allow a labourer to extricate an eel he found, which he proposed to take home and eat — after skinning it alive in the traditional canal manner. Notwithstanding this interruption the paddles were eventually 'fitted around' by 12.30. The process for 'fitting around' a paddle is that the nuts holding the paddle-rod to the paddle are undone, the paddle rod lifted out of the way slightly, the one paddle slide removed by knocking out the cotter pins and pulling it away. The paddle is then removed from the frame and placed on a 'horse box', generally cleaned up and inspected, the areas of greatest wear being fairly apparent. The paddle frame is then wiped clean and raddled, the paddle — a weight of about 56lb — being placed back and moved against the raddle. In theory, if it is a perfect fit, an area of three inches around the face of the paddle will be red. In the case of these two paddles the outside one was worn slightly but only took about ten minutes adzing and three placings against the paddle frame to get a reasonably good fit, but the inside paddle was very badly worn in the middle and took about 35 minutes. It is understood that chippies' rheumatism, common to most canal carpenters, was probably caused by holding paddles in place with the knee — the paddles are, of course, soaking wet, muddy and covered in lichenous growth. This job required two chippies, two labourers, the pump-man to watch from above and the eel-eater likewise.

During this time one other labourer was occupied in scooping the water out of the *Leo* prior to refloating, while the foreman was lifting the planks at Hammonds Bridge.

The afternoon was spent loading both craft with all loose material, the flat B67 towing *Leo* down to Stoke Prior Wharf where both craft were tied up for the night. The men did not leave the site until just after five. Some delay occurred due to the presence of craft moored against the towpath, but after removal of the last set of planks at the head of Lock 7 and removal of the chains which prevented egress of craft at this lock the stoppage was officially declared over.

Unfortunately, although this was the official end of the stoppage, further work was necessary on the site, for apart from dismantling the gantry and reloading and moving the craft it was found that the rubber inserts on the gates still did not abut correctly to the quoin and had to be removed and reset, which took the carpenters a few days. At Lock 26 a severe leak was found in the field behind the towpath. It came from the lock chamber, where it was apparent that some brick and stone courses had shifted, either from the digger moving across the lock or from its bucket having caught on the brickwork. The remedial works, apart from involving a large quantity of material, took a couple of workmen three weeks to complete.

No attempt can be made at costing this job, although the labour cannot, even with the then labourers' wages of £15.37½ per week, have been less than £500.

APPENDIX 2

A.C. Lisle seems to have been promoted between 1935 and 1941 for writing here he has become the Assistant General Manager and his paper has improved from the basic 'Port of Gloucester' style he used for most of the correspondence in chapter 8.

Dear Spiers, I have been asked by the Birmingham Canal Coal Committee to furnish them with certain information regarding consumers of coal on the W&B Canal. I enclose two copies of the form shewing the information desired, and I should be obliged if you could fill in the columns no. 1-5 inclusive, so far as you are able to do so, and return one of the forms to me as early as possible. *4th July 1941*

Unfortunately, it has not proved possible to find a copy of the original form of the type Mr Spiers had to fill in, but we do have parts of various draft replies he attempted, although it is apparent that it took a long time to garner the information for one of his originals is dated October October 1941. Initially, Mr Spiers seems to have used eight columns although reducing this in the later attempt, but these do show how much information he was trying to collate and are reproduced for interest.

1. Name of firm.
2. Full receiving capacity of Canal wharves per week (7 days) in tons.
3. No. of hours working per week (7 days) subdivided into day and night.
4. Conditions for unloading barges.*
5. Any mechanical devices be provided.
6. Could mechanical devices be provided?
7. Is labour available for dealing with increased quantities by canal.
8. By whom would such labour be provided.

*Odd the use of this word on a predominantly 'narrow' canal,

Consumer	Wharves: Remarks	Conditions	Dredging
Noars Salt Ltd, Commercial street	Formerly coal retailers, Wharf not now used	Dredging required	6 loads
Davenports Brewery	100 tons per 7-day week. Private only. Cannot be removed. Manual discharge.	In order	
Queen's Hospital	120 tons per 7-day week as Davenports	In order	
John & E. Sturge		Dredging required	4 loads
Wheeley's Road Wharf	Formerly occupied by H.Kings, retailers. Wharf now fenced from the canal.	Dredging required	6 loads
Birmingham Hospital Centre	LMS railway runs between canal and hospital. New wharf would be required and overhead conveyor or coal might be unloaded at Goodman's wharf.		
Birmingham University Wharf	Not now used. Much material dumped from road (Pritchetts Lane) would have to be removed to bring wharf back into use ? Goodman's wharf might be used.		6 loads
Boxfoldia, Selly Oak H.Ward, Selly Oak	Coal was unloaded at north end of these works when occupied by Cycle Components. The coal was fed into a chute running down the embankment which is high (30 feet?). Wards air raid shelters erected on top of embankment would make unloading difficult.		
Goodman & Co.	Can this wharf be used as an unloading centre for Boxfoldia, Wards and ICI Metals? Hospital and University?	Dredging required	6 loads
ICI Metals Ltd	Canal basin filled in. Goodman's wharf might be used. Quarter of mile away.		
Patent Enamel Co.	Canal basin. Dredging required	Dredging required	10 loads
Cadbury Bros., Bournville	In use. 250 tons maximum in 7-day week. Manual discharge loaded into trucks. Grab occasionally available.	In order	
Sparreys Wharf (Public Wharf) Bournville	Might be used by local (Stirchley) retailers	Dredging required	4 loads
Birmingham Corporation Yard, Alexandra Road (off Mary Vale Road)	New wharf required	New wharf and dredging required	6 loads
Ten Acres & Stirchley Co-operative Society	250 tons a week. Manual discharging	In order	
E. Showell & Sons Stirchley	New wharf would be required and conveyor to top of bank. Sparrey's wharf might be used.		
Guest, Keen & Nettlefolds, Stirchley	In use. 250 tons maximum. Storage space small	In order	
Breedon Cross Wharf (Public Wharf)	Wharf occupied by H. Head, but could be used for unloading but not for storage under present conditions.	Dredging required	4 loads
R.J.Hunt, Lifford Foundry	New wharf and dredging required, or Breedon Cross wharf used. *Coke chiefly*	New wharf and dredging required	6 loads
Birmingham Corporation Destructor	Concrete wall along tow path side. Breedon Cross wharf to be used. *Not really possible.*		
Slough Estates Factory Centre, Lifford Lane	Canal basin requires dredging. About 35 firms occupy the site.	Dredging required	6 loads
Kings Norton Metal Co.	Nil. No wharf. Breedon Cross three quarters mile away.		
Kings Norton Paper Mills	In order. 25 tons maximum, but no spare storage space.		
Kings Norton Brick Company	Unavailable for canal-borne coal	Dredging required	8 loads at least
J.Forbes Wharf Kings Norton Wharf South side of bridge	Formerly retailer. This and K.N. Wharf might be brought back into use, though K.N.Wharf has a bad draw in.	Dredging required	4 loads each
Hopwood Wharf Public Wharf	Might be used by Barnt Green retailers (F&M Dixon)	Dredging required	4 loads
Bittell Arm Wharf	as above (but much dredging required to make navigable.	Dredging required	80 loads *(was 8)*
Alvechurch Brickworks	Not working	Dredging required	8 loads
Scarfield Wharf, Alvechurch	Might be used by Alvechurch retailers	Dredging required	4 loads
Tardebigge Old Wharf Tardebigge New Wharf	Either might be used by Redditch & Plymouth Estates New wharf probably best wharf for Bromsgrove district	Dredging required (Old Wharf) In order (New)	6 loads
Tardebigge Half Way	Nearest Wharf to Bromsgrove, although New Wharf might be convenient	Dredging required	6 loads

Gloucester occasionally used it, probably as a general boat description, and although the Worcester & Birmingham was built to wide boat dimensions on the lock free upper pound, elsewhere Spiers writes about 'long' or 'narrow' boats. Was this a question on the form from the Birmingham Coal Committee perhaps?

The table shown represents a slightly simplified fusion of the inspectors various efforts (or those that are available) and, in the main, is transcribed from faded pencil entries:

Consumer	Wharves: Remarks	Conditions	Dredging
Stoke Pound Wharf (Bates Wharf)	Not in use	Dredging required	4 loads
Stoke Wharf (F.Gaylor)	Not in use	Dredging required	6 loads
Mula Chemical Co	Unavailable for canal borne coal	Dredging required	4 loads
Stoke Works (I.C.I. Salt) Hanbury Brick Yard	Canal basin unusable Might be used by Droitwich retail coal mechants	Dredging required Dredging required	6 loads 6 loads
Hanbury Wharf (public Wharf)	" "	Dredging required	6 loads
Dunhampstead Wharf	might be used by local retail coal merchants	Dredging required	6 loads
Tiberton Wharf	" "	Dredging required	6 loads
Cadbury Bros, Blackpole	In order.		
I.C.I. Ltd	Unavailable for public use		
Barkers Brick Yard (elsewhere Bakers Brick Works)	(Added in a different hand 'now electrified')	Dredging required	6 loads
Lowesmoor Wharf (E.Jackson & J.Smith Retailers)		One arm requires dredging and sunken boat raised.	6 loads
Worcester Gas Co	NIL Structural alterations required	In order	
South Wales Cannock Chase Coal & Coke Co	Would be supplied through Lowesmoor		
Heenan Froude's (ie Heenan & Froude)	Would be supplied through Lowesmoor Coke Chiefly	No Wharf	
Worcester Union Workhouse (Midland Road)	Would be supplied through Lowesmoor	Not on canal	
Lea & Perrins (Worcester sauce) (Midland Road)	Would be supplied through Lowesmoor	Not on canal	
Hardy & Padmore (Worcester)	Coke chiefly	Not on canal	
Worcester co-operative Society (Sidbury)	Wharf known as Clare St Wharf and could be re-opened by removing brick boundary wall	Dredging requ'd	6 loads
Worcester Royal Porcelain Co	500 tons per week. Private only	Dredging required	6 loads
T.S.Townsend & Son (Townsend's Mill)	250 tons per week. Private only	In order	
L.Baggott & Co	Dredging requ'd. Coke chiefly	Dredging requ'd	6 loads

Not included in the above although using the canal are Birmingham Batteries & Smart's Brickworks whose wharves are on the B.C.N. (Birmingham Canal Navigations). In an emergency it might be possible to supply Worcester Electricity Works from the river.

Wharves 90ft long total 8' 0" x 9" 3" timber. 35ft per yard. 1050ft per wharf = 200 cu.ft. at £5.5.0
          per standard of (?) 16 cu.ft = £66 say £70
          10 men 12 days   = £60
Dredging 30 yard x 1 yd deep x 3 yds wide = 90 cu.yd, say 120 tons = 6 boat loads (3 men) at £5 per ton
                                                      = £30
Iron 3 cwt @ 6d (2½) per lb   = £8
                                         = £168 (presumably per wharf re-opened.)

Looking north toward the tunnel at Tardebigge Maintenance Yard in 1972. MB Coleshill ex-GUCCo with the bows of the ex-FMC motor 'Bramble'; mill on the right, with the white painted 'Pixie' house on its end being a workman's one-bedroom dwelling. Manual crane on the right.

Left: Bilford Top Lock No.8. At one time the lock-keeper and his wife fell out and the house was divided into two halves. Nonetheless she continued to cook his meals leaving them on the dividing wall. The contrast between the two halves was unbelievable for the lady was houseproud to the nth degree, whereas the lock-keeper was none too fussy. The boat is also interesting as Ken Mullings built it in his garden as a 20' (6.1m) cruiser, subsequently extending it to 60'. Photograph 1977. Right: Bittell Reservoir attendant's cottage from on board a tug. The feeder to the reservoir passes in front of the house alongside the mud boats and the dwelling actually stands on an island. 1971.

Blackpole wharf, one-time Cadburys loading bay 1972.

A rather attractive and quite unusual photograph supposed to have been taken around 1910 at West Stockwith, the junction of the Trent with the Chesterfield Canal. All three craft are preparing to work down the Trent and while 'Rose' is a fairly usual sailing boat, the middle craft is an 'iron-pot' of an unorthodox design, presumably used for dredging as her 'mast' appears to be more of a boom. The narrow boat 'Shamrock' is typical of craft used on a river navigation insofar as instead of T-studs for tying up she has heavy barge-style 'bitts'. The mast is lowered and raised by windlasses and the whole tackle looks seamanlike — her master was, without doubt, a 'Turnpike Sailor'!

Appendix 3
Extracts from a Trent Lock gauging register 1855-1856

All boats' dunnage includes jury mast and line. Headfast and sternfast lines, fire stove and one or more shafts, plus:

(1) includes "she has side cloths fitted to her gunnels"

Tonnage

Register Number	Date Weighed	Fleet Number	Owner	Built	at	First Owner	Purchased	Traffic Usage	Length	Beam	Maximum Capacity	Draught	Dunnage	Notes
	1855													
1783	11 Dec	3	Thomas Walker Derby	NK	NK	NK	1855	Manure on Derby Canal	70'0"	6'5"	24	40.61"	3 deal planks, 2 wheelbarrows	No floor
1784	17 Dec	8	West Hallam Iron Works	NK	NK	NK	1846	Metal to Bilston	71'2"	6'10"	29	40.17"	4 deal planks	
1785	17 Dec	2	West Hallam Iron Works	NK	NK	NK	1846	Metal to Bilston	71'5"	6'10"	31	41.04"	4 deal planks	No floor
1786	18 Dec	1	Benjamin Goodman Berkby Wharf	NK	NK	NK	1846	Mountsorrel Stone to London	70'2"	6'9"	26	39.57"	2 wings, 5 deal plank 2 standards	No floor (1)
1787	18 Dec	2	Benjamin Goodman Berkby Wharf	NK	NK	NK	1846	Mountsorrel Stone to	70'4"	6'6"	30	42.29"	2 wings, 4 footing planks, 2 standards	No floor (1)
	1856													
1788	5 Jan	1	W&I Freeman Westminster	1836	Berkhampstead	Grand Junction Canal Company	1854	Stone to London	70'9"	6'9"	28	41.87"	2 wings, 5 deal planks 2 standards	No floor
1789	5 Jan	2	W&I Freeman Westminster	1842	Berkhampstead	Grand Junction Canal Company	1854	Stone to London	70'8"	6'9"	29	43.99"	2 wings, 1 cover	No floor (1)
1790	24 Jan	3	Thomas Parker Derby	NK	NK	NK	1855	Coal to Derby	69'6"	6'8"	24	40.18"	1 pole, 3 deal planks	"rather leaky"
1791	11 Feb	3	Joshua Street Borrowash	NK	NK	NK	1854	Coal to Derby	72'2"	7'0"	30	40.64"	3 deal planks	No floor
1792	18 Feb	3	Thomas Thornicroft Leicester	NK	NK	NK	1852	Coal to London	70'6"	7'0"	29	40.45"	2 wings, 4 footing planks, 2 standards	No floor (1)
1793	18 Feb	1	Thomas Thornicroft Leicester	NK	NK	NK	1853	Coal to London	70'8"	7'0"	29	39.89"	4 footing planks, 2 standards	No floor "very leaky"(1)
1794	12 June	9	High Peak Railway	NK	NK	NK	1854	Coal trade upon the Cromford	68'1"	6'5"	25	41.54"	1 deal plank	No floor - ex-Nathaniel Wheatcroft Jnr. A very small boat
1795	14 July	3	George Smedley Loughborough	1845	Loughborough	Joseph Henson	1855	Coal trade to Loughborough	71'9"	13'9"	49	39.46"	5 poles, 2 deal planks 1 wind rope, 4 ice planks, 1 fire stand	Ex-no.1662. This was a re-weigh. "The length of the forehold is 21'3" and hinderhold 24'3" and whole length, including the midship beam, 49'10"..."
1796	30 Sept	4	Joseph Byatt Derby	1826	Middlewich	Mr Barrows	1843	Coal trade to Derby	69'9"	6'11"	23	39.22"	1 deal plank	
1797	30 Sept	9	Joseph Byatt Derby	1843	Braunston	Pickford&Co	1853	Coal trade to Derby	69'10"	6'5"	22	37.26"	1 deal plank	No floor
1798	12 Dec	1	S&P Potter Ilkeston	1856	Trent Lock	S&P Potter	New	Coal trade to Bottesford	70'6"	6'9"	31	41.97"	4 footing planks, 2 standards	No floors. This pair of boats were identical
1799	12 Dec	2	S&P Potter Ilkeston	1856	Trent Lock	S&P Potter	New	Coal trade to Bottesford	70'6"	6'9"	31	41.97"	4 footing planks, 2 standards	
1800	17 Dec	1	James Newton Loughbrodge	1830	Birmingham	Mr MacDonald Buckingham	1852	Coal trade to Uxbridge	70'7"	7'0"	29	42.23"	4 footing planks, 2 standards	No floor (1)
1801	17 Dec	2	James Newton Loughbrodge	NK	NK	NK	1854	Coal trade to Uxbridge	71'0"	6'10"	29	40.88"	4 footing planks, 2 standards	No floor (1)
	1857													
1802	7 Dec	-	William Dawson Ilkeston	NK	NK	NK	1857	Coal trade to the Grand Junction Canal	71'0"	7'0"	29	42.11"	4 footing planks 2 standards, 2 wings	No floor (1) "Found rather leaky"
1803	12 Dec	-	West Hallam Iron Works	NK	NK	NK	1856	Iron trade to Birmingham	71'7"	6'10"	32	41'48"	6 footing planks	No floor. A later pencilled note adds: "one ton down".
	1856													
1804	18 Jan	-	Charles Woodhouse Loughborough	NK	NK	NK	1856	Coal trade to the Union Canal	70'0"	6'8"	27	40.02"	4 footing planks, 3 standards, 2 wings	No floor, note (1), "found weak and leaky" The 'Union Canal' was, presumably, the Leics & Northants (Old) Union.
1805	25 Jan	4	West Hallam Iron Works	NK	NK	NK	1856	Iron trade to Birmingham	71'4"	6'11"	30	41.07"	5 footing planks 3 standards	No floor
1806	26 Jan-		George Evans Ilkeston	NK	NK	NK	1857	Plaster to Ilkeston	70'8	7'1"	29	41.75"		No floor. "found weak and leaky". (one wonders about the carriage of plaster in such a poor boat).
1807	24 Feb	1	West Hallam Iron works	NK	NK	NK	1856	Iron trade to Birmingham	70'3"	6'10"	31	42.44"	4 footing planks 3 standards	No floor
1808	26 Feb	-	James Newton Loughborough	1857	Trent Lock	James Newton	New	Coal to Uxbridge	70'6"	6'7"	29	41.21"	4 footing planks, 3 standards, 2 wings.	
1809	9 July	2	Thomas Parker Derby	NK	NK	NK	1853	Coal to Derby	71'0"	6'10"	29	41.68"	1 deal plank	No floor. "found to be very weak and leaky". Note (1)
1810	13 Oct	70	Grand Junction Canal Company	1837	Tipton	Whitehouse & Sons	1849	Trade to Nottingham	70'0"	6'7"	20	36.58"	6 standadrds, 4 footing planks	"one ton down".
	1856													
2019	28 Feb	1	Samuel Smart Nottingham	1835	Nottingham	Samuel Barnsdall	NK	Getting and carrying gravel to Nottingham	72'6"	14'0"	53	39.91"	2 planks	
2035	16 July	-	Sanitary Committee Nottingham	1839	Loughborough	Sutton & Co Shardlow	1866	Manure	72'3"	14'1"	50	41.44"		"A new concrete floor was put in this boat and she was found 'very leaky'.
	1856													
2029	17 Jan	2	Henry Wilson Cropwell	NK	NK	NK	1878	Coal and stone to the Grantham Canal	70'0"	6'6"	23	39.74"	4 footing planks, 3 standards	
2033	5 April	1	Kempson & Howell Pye Bridge	NK	London	Mr Dutton	1878	Gas tar from Grantham to Pye Bridge	72'2"	6'7"	25	42.47"	1 footing plank	"Decked boat. The length of the hold is 47'10"; divided into three compartments for storing gas tar." A pencilled note adds "down 2 tons, May 30/95
2035	16 July	-	Sanitary	1817	Loughborough	William	NK	Manure	72'8"	14'0"	53	40.55"		"She was found very leaky". Apart from the age of the boat (61 years) it is interesting to see her master, Job Samples, was also the master of 2033, a year earlier. Did 2033 break up?

Appendix 4
Shared Boat Ownership

CANAL boat ownership has been, and is, an expensive activity, but something that gives a certain flexibility to one's activities (writes John Heath). In recent years schemes have evolved to minimise the initial expense of purchase, and the sharing of the running costs of a boat. Some five or six shared ownership schemes, whereby groups of about twelve people purchase and run a boat between them, have been set up in the last few years. In some of the schemes, the owners are responsible for maintenance, while in others the selling company undertakes this for a fee. Initially the schemes prospered, but it would appear that the extent of such boat ownership is limited, and a drawback of the schemes is that owners are restricted to taking the same holiday each year from the same marina.

Shared ownership has had the effect of taking regular canal boat hirers out of the market, and hirers are, as a result, 'feeling the pinch'. Likewise prospective outright buyers are fewer in number and therefore less boats are now being built, though the recession has had its impact.

An alternative to owning a boat was started in late 1992 with the establishment of Countess Cruises Club, initially based at the Festival Park Marina at Etruria (Stoke-on-Trent), to be followed in the near future with the Chirk Marina, near Llangollen. In 1994 there are four boats, two four berth, a six berth and an eight berth.

The Countess Cruises Club is run as a timeshare, weeks being purchased and an annual maintenance charge being levied. The weeks purchased are 'float-time', that is they are not fixed in the calendar, and use is by negotiation. This means that the initial expense of ownership is greatly reduced and the annual maintenance costs are more widely shared. Such an arrangement permits the owner of a week to exploit the advantages of the world's largest timeshare exchange organisation giving access to over 2,500 resorts worldwide. Exchanges have resulted in the boats being used in the first year of operation by families visiting the United Kingdom from USA, Mexico, Malaysia, Australia and New Zealand, Germany, South Africa and Zimbabwe. Such visitors would, in the past, have been unlikely to explore a part of the English canal system, and even less likely to have visited Stoke-on-Trent — a revelation!

The ultimate aim is to have some twenty boats catering for about one hundred visitors/boaters weekly over the forty-six week season.

Above and below: The pleasure of shared boat ownership enables participants to enjoy regular boating holidays at minimal expense.